Competing Motives in the Partisan Mind

Series in Political Psychology

Series Editor
John T. Jost

Editorial Board
Mahzarin Banaji, Gian Vittorio Caprara, Christopher Federico, Don Green, John Hibbing, Jon Krosnick, Arie Kruglanski, Kathleen McGraw, David Sears, Jim Sidanius, Phil Tetlock, Tom Tyler

Image Bite Politics: News and the Visual Framing of Elections
Maria E. Grabe and Erik P. Bucy

Social and Psychological Bases of Ideology and System Justification
John T. Jost, Aaron C. Kay, and Hulda Thorisdottir

The Political Psychology of Democratic Citizenship
Eugene Borgida, Christopher Federico, and John Sullivan

On Behalf of Others: The Psychology of Care in a Global World
Sarah Scuzzarello, Catarina Kinnvall, and Kristen Renwick Monroe

The Obamas and a (Post) Racial America?
Gregory S. Parks and Matthew W. Hughey

Ideology, Psychology, and Law
Jon Hanson

The Impacts of Lasting Occupation: Lessons from Israeli Society
Daniel Bar-Tal and Izhak Schnell

Competing Motives in the Partisan Mind
Eric W. Groenendyk

Competing Motives in the Partisan Mind

How Loyalty and Responsiveness Shape Party Identification and Democracy

Eric W. Groenendyk

OXFORD
UNIVERSITY PRESS

OXFORD
UNIVERSITY PRESS

Oxford University Press is a department of the University of Oxford.
It furthers the University's objective of excellence in research, scholarship,
and education by publishing worldwide.

Oxford   New York
Auckland   Cape Town   Dar es Salaam   Hong Kong   Karachi
Kuala Lumpur   Madrid   Melbourne   Mexico City   Nairobi
New Delhi   Shanghai   Taipei   Toronto

With offices in
Argentina   Austria   Brazil   Chile   Czech Republic   France   Greece
Guatemala   Hungary   Italy   Japan   Poland   Portugal   Singapore
South Korea   Switzerland   Thailand   Turkey   Ukraine   Vietnam

Oxford is a registered trademark of Oxford University Press in the UK and certain other
countries.

Published in the United States of America by
Oxford University Press
198 Madison Avenue, New York, NY 10016

Library of Congress Cataloging-in-Publication Data
Groenendyk, Eric W.
Competing motives in the partisan mind : how loyalty and responsiveness shape party
identification and democracy / Eric W. Groenendyk.
    pages cm. — (Series in political psychology)
Includes bibliographical references.
ISBN 978–0–19–996980–7 (hardcover); 978–0–19–026430–7 (paperback)
1. Party affiliation.   2. Political parties.   3. Voting.   4. Democracy.   I. Title.
JF2071.G76 2013
324.201'9—dc23
2013005545

To my family, whose impassioned political discussions inspired me and whose love and support made this book possible.

Preface

This book has been long in the making. In some sense, data collection really began decades ago around my family's dinner table. Epic political debates were part of the festivities when we all got together for holiday gatherings. At some point between turkey and pumpkin pie, discussion would inevitably turn to politics, decibel levels would begin to rise, and family members would divide along a predictably partisan cleavage. For my poor mother, who had inevitably spent hours preparing a beautiful meal, this was all quite stressful and unfortunate (though this never prevented her from joining in). But for me, it was exciting! My mild-mannered, middle class, Midwestern family was not the type to engage in heated arguments. But when it came to politics, all bets were off. Though the Republican and Democratic factions were almost identical in terms of socioeconomic status, race, religion, ethnicity, and virtually every other dimension one can imagine, they somehow managed to disagree passionately on nearly every political issue. It was almost as if they felt compelled to disagree, and everyone (except my poor mother) loved every minute of it.

By the time I eventually entered graduate school at the University of Michigan, I had a pretty strong sense that I wanted to study political psychology. As an undergraduate, I had written an honors thesis comparing the effects of interest group–sponsored ads with those of candidate-sponsored ads, and I had become quite interested in information processing and persuasion. Initially, however, I had no interest in taking on the subject of party identification. In fact, I viewed the party identification debate as a can of worms that I didn't want to open. But, as I continued my studies, I found myself returning to party identification time and time again. It was not until well after I had collected the data for the experiment reported in Chapter 2 and begun writing the National Science Foundation grant proposal that would eventually fund much of the research for this book that I finally recognized the project was really about the motivations underlying party identification. Without realizing it, I had begun a 7-year investigation into my family's dinner table debates. As it turned out, what I had initially believed to be a number of disparate concerns came down to two closely related questions: How could party allegiances create such a fierce divide within my mild-mannered, middle-class Midwestern family? And if these allegiances could have such an effect on my family, could party cues really serve as efficient shortcuts for voters attempting to decide how to vote?

Writing this book has been a fantastic and rewarding experience. The moments of revelation made the hours of frustration worthwhile, and the wonderful conversations with friends and colleagues in Ann Arbor, in Memphis, and at conferences around world made the process fun and enlightening. Several people deserve special thanks for their help along the way. First, I thank the members of my dissertation committee (Ted Brader (co-chair), Nick Valentino (co-chair), Vince Hutchings, Don Kinder, and Norbert Schwarz) for all of their valuable advice during the development of this project. Nick and Ted have been mentors since my undergraduate days, and without the encouragement and careful feedback they provided on numerous drafts of the manuscript, it would not be nearly the product that it is today. In fact, it may never have gotten off the ground in the first place if Nick had not inspired me to pursue a career in political science and Ted had not given me work as a research assistant before I began graduate school. I will be forever indebted to them both.

In addition, I want to acknowledge my brilliant friends in graduate school—especially Antoine Banks—who helped me work out my ideas over countless cups of coffee, pints of beer, lopsided games of one-on-one basketball, and 2-hour phone conversations. My wonderfully supportive colleagues at the University of Memphis also deserve thanks for their encouragement and help in refining this project as it transitioned from a dissertation into a book. I also thank Abby Gross, John Jost, and the book's anonymous reviewers for their helpful feedback and guidance as I learned about the publication process. Adam Hogan, Ashley Jardina, David Plunk, and the staff at YouGov/Polimetrix deserve thanks for their excellent research assistance, and the National Science Foundation, Gerald R. Ford Fellowship Program, Marsh Center for Journalistic Performance, and Rackham Graduate School deserve acknowledgement for assistance in funding this project.

Finally, I thank my family for the support, encouragement, and inspiration they provided. From the political discussions on the porch with my Dad (Gary), to the stressed-out phone conservations with my Mom (Jill), to the methodological consultations during car rides home with my sister (Allison), I cannot imagine what this book (or I) would be without them.

August 17, 2012

Contents

Introduction

The language and imagery of sports abounds in American politics. From the start of the "race to the White House" to the "passing of the baton" from one president to the next, each campaign is a match in the ongoing competition between America's two parties. Along the way, fans cheer, wave signs, and even paint their faces, while, in an awesome barrage of mixed sports metaphors, candidates "throw their hat into the ring," "compete in the horse race," "score points with voters," and occasionally "play hardball." Each side even has a mascot (elephants versus donkeys) and a team color (red versus blue). Like box scores, the latest tracking polls appear in the morning paper, and political pundits, like ESPN personalities, spend each day on cable television and talk radio endlessly debating which team will come out on top when the campaign season concludes. In the end, politics becomes sport, and this seems to be just the way we like it. After all, government and media are obliged to give the fans what they want.

But why is it that we get so caught up in the game? The answer is simple: At its heart, politics *is* a competition, and political parties *are* essentially teams. Therefore, in politics, as in sports, citizens get swept up in the competition, rallying behind the Red Elephants or the Blue Donkeys just as they rally behind the Red Sox or the Blue Jays. While this political fandom may seem innocuous enough, it has vital consequences for democratic accountability.

In stark contrast to the notion of politics as a sporting arena, scholars often draw analogies between politics and the marketplace. Just as firms supply products to fulfill consumer demands, parties supply policies to fulfill voter demands. Like consumers, voters are assumed to be selective, so parties are forced to compete for vote share. This competition not only ensures that parties respond to voters' demands but also encourages policy innovation as each party attempts to gain an electoral advantage. In short, these theories suggest that we are able to achieve democratic accountability because voters demand quality from parties and respond to changes in their policy offerings. However, the implications change dramatically when voters act more like sports fans than consumers. If party loyalty gets in the way of citizens' willingness to respond to changes in parties' policy offerings, then accountability is clearly lacking.

Although brand loyalties are common in the marketplace, they differ markedly from the party loyalties we see in politics. For example, many consumers buy iPhones, iPods, and iPads because they associate the Apple brand with quality. Hence, the brand serves as a helpful shortcut for consumers as they make purchasing decisions. Consumers can be reasonably confident that they are getting a good product when they see the Apple logo, so they need not spend hours reading product reviews. Of course, if Apple were to start producing defective products, this brand loyalty would quickly erode. This would occur because consumers feel the consequences of their purchasing decisions. The same is not true in politics. As Caplan (2007) explains:

> *Democracy is a commons, not a market.* Individual voters do not "buy" policies with votes. Rather they toss their vote into a big common pool. The social outcome depends on the pool's average content (p. 206).

In other words, each citizen has only one vote to cast. Therefore, unlike a purchasing decision, an individual's voting decision has very little impact on the product she actually receives. Regardless of whether she supports the Republican or the Democrat, she knows that her vote is extremely unlikely to affect the outcome of the election. Therefore, unlike consumers with brand loyalties, voters have relatively little incentive to change their party loyalties to reflect variation in the desirability of the products parties offer. In fact, the more the Republican and Democratic parties seem like rival teams, the more likely partisans will be to cling to their allegiances regardless of what the parties offer. Thus, while brand loyalties help consumers make efficient decisions, party loyalties may actually lead voters astray.

With party elites more polarized than they have been in decades (see McCarty, Poole, & Rosenthal, 2006; Theriault 2008), the line dividing the parties is clearer than ever and the rivalry more heated. Although many of America's foremost political scholars once advocated stronger and more internally cohesive parties as a remedy for democracy's ills, many contemporary observers have come to question this wisdom. Proponents of the "responsible parties thesis" reasoned that, if parties could maintain greater discipline over their members, voters would see a greater distinction between parties and have an easier time holding them accountable for their policies (see Ranney 1954). However, now that the parties have achieved greater internal cohesion, it appears that proponents of the responsible parties thesis overlooked the "partisan rancor," "political polarization," and "policy stasis" inherent in such a system (Rae, 2007). In short, they failed to recognize that a clearer delineation between choices also means a clearer distinction between teams. The challenge for contemporary scholars is to determine how party competition plays out in the mind of the voter, because our assumptions about the mind of the voter shape our understanding of democracy.

This book develops a theory of party identification in which individuals have potentially competing motives. On one hand, they feel duty-bound to hold parties accountable, but they are also driven to maintain their party allegiances. Whether parties help guide citizens to sound decisions or undermine democratic accountability depends on which motive wins out.

THE FAN

In politics, as in sports, loyalty is imperative once a person declares his or her allegiance to a team. True devotees hate "fair-weather fans." If you grew up on the North Side of Chicago, you probably root for the Cubs—as your parents did before you and your children will after you—despite the Cubs' century-long losing streak. Fans may admit that rival teams possess more attractive qualities (exciting players, a more stimulating style of play, greater physical or mental toughness), but team loyalties tend not to be rooted in these types of evaluations. Instead, fans' allegiances develop out of regional, cultural, and familial traditions.

At the end of every season, frustrated fans of teams such as the Chicago Cubs feel like giving up on their franchise. They feel as though they simply cannot bear the pain of supporting such an awful team for another year. But the next season, when springtime rolls around, they find themselves right back in the stands cheering for their team and hoping once more that this might be their year. When it comes down to it, they simply cannot bring themselves to root for someone else. They grew up as fans of the team and they will probably always root for their team, because it is part of who they are. When they don their sweat-stained Cubs cap, they feel a connection to their family, their community, and the generations of Cubs fans who suffered before them. When the team occasionally wins a game, it feels like a personal victory, and when they lose a game, it feels like a personal loss. The team's embarrassments are their embarrassments, and when they discuss sports with others, they refer to the team as "we," as in "We lost again."

Readers familiar with identity research may recognize these attributes. To refer to one's group as "we," to feel wins and losses for one's group as wins and losses for the self, and to experience group embarrassments as personal embarrassments are all tell-tale signs of social identification (Greene, 1999).

In other words, part of a fan's identity is wrapped up in his or her sense of association with the team. Even if fans evaluate rival teams more positively than their own, their team identity is part of who they are, for better or worse.

Like identification with a sports team, identification with a political party entails much more than being fond of or agreeing with a party. It means seeing one's self as a Republican or a Democrat. Although the concepts of attitude and identity are often used interchangeably in the political science literature, attitudes toward parties are nonetheless conceptually distinct from identification with a party (Green, Palmquist, & Schickler, 2002; Groenendyk, 2012; Rosema, 2006). Whereas attitudes are *evaluative* in nature (Eagly & Chaiken, 1993), identities are rooted in *self-conceptualization* (Monroe, Hankin, & Vechten, 2000).[1] In short, an important distinction exists between *liking* and *being*. In fact, this was the reason for conceptualizing partisanship as an identity in the first place (see Campbell, Converse, Miller, & Stokes, 1960; Campbell, Gurin, & Miller, 1954).

> In characterizing the relation of individual to party as a psychological identification we invoke a concept that has played an important if somewhat varied role in psychological theories of the relation of individual to individual or of individual to group. We use the concept here to characterize the individual's affective orientation to an important group object in his environment.... We have not measured party attachments in terms of the vote or evaluation of partisan issues because we are interested in exploring the influence of party identification on voting behavior and its immediate determinants. When an independent measure of party identification is used it is clear that even strong party adherents at times may think and act in contradiction to their party allegiance (Campbell et al., 1960, pp. 122–123).

The distinction between attitude and identity plays out in important ways as we observe public opinion and political behavior. Being part of one's self-concept, an identity is something one is motivated to defend. Like our sports team loyalties, we tend to inherit our party identities from our families and our communities, and party images are often interwoven with our understanding of local culture and history. For many years, being a "true Southerner" meant being a Democrat, almost regardless of one's issue positions, and this is only one of numerous examples in which regional, cultural, racial, religious, and occupational identities have become entwined with party identification. Because party identity has such deep roots, change does not come easily. Like

---

1. For this reason, the terms *attitude* and *evaluation* will be used interchangeably throughout this book.

the sports fans described earlier, partisans may find that their political attitudes increasingly conflict with their identity, yet they continue to feel the
pull of their party. Whether this pull is sufficient to compel continued loyalty
depends on the strength of one's competing motives.

THE GOOD CITIZEN

Throughout American history, politics and government have been shaped by
tensions between party loyalty and the ideals of objectivity and pragmatism
(Schudson, 1998). Although partisans often act like sports fans, they view
themselves quite differently. No one wants to admit that their team loyalty
clouds their evaluations, and few are willing to confess their motivation to
maintain their party identity even when they disagree with their party's policies. Rather than viewing themselves as fans, they see themselves as good
citizens bound by civic duty to evaluate parties objectively. To maintain this
self-image, they must sustain the belief that their party identity is grounded
in reason and not mere affect. Of course, psychological conflicts are bound to
arise as *the good citizen* and *the fan* attempt to coexist within the mind of the
partisan.

   For example, imagine a Democrat who, along with then-candidate Barack
Obama, opposed mandatory healthcare coverage for individuals during the
2008 presidential primaries. This was one of the few substantive differences
between the platforms of Hillary Clinton and Obama. Our Democratic partisan has thought a lot about this issue and has become committed to her
position. However, by 2010, she discovers that her party—including President
Obama—has unified in favor of an individual mandate. She now faces a
dilemma. She may regain cognitive consistency by changing either her attitude or her party identity to match the other, but neither option is particularly
attractive. To knowingly change her attitude about mandatory healthcare coverage to reflect her Democratic identity would constitute partisan bias and
thus violate norms of political objectivity and pragmatism. On the other hand,
to weaken her Democratic allegiance to reflect her disagreement would also
entail a psychological cost. Thus, the optimal solution is to find some way
to justify maintaining her Democratic identity despite the disagreement (see
Abelson, 1959).

   Of course, partisans need to be both motivated and able to construct these
types of justifications. A partisan may lack the cognitive resources necessary
to justify continued identification with her party, or her partisan motivation
may simply be insufficient to warrant the effort. If either of these is the case,
she will likely update her identity to reflect the disagreement with her party.

A number of works suggest that at least some partisans update their party identity to reflect their political evaluations some of the time (Allsop & Weisberg, 1988; Brody & Rothenberg, 1988; Carsey & Layman, 2006; Dancey & Goren, 2010; Fiorina, 1981; Franklin, 1984, 1992; Franklin & Jackson, 1983; Highton & Kam, 2011; Jackson, 1975; Lavine, Johnston, & Steenbergen, 2012; MacKuen, Erikson, & Stimson, 1989; Markus & Converse, 1979; Page & Jones, 1979). Even Campbell and colleagues, who stressed the enduring nature of party identification, acknowledged that it is "firm but not immovable" (Campbell et al., 1960, p. 148). Thus, the challenge is to determine the conditions under which partisans are more likely to change their identity to reflect disagreements with their party and those under which they are more likely to rationalize away disagreements to maintain their party allegiance.

For decades, the party identification literature has been preoccupied with the question of whether party identification is predominantly stable or inherently changeable. By developing a *dual motivations theory* of party identification, this book attempts to push the debate toward the more pertinent underlying question: When is party identification more likely to help and when is it more likely to hurt democracy? The answer lies in examining voters' motivation to hold parties accountable versus their motivation to maintain their team allegiances. Party identification has the potential to help citizens navigate their way through politics, but this requires a willingness to update their party identity. If they do so, their party identity will serve as a running approximation of their evaluations and thus function as an efficient information shortcut.[2] If they fail to update, then their party identity will likely lead them astray.

PLAN OF THE BOOK

This book is organized around a series of predictions—each of which is the focus of at least one chapter. These predictions are derived from the dual motivations theory of party identification developed in Chapter 1. The dual motivations theory posits that two competing psychological forces shape party identification: partisan motivation and responsiveness motivation. On one hand, partisans are driven to maintain party loyalty, but on the other hand, they are motivated to be responsive to their political environment. When individuals disagree with their party, they will attempt to develop justifications

---

2. Because citizens possess incomplete information, they will often make errors in choosing the party with which to align themselves. However, errors attributable solely to incomplete information can be assumed to be random and therefore to cancel out in the aggregate (see, for example, Page & Shapiro, 1992).

for maintaining their party allegiance despite that disagreement.[3] Party identification change occurs when a justification cannot be found or if responsiveness motivation is simply too high.

Chapters 2 and 3 provide evidence of partisan motivation. Although verification of partisan stability is easy to come by, there is relatively little evidence to suggest that this stability is actually driven by partisan-motivated reasoning (Green et al., 2002). I look for evidence of party identity justification as an indicator of the influence of partisan motivation. If individuals attempt to rationalize away disagreement with their party, we can be assured that partisan motivation does exist. Otherwise, there would be no reason to produce such justifications. Chapter 2 focuses specifically on the notion of "lesser of two evils" identity justification. As partisans' attitudes toward their own party wane, they may nonetheless justify continued identification with that party if their attitudes toward the other party remain even more negative. Chapter 3 investigates identity justification via issue reprioritization. When partisans come to evaluate their party negatively on a particular issue dimension, they may simply reweight their priorities in favor of issues on which they do agree with their party.

Chapter 4 considers whether partisan stability is actually contingent on one's ability to justify his or her party identity. If partisan stability is contingent on the ability to justify maintaining party identity, then, absent the ability to justify one's identity, we should see evidence of party identification change.

Chapter 5 investigates the psychological tension between partisan motivation and responsiveness motivation within the context of public opinion surveys. Whereas much of the existing literature on party identification debates whether partisans update their identity to reflect their evaluations or whether such findings result from measurement error, Chapter 5 seeks a partial reconciliation. Surveys create psychological tension by making inconsistencies between party identification and political attitudes salient. Because respondents feel a need to maintain cognitive consistency without violating

---

3. Throughout this book, disagreement will be operationally defined as taking an issue position closer to that of the opposition party than to one's own party. People sometimes take positions that are more ideologically extreme than that of their party, and this may be reasonably characterized as disagreement with one's party. However, because this position is still closer to the position of their own party than to that of the opposition party, this type of disagreement causes relatively little cognitive dissonance (and therefore relatively little pressure to adjust one's identity). For the purposes of this book, such people are considered to be in agreement with their party.

norms against overt partisan bias, they update their identity to reflect their evaluations. However, these changes are undone as individuals rationalize away the inconsistency and seek new justifications for their original identity over the course of the survey. Therefore, variation that might otherwise be called measurement error offers important insights into the dynamics of party identification. The psychological tensions at play within the survey context are the same as those that exist in the real world.

Chapter 6 asks, regardless of how motivated people are to change their party identity, what is the root of this responsiveness motivation? Do partisans change their identity because they wish to identify with the party that offers them the most policy benefits, or do people update their identity in order to conform to norms of civic duty and pragmatism? In other words, is partisan updating instrumental to the attainment of policy benefits, or does partisan updating result from the need to express one's pragmatism?

Finally, Chapter 7 discusses the implications of the dual motivations theory for understanding of the role of party identity in democracy. Particular attention is paid to the efficiency of party identification as a voting heuristic, implications for parties' institutional role in government, and what to make of the polarized state of contemporary American politics.

Competing Motives in the Partisan Mind

CHAPTER 1

A Dual Motivations Theory

If we know one thing about voter behavior, it is that most citizens vote their party identity most of the time. By and large, Republicans vote for Republican candidates, and Democrats vote for Democratic candidates. In fact, studies show that party identification is the most powerful predictor of Americans' voting behavior (Campbell, Converse, Miller, & Stokes, 1960; Lewis-Beck, Jacoby, Norpoth, & Weisberg, 2008). However, the implications of this empirical regularity continue to vex scholars. Does party identification serve as an efficient shortcut that helps voters with incomplete information make vote choices that nonetheless reflect their interests? Or does it function as a filter that motivates people to disregard disagreements with their party so that they may remain loyal to their team?

Political parties simplify politics by narrowing the set of choices for democratic citizens. Because voters have relatively little time or incentive to gather information about politics (Downs, 1957), such a shortcut or "heuristic" may play an important role in supplementing voter competence. As long as citizens identify with a party that reflects their interests, party cues will help guide them to candidates who will represent those interests. In other words, even without much information, party identification may allow citizens to vote as if they were relatively well-informed.

However, while voters need not be particularly attentive to politics for party identification to function as an efficient shortcut, they must be *motivated* to identify with the party that best represents their policy interests and therefore *willing* to update their party identity to reflect their disagreements and negative evaluations. If party loyalties instead motivate citizens to maintain their identity despite disagreements and negative evaluations, party identification no longer approximates voters' policy interests and therefore ceases to function as an efficient shortcut.[1] In fact, it represents a biased approximation

---

1. Although we tend to think of the two major parties as standing for particular issue positions and ideologies, there is no reason this must be true. In fact, party platforms have evolved considerably over time as new issues have arisen and

of voters' interests and causes ostensibly competent citizens to favor candidates they might otherwise oppose. In short, we must understand what *motivates* partisans if we hope to understand whether our most powerful predictor of political behavior helps or hinders voter competence. The stakes of this debate could not be higher. After 50 years, the question remains whether party identification facilitates democratic accountability or undermines it.

THE NATURE AND STABILITY OF PARTY IDENTIFICATION

The dispute over the nature and stability of party identification is longstanding. For years, scholars have debated whether partisanship is better characterized as a highly stable socialized identity (Campbell et al., 1960; Green, Palmquist, & Schickler, 2002; Green & Palmquist, 1990, 1994; Miller, 1991; Miller & Shanks, 1996) or as a readily updated summary measure of political attitudes[2] (Achen, 1992, 2002; Allsop & Weisberg, 1988; Brody & Rothenberg, 1988; Fiorina, 1981; Franklin, 1984, 1992; Franklin & Jackson, 1983; Jackson, 1975; MacKuen, Erikson, & Stimson, 1989; Page & Jones, 1979; Weinschenk, 2010). Originally, party identification was thought to be virtually immune to influence (Campbell et al., 1960). It affected voting behavior and political

---

each party has attempted to outflank the other in an effort to build a winning coalition (for examples, see Sundquist, 1983; Carmines and Stimson, 1989). As Aldrich (1995) explains, parties exist to win elections. To the degree that parties stand for particular sets of issue positions or ideologies, it is only to fulfill voter demands. The institutional structure of American politics forces elected officials to adapt, because those who are not willing to give voters what they want will be replaced by someone who is. Thus, candidates who offer winning policy packages (whatever those may be) gain control of party brands. The effectiveness of this system hinges on voters' motivation to voice clear policy demands. If voters become committed to party labels rather than to a set of issues or an ideology, accountability disappears. Moreover, even if voters attempt to hold parties accountable on the basis of ideology, accountability is lost if voters rely on party cues to signal "what goes with what." In such cases, the logic of accountability becomes circular.

2. Throughout this book, the terms "attitude" and "evaluation" will be used interchangeably, but, as discussed later, both of these terms are considered distinct from "identity." Attitudes are, by definition, evaluative in nature (Eagly & Chaiken, 1993), whereas identities are rooted in self-conceptualization (Campbell et al., 1960; Campbell, Gurin, & Miller, 1954; Green et al., 2002; Monroe, Hankin, & Van Vechten, 2000).

attitudes across the board, yet nothing seemed to affect party identification. According to the classic Michigan model, party identification develops early in life and remains highly stable thereafter. Because partisanship constitutes an identity, partisans feel an affective attachment and a motivation to maintain their party loyalty. When attitudes and party identity come into conflict, the inconsistency is almost always resolved in favor of the latter. Therefore, party identification is characterized as a "perceptual screen" through which disagreeable information is filtered out.

More recently, however, "revisionist" researchers have shown that individuals' policy positions (Carsey & Layman, 2006; Dancey & Goren, 2010; Franklin, 1992; Franklin & Jackson, 1983; Jackson, 1975; Highton & Kam, 2011; Lavine, Johnston, & Steenbergen, 2012), retrospective performance evaluations (Fiorina, 1981; Weinschenk, 2010), candidate evaluations (Page & Jones, 1979), and past votes (Markus & Converse, 1979) affect individuals' party identities. Such findings are bolstered by studies showing variation in party identification over time at the individual level (Brody & Rothenberg, 1988) and at the aggregate level (Allsop & Weisberg, 1988; Box-Steffensmeier & Smith, 1996; MacKuen et al., 1989). In contrast to the Michigan model, revisionist models often characterize party identification as a "running tally" of political evaluations (Fiorina, 1981). In doing so, revisionists are able to explain why party identification tends to stabilize in adulthood despite partisans' lifelong openness to change. In this framework, also known as Bayesian learning, the stability of party identification increases as individuals gain confidence in their understanding of the parties' positions relative to their own (Achen, 1992, 2002; Franklin, 1984). In other words, and perhaps counterintuitively, revisionist theories suggest that partisan stability results from a willingness to update one's identity in response to new information. As more and more knowledge is accumulated about the parties' positions, each additional piece of information has a smaller effect on party identity. Therefore, motivated reasoning and identity defense need not play any role at all.

Swimming against the revisionist tide, Donald Green and colleagues have found that party identification change all but disappears when random measurement error is taken into account (Green & Palmquist, 1990, 1994; Green et al., 2002).[3] They argue that party identification change, rather than fluctuating with short-term forces as revisionist works contend, occurs very

---

3. But see Lavine et al. (2012), who show that ambivalent partisans change their identity to reflect their issue positions even after accounting for measurement error. Under this model, partisan defenses wear down after extended periods of ambivalence.

gradually, if at all, as party images slowly evolve (Green et al., 2002). In making this claim, they stress the vital distinction between evaluation and identification. As they see it, identities remain stable because they are rooted in the way people think of *themselves* rather than in how they evaluate parties. Thus, partisans may hold attitudes that conflict with their identity without feeling any pressure to update their identity, as revisionists argue, or to defend their identity, as the Michigan model argues.

> Like those scholars who emphasize the rational underpinnings of public opinion, we are skeptical of the notion that partisans ignore or reinterpret discordant information....People may assimilate new information about the parties and change their perceptions of the parties without changing the team for which they cheer....As people reflect on whether they are Democrats or Republicans (or neither), they call to mind some mental image, or stereotype, of what these sorts of people are like and square these images with their own self-conceptions (Green et al., 2002, pp. 7–8).

In short, Green and colleagues disagree with revisionists regarding the effect of attitudes on party identification, but they agree that motivated reasoning has little or no role to play. Rather than defending their party identity, citizens are highly responsive to new information and willing to objectively evaluate the world around them (Gerber & Green, 1999; Green et al., 2002). Revisionist models simply argue that partisans update their identity to reflect these evaluations, whereas Green and colleagues contend that party identification is unaffected by evaluations.

Despite these claims, there exists a good deal of evidence to suggest that partisans engage in motivated reasoning to avoid holding attitudes that conflict with their party identity. For instance, Goren (2002, 2007) found that partisans hold candidates of the opposing party to higher character standards than they hold their own party's candidates.[4] Partisans also blame the opposition party for poor performance while allowing their own party to avoid accountability (Lebo & Cassino, 2007; Malhotra & Kuo, 2008; Rudolph 2003, 2006; Tilley & Hobolt, 2011). They also evaluate the state of the economy more favorably (Bartels, 2002; Duch, Palmer, & Anderson, 2000; Gerber & Huber, 2010) and perceive fewer military casualties to have occurred when their own party is in power (Berinsky, 2009).[5] In addition, partisans tend to take the issue positions of their party even when those positions conflict with

---

4. Also see Fischle's (2000) demonstration of how individuals' feelings toward Bill Clinton affected their response to the Lewinsky scandal.
5. But see Lewis-Beck, Nadeau, and Elias (2008).

their own ideology (Cohen, 2003). Party identification even shapes the values citizens endorse (Goren, 2005; Goren, Federico, & Kittilson, 2007). And these microlevel processes do not appear to wash out when opinions are aggregated (Bartels, 1996; Zaller, 1992). In short, these studies suggest that partisans are motivated to maintain their team loyalty by avoiding disagreement with their preferred party, just as the Michigan model originally argued.

Therefore, despite important strides toward understanding the nature of party identification, the field remains far from consensus. Party identification appears to be quite stable, but perhaps not entirely stable. Party identities may be largely devoid of issue content, or they may constitute running tallies of objective political evaluations. Thus, party identification may act as a drag on democratic accountability, or it may function as a highly efficient information shortcut.

This book's dual motivations theory of party identification offers a framework through which these competing approaches may be reconciled.[6] On one hand, individuals are motivated to make accurate evaluations, but on the other hand, they are motivated to reach conclusions that favor their party. With this approach, party identification can be seen as the outcome of a *process* through which individuals attempt to reconcile potentially competing motives. Rather than assuming that partisans are simply driven to identify with the party that offers the most preferable policies or positing that partisans are solely driven to maintain their party loyalty, the model allows partisans to feel conflicted. The stability and heuristic value of a person's party identity at any given time is determined by the resolution of this motivational conflict. Partisans must be able to justify continued identification with their party or else change their party identity to reflect their disagreements. If a partisan is able to avoid updating her party identity to reflect her disagreements, then her party identification loses its efficiency as an information shortcut.

By characterizing party identification in this way, it is possible to generate falsifiable hypotheses regarding the conditions under which partisans are likely to defend their identity and those under which they are likely to change

---

6. The dual motivations approach should not be confused with dual processing models of cognition. Whereas dual processing models focus primarily on the amount of effort an individual puts into evaluation (see Eagly & Chaiken, 1993; Petty & Cacioppo, 1986), dual motivations models focus on where that effort is directed (i.e., accurate evaluation versus desiring a particular evaluative outcome) (see Kunda, 1990). Therefore, although the two types of models are entirely compatible (see Eagly & Chaiken's [1993] discussion of motivation and attitude defense), readers should be careful not to confuse the two approaches.

their identity to reflect their evaluations. Thus, the dual motivations approach facilitates investigation of the central normative question underlying the party identity debate: Does party identification facilitate voter competence, does it undermine voter competence, or is the answer conditional?

Given the polarized state of contemporary American parties (see McCarty, Poole, & Rosenthal, 2006; Theriault, 2008), one of the biggest debates inside and outside the academy concerns what effect this polarization is having on the electorate (Abramowitz, 2010; Abramowitz & Saunders, 2008; Baldassarri & Gelman, 2008; Fiorina, Abrams, & Pope, 2008, 2011; Hetherington, 2001; Levendusky, 2009, 2010; Rae, 2007; Sniderman & Stiglitz, 2012). Is the system in need of reform, or does polarization facilitate responsible party government? Much depends on the motivational assumptions underlying the model. On one hand, internally cohesive and ideologically distinct parties provide voters with clear alternatives (APSA Committee on Political Parties, 1950a, 1950b, 1950c; Hetherington, 2001; Levendusky, 2009, 2010; Ranney, 1954). Such clarity is ideal if one views party identification as a running tally of political evaluations (Achen, 1992, 2002; Fiorina, 1981). When parties take clear and unambiguous stands, citizens can be sure that they have aligned themselves with the party that best represents their interests. If that party then fails to follow through on its campaign promises, voters can realign themselves accordingly.

On the other hand, if one views party identification as a perceptual screen (Campbell et al., 1960), internally cohesive and ideologically distinct parties are substantially less desirable. Clearer distinctions make for clearer rivalries (Sherif, 1956), so partisans will only become more resistant to any information that conflicts with their party identity. And, absent debates between intraparty factions, citizens can blindly follow party cues without ever being forced to weigh policy alternatives or consider the direction their party is moving (see Baldassarri & Gelman [2008] for a related discussion of polarization and pluralism). In short, the logic of responsible parties either holds or gets completely turned on its head, depending on our assumptions regarding citizens' motivations.

The dual motivations approach also provides new insights into the process of political socialization. Scholars have long debated why partisan strength and stability increase with age (Converse, 1969, 1976; Franklin & Jackson, 1983; Jennings & Niemi, 1981). On one hand, partisan stability may result from the accumulation of information about what the parties stand for (Achen, 1992, 2002; Franklin, 1984; Gerber & Green, 1998). On the other hand, party loyalties may simply "crystallize" with age and experience (Alwin & Krosnick, 1991; Brader & Tucker, 2001; Converse, 1969, 1976; Sears & Levy, 2003) as individuals are exposed to successive campaigns (Sears & Valentino, 1997; Valentino & Sears, 1998).

The dual motivations theory suggests another potential stabilizing mechanism: Partisans may become better at justifying their identity as they mature and gain experience with politics. This notion comports well with work by Stoker and Jennings (2009), who sought to explain how partisans have become so polarized (or at least sorted by ideology). They argue that, after party identity becomes crystallized, adult partisans bring their issue positions into increasingly closer alignment with this identity. Given reasonably stable party platforms, this leads partisans to sort themselves into increasingly distinct teams (see also Levendusky, 2009).

This pattern has troubling implications. First, it suggests that the system lacks short-term accountability. Because party identities are thought to drive issue positions rather than vice versa, "Changes in the positions taken by the political parties will, eventually, be reflected in the public, but only after many years and perhaps decades have passed" (Stoker & Jennings, 2009, p. 632). Second, if partisans get better at justifying their identity as they gain experience with politics, the most sophisticated partisans should be best at rationalizing away disagreements (see also Gaines, Kuklinksi, Quirk, Peyton, & Verkuilen 2007; Zaller, 1992). This leads to the counterintuitive and perhaps distressing conclusion that democratic accountability hinges disproportionately on the least experienced and most impressionable citizens.

MOTIVATED REASONING

Psychologists have long been interested in how motivation affects attitudes. Early research spoke to the potential for attitudinal durability even in the face of massive countervailing evidence (Festinger, Rieken, & Schachter, 1956). These studies revealed that individuals are innately driven to maintain cognitive consistency (Festinger, 1957). More recently, research into cognitive dissonance has been incorporated into a more general theory of motivated reasoning (Kunda, 1990). Motivated reasoning theory posits that individuals are driven by two competing forces: accuracy motivation and directional motivation (see Kunda, 1990, 1999; Lodge & Taber, 2000, 2013; Taber, Lodge, & Glather, 2001). Often, individuals have a vested interest in arriving at a particular conclusion. For example, when evaluating sports teams, fans tend to be motivated to see qualities in their favored team and faults in the opposition. This is an example of directional motivation. However, this drive may be offset by a competing motivation to reach an accurate evaluation—particularly if there is something at stake. For instance, if an individual is evaluating sports teams in order to decide on which team to place a wager, the motivation to see one's favored team in a positive light would almost certainly be tempered by the incentive to win the wager.

A recent voting experiment illustrated how this type of incentive structure can affect political behavior. Bassi, Morton, and Williams (2011) assigned participants to arbitrary groups in the tradition of the "minimal groups" paradigm (see Tajfel, Billig, Bundy, & Flament, 1971). The idea behind this method is to induce group identification that is empty of content. After being assigned to a group, participants were asked to participate in a series of voting games. In these games, the researchers varied the information participants received about other voters and the size of the payoffs they could expect to obtain. They found that the "minimal group identities" of participants influenced their voting behavior, especially when voters' actions were seen as less consequential (either because they lacked sufficient information to make a strategic choice or because they expected only a small payoff). These results illustrate the tradeoff between directional and accuracy motivation as well as the power of identity in shaping these motives.

In addition to material incentives such as wagers and voting game payoffs, research has also shown that accuracy motivation can be triggered when people expect to have to justify their evaluations to their peers. Experimental evidence suggests that individuals engage in more thorough processing (Tetlock & Kim, 1987) and show less bias (Kunda, 1990) when they expect to be held accountable for the positions they take. Likewise, people who participate in deliberative forums where they are encouraged to think pragmatically show effects similar to those of counterparts in laboratory experiments designed to induce social accountability (Barabas, 2004). Such results indicate that there is value in the *appearance* of pragmatism. Regardless of whether they can expect their evaluations to be consequential, individuals need to prove to themselves and their audience that their positions are well-reasoned. "Failure to behave in ways for which one can construct acceptable accounts leads to varying degrees of censure—depending, of course, on the gravity of the offense" (Tetlock, Skitka, & Boettger, 1989). Therefore, just as material incentives may increase accuracy motivation, the incentive to conform to societal norms of pragmatism may also increase accuracy motivation. As Kuklinski, Quirk, Jerit, and Rich (2001) explain, citizens' actions are so unlikely to affect the outcome of any given election that democracy provides individuals with relatively little incentive to weigh issues carefully. Thus, to the degree they are motivated to think carefully, they must be responding to pleas for responsible decision-making. In other words, they must be conforming to norms of civic duty rather than acting on self-interest.

Mutz (1998) expands on this social accountability effect by suggesting that individuals engage in "internalized conversations with perceptions of collective opinion" (p. 23). In an era of 24-hour news and constant public opinion polling, social pressures can be felt even without interpersonal communication.

> When they [citizens] learn that a particular candidate or issue is popular or unpopular, their implicit interaction[s] with these generalized others prompt them to alter or refine their own political views (Mutz, 1998, p. 23).

In short, individuals may feel social pressure to conform to norms of pragmatism even if they do not anticipate having to directly discuss their opinions with their peers.

However, experimental research also shows that, once individuals commit to a position on a political issue, they devote the bulk of their mental effort to justifying that position rather than reexamining it (Tetlock et al., 1989). People are motivated to defend their positions because they "do not want to appear to lack the courage of their convictions" (Tetlock et al., 1989, p. 633). In other words, once a person commits to a particular position, directional motivation takes hold. This strategy allows individuals to appear pragmatic and justified in their position without "flip-flopping."

Investigations in neuroscience support the idea that directional motivation influences the way people process political information. When individuals encounter information that is threatening to their favored candidate, regions of the brain associated with emotion and motivation become activated while regions associated with "cold" reasoning and emotion regulation remain inactive (Westen, Blagov, Harenski, Kilts, & Hamann, 2006).

Similarly, social psychologists have found that directional motivation biases the cognitive processes involved in judgment formation. For example, when led to believe that a particular self-concept (introversion or extroversion) was related to academic success, subjects in a series of experiments came to see themselves as possessing the desired trait (Kunda & Sanitioso, 1989). Analysis of memory-listing and response time data showed that these self-assessments result from biased memory search (Sanitioso, Kunda, & Fong, 1990). The same process may be at work when it comes to stereotyping. Fein and Spencer (1997) found that, after having their self-image threatened by negative performance feedback, individuals became more likely to derogate a stereotyped outgroup in order to facilitate a favorable social comparsison. This act of derogation raised their self-esteem back up to its baseline level.

In short, research shows that the need to see one's self in a favorable light leads individuals to unconsciously access memories and stereotypes that support desired conclusions. These directional biases should be most pronounced when accuracy motivation is low. However, directional motivation can exert an influence even when accuracy motivation is high as long as it can be justified. "When one wants to draw a particular conclusion, one feels obligated to construct a justification for that conclusion that would be plausible to a dispassionate observer" (Kunda, 1990). In other words, directional motivation is capable of exerting a powerful influence on reasoning, but this influence is contingent on one's capacity to justify or rationalize that judgment.

COMPETING MOTIVES UNDERLYING PARTY IDENTIFICATION

By applying motivated reasoning theory to the literature on party identification, it is easy to see how a dual motivations theory may help us to understand the conditions under which party identification changes or remains stable. In *The American Voter* (Campbell et al., 1960), party identification is portrayed as a source of directional motivation. People feel this directional motivation because group identification provides symbolic and expressive rewards (see Akerlof & Kranton, 2000). Just like sports fans, partisans take pleasure in cheering on their team, *not* because they believe their cheers will affect the outcome of the game, but because it fulfills their basic human need to belong (Baumeister & Leary, 1995; Van Vugt & Hart, 2004; Van Vugt & Shaller, 2008) and because a victory for the group is felt as a victory for the self (Greene, 1999, 2004). As Darwin (1890) originally explained, the need to form and maintain group allegiances stems from the evolutionary advantage it provides.

> With those animals which were benefited by living in close association, the individuals which took the greatest pleasure in society would best escape various dangers, while those that cared least for their comrades, and lived solitary, would perish in greater numbers (Darwin, 1890, p. 105).

In short, to rationalize away disagreements with one's own party may appear irrational, but this motivation is highly advantageous from an evolutionary standpoint. Strong group bonds facilitate survival. Given the present context, I will refer to this specific type of directional motivation as *partisan* motivation.

In contrast to the Michigan model of party identification, revisionist models assume that party identification is driven largely by accuracy motivation—or the desire to hold an identity that accurately reflects one's positions relative to those of the respective parties. Identification with the "correct" party is considered to be instrumental to the maximization of policy benefits and therefore desirable (Achen, 1992; 2002; Shively, 1979). Under such models, individuals identify with the party that offers the most favorable policy proposals and vote for that party in order to increase the likelihood that its policies will be implemented. Although there is significant variation in the scholarship generally considered under the umbrella of "revisionist work," scholars of the revisionist camp share the view that partisans are responsive to their information environment. Therefore, I will refer to the drive for accuracy in party identification as *responsiveness* motivation.

Again, it is worth calling attention to the contrasting portraits of the partisan drawn by the Michigan model versus the revisionist model. On one hand, we have the fan whose motives are *partisan* through and through. The fan is hopelessly blinded by his own biases, because he derives his utility from his team allegiance. He wants his team to win year in and year out regardless of the team's composition or style of play. His affection is unconditional. On the other hand, we have the good citizen whose party identity is purely a reflection of her ongoing political evaluations. The good citizen is *responsive* to the information she receives, because she is motivated to hold her party accountable. Her party identity may be stable, but this commitment is conditional. If the party fails to live up to her expectations, she will change her allegiance without hesitation. Thus, in the absence of other information, she can trust that her party identity will function as an efficient shortcut and reliably guide her to candidates who share her issue positions.

Both images seem caricatured. The dual motivations theory attempts to meld insights from the two approaches, allowing the fan and the good citizen to coexist in the mind of the partisan. In this model, partisans have both *responsiveness* motivation and *partisan* motivation. The probability of changing one's party identity to reflect a given evaluation is modeled as a function of one's *responsiveness* motivation relative to *partisan* motivation.

A Dual Motivations Model

Although it is important to maintain the conceptual distinction between identities and attitudes (Green et al., 2002; Groenendyk, 2012; Rosema, 2006), individuals may nonetheless feel psychological pressure to maintain consistency between their attitudes and their identity when discrepancies between them become salient (Campbell et al., 1960; Groenendyk, 2012). In its simplest form, party identification at a given time (P_t) can be modeled as a function of past party identification (P_{t-1}) and evaluations (E_t) based on party performance and issue positions:

$$P_t = B_0 + B_1 E_t + B_2 P_{t-1} + u_t \tag{1}$$

However, the central question is not whether political attitudes cause changes in party identification but whether inconsistencies between evaluations and party identification weaken one's identity. This is an important distinction, because it is not disputed that agreement with one's party may strengthen party identification. The crux of the debate pertains to whether party identification acts as a "filter" for disagreeable information or whether disagreement with one's party weakens party identification (Campbell et al., 1960). Even in a perfectly biased world where partisans filter out all information that conflicts with their party identity, individuals may nonetheless update their identity to reflect their attitudes when they agree with their party. This fits the known pattern whereby party identification becomes stronger with age and experience (Alwin & Krosnick, 1991; Brader & Tucker, 2001; Converse, 1969, 1976; Sears & Levy, 2003; Stoker & Jennings, 2009). In short, a demonstration that party identification changes with attitudes is not necessarily evidence against partisan filtering. In fact, given that the standard scale runs from strong Republican to strong Democrat, shifts in party identification may result from weakening of identification with one party, strengthening of identification with the other, or both. Therefore, the key question is not just whether party identification changes with attitudes, but whether, when individuals become aware of inconsistencies between their attitudes and their party identity, they report weaker identification. To this end, party identification (P_t) is replaced with strength of party identification (S_t) in the model, and partisans who cross over from one party to the other are coded as having a strength of zero.[7] Evaluation (E_t) is replaced with agreement (A_t) and disagreement (D_t) with one's party.

$$S_t = B_0 + B_1 A_t + B_2 D_t + B_3 S_{t-1} + u_t \tag{2}$$

Turning to the motivational element of the model, individuals have both responsiveness motivation (R) and partisan motivation (M). When a partisan agrees (A) with her party, partisan motivation (M) only serves to reinforce

---

7. By "crossing over from one party to the other," I mean those partisans who report identifying with or leaning toward one party at time t-1 and then report identifying with or leaning toward the other party at time t.

responsiveness motivation (R). However, when disagreements arise, partisan and responsiveness motives come into conflict. The amount of influence exerted by partisan motivation is subject to the ability to justify (J) one's party identity. In other words, individuals must be able to rationalize their biases. Whereas the M-term accounts for an individual's *motivation* to maintain her party identity, the J-term accounts for her *ability* to justify acting on that motivation.[8] Partisan motivation may be powerful, but individuals must be able to maintain their sense of pragmatism (Campbell et al., 1960; Kunda, 1990).[9] Therefore, in addition to having the motivation, one must have the ability to justify continued identification. Adding in the motivational and justification components, party identification strength (S_t) can be modeled as follows:

$$S_t = B_0 + B_1 A(R + MJ) + B_2 D(R - MJ) + B_3 S_{t-1} + u_t \tag{3}$$

Because motivations cannot be measured directly, there are no coefficients associated with these terms in the model. They only serve to inflate or deflate the effects of agreement and disagreement on party identification strength. However, reasonable proxies for the J-term (ability to justify party identity) do exist, such as experience with politics, political sophistication, and other indicators of cognitive resources. Because the influence of partisan motivation (M) is contingent on the ability to justify partisan outcomes (J), explicit inclusion of J in the model makes it possible to estimate the effects of agreement (A) and disagreement (D) when J, and therefore M, are equal to zero.

If partisan stability turns out to be contingent on the ability to justify maintaining one's identity, partisan motivation will have an important role to play in stabilizing party identification: Evidence of identity defense suggests a motivation to defend. Another way to think about this is that such a result would indicate a cost to partisan updating—specifically, the cost of forgoing

8. This book remains agnostic with regard to whether such processes must be conscious. Presumably, with rehearsal, justifications become automatic and occur outside of consciousness (Bargh & Chartrand, 1999). This may help to explain why increased partisan stability and partisan strength are observed with increased age. Still, this issue remains outside the scope of this book.

9. Lavine et al. (2012) argue that, after extended periods of partisan ambivalence, people lose their motivation to justify continued identification, and party identification changes. At least in this respect, their theory is entirely consistent with this book's dual motivations approach.

benefits that flow from loyal partisanship.[10] Interestingly, this frame suggests a familiar concern for those acquainted with the "paradox of voting": If there is a cost to updating one's party identity, are the benefits of updating sufficient to outweigh this cost?

To answer this question, we must consider what the possible benefits of partisan updating may be. In other words, what incentives underlie responsiveness motivation? Although partisan motivation clearly stems from the value of expressing partisan loyalty, responsiveness motivation is potentially rooted in both instrumental incentives and expressive incentives. Shively (1979) theorized that party identification is *instrumental* to attaining policy benefits, and this assumption underlies much of the revisionist scholarship on party identification. As long as citizens are willing to update their party identity when they receive credible information, party identification may serve as an efficient shortcut, helping individuals who possess incomplete information to vote approximately as if they were well-informed about the candidates' positions (Brady & Sniderman, 1985; Huckfeldt, Levine, Morgan, & Sprague, 1999; Popkin, 1991; Schaffner & Streb, 2002; Shively, 1979; Tomz & Sniderman, 2005).

In considering the degree to which responsiveness motivation stems from such instrumental concerns, it is essential to consider the expected benefit of one's actions relative to their costs. Anthony Downs (1957) famously points out that the probability that a given individual will cast the decisive vote in any major election is approximately zero. Therefore, the policy benefits to be gained from voting "correctly" approach zero. It follows that, as the size of the electorate increases, the expected policy benefits to be gained from responsive partisanship are also vanishingly small. If there are costs associated with partisan disloyalty, it stands to reason that partisan responsiveness is not driven by the quest for policy benefits. This raises the question of whether responsiveness motivation should lead to any amount of party identification change. As Caplan (2007) argues, "irrationality" can be "rational." With so little to be gained from voting "correctly," individual voters may as well do whatever makes them feel good. If this means disregarding credible information and ignoring disagreements in order to reap the benefits of continued party

---

10. These costs are not necessarily constant across changes in party identification. To shift from being a weak identifier to being an independent leaner may be more costly than shifting from a strong partisan to a weak partisan position or from being a partisan leaner to being a pure independent. This amounts to different-sized intervals between levels of party identification and is accounted for in the analyses that follow by the use of ordered probit regression.

identification, then such behavior can be seen as perfectly rational (Akerlof & Kranton, 2000). Yet, partisans appear more responsive than this (Allsop & Weisberg, 1988; Brody & Rothenberg, 1988; Carsey & Layman, 2006; Fiorina, 1981; Franklin, 1984, 1992; Franklin & Jackson, 1983; Jackson, 1975; Highton & Kam, 2011; Lavine et al., 2012; MacKuen, et al., 1989; Markus & Converse, 1979; Page & Jones, 1979), and even the most ardent proponents of stable party identification acknowledge that it would be folly to argue that identities never change (Campbell et al., 1960; Converse & Markus, 1979; Green et al., 2002). What then might explain the motivation to bring one's party identity into alignment with one's disagreements?

I hypothesize that responsiveness motivation is driven by the need to express one's pragmatism and lack of bias, thereby conforming to norms of civic duty. In other words, partisan responsiveness may offer *expressive* rewards.[11] Individuals have an incentive to see themselves as good, unbiased citizens whose party allegiances are grounded in the issues (Campbell et al., 1960; Kunda, 1990). Reinforcing this notion, Kam (2007) found that when citizens were provided subtle reminders of civic duty, they were more likely to learn where candidates stood on issues and search for information in an open-minded way. Schudson (1998) traces this norm back to the nation's founding but argues that its importance was renewed during the Progressive Era. He explains that, in the backlash against the party machines of the late 19th century, "the new model of citizenship called for a voter more intelligent than loyal" (p. 182). In short, there is reason to believe that partisans may update their identity to demonstrate their pragmatism and lack of bias even if the expected policy benefits of partisan updating are very small. They do this because "good citizens" consider the issues and not just the party.

Readers familiar with the "paradox of voting" literature will recognize that this reformulation of responsiveness motivation builds directly on the voter calculus model proposed by Riker and Ordeshook (1968), in which the *expressive* value of affirming one's civic duty is captured by the (in)famous "D-term." According to Riker and Ordeshook, if these expressive benefits are high enough to offset the cost of voting, then voters will turn out on election day.[12] Riker and Ordeshook model the rewards to be derived from voting as a

---

11. See Fiorina (1976) and Schuessler (2000) for extensive discussions of instrumental versus expressive utility.
12. Although individuals' misperceptions of their potential for influence (p) may increase the influence of B, empirical investigations suggest that one's sense of civic duty is the dominant driver of turnout in this model (Barry, 1970; Riker & Ordeshook, 1968).

function of the probability of casting the decisive vote (p), the policy benefits to be gained by the preferred party winning (B), the cost of turning out to vote (C), and the expressive benefits of voting (D):

$$Rewards = pB - C + D \tag{4}$$

To apply this logic to party identification, responsiveness motivation can simply be substituted for rewards in the Riker and Ordeshook model. However, the D-term is meant to capture a somewhat broader concept of civic duty—not just the value of turning out to vote but the importance of considering the issues in an unbiased and pragmatic manner. Dalton (2008) refers to this aspect of citizenship as "autonomy."[13] In my model, responsiveness motivation (R) is derived from the probability of one's vote determining the outcome of the election (p), the policy benefits associated with the preferred election outcome (B), and the expressive benefits that come from seeing oneself as an unbiased and pragmatic citizen—an aspect of civic duty (D).

As noted earlier, the cost of partisan updating flows from partisan motivation (M). To act on responsiveness motivation (R) and update one's party identity to reflect disagreement (D) entails incurring the costs of disloyal partisanship (or forgoing the benefits of acting on one's partisan motivation). Therefore, C is replaced with M in the party identification model. In the case of agreement (A) with one's party, to act on one's responsiveness motivation (R) also means acting on one's partisan motivation (M), so M is added (as a benefit) rather than being subtracted (as a cost). Substituting for R in the full model yields the following:

$$S_t = B_0 + B_1 A_t (pB + D + MJ) + B_2 D_t (pB + D - MJ) + B_3 S_{t-1} + u_t \tag{5}$$

In summary, both responsiveness motivation (R) and partisan motivation (M) have the potential to influence the strength of one's party identification (S_t). To the degree that responsiveness motivation has an influence, agreement (A) and disagreement (D) will both affect party identification. And to the degree that partisan motivation has an influence, disagreement will affect party identification less. Since the probability of influencing policy (p) is expected to be low, responsiveness motivation is expected to primarily be a function of one's

---

13. In his analysis of data from the 2004 General Social Survey (GSS) and the 2005 Citizens, Involvement, and Democracy Survey (CDACS), Dalton found that Americans' ideas about what it means to be a good citizen loaded onto two distinct dimensions—one that picked up norms of participation and deference to the law and another that captured several constructs including autonomy.

desire to appear as a good, pragmatic citizen (D) (Barry, 1970). However, if an individual can convince herself through rationalization and justification (J) that her partisan motives (M) are rooted in pragmatism, then disagreement will not undermine party identification. Next, I outline specific hypotheses derived from the theory.

HYPOTHESES

The Michigan model of party identification suggests that partisan stability stems from motivated psychological processing—the famous perceptual screen (Campbell et al., 1960). More recently, however, revisionist scholars have demonstrated that partisan stability can be theoretically accounted for through a simple Bayesian learning model—without partisan motivation playing a role (Achen, 1992, 2002). As was suggested earlier, to accept this account of partisan stability is not merely a move toward parsimony but a significant theoretical departure from the Michigan model with enormous normative implications. Under this revisionist model, party identification functions as a perfectly efficient shortcut, and the powerful influence of partisanship on virtually all aspects of political life is of no concern. This places the onus on proponents of the Michigan model to demonstrate the existence and impact of partisan motivation. To demonstrate the stability of party identification is not enough to prove the existence of partisan motivation, because such findings can be explained through Bayesian learning. If partisan motivation has an influence, we should see evidence of this motivation.

Classic work on cognitive dissonance suggests that individuals attempt to reduce cognitive dissonance via a process known as "bolstering" (Abelson, 1959; Festinger, 1957). This involves justification of an attitude, behavior, or group association by calling to mind consonant attitudes to offset dissonant attitudes. To borrow Festinger's classic example, a smoker may call to mind the pleasure she gets from smoking because her behavior is dissonant with her knowledge of the dangers associated with smoking. She could instead reduce the dissonance by quitting her habit, but this would require great effort. Similarly, a partisan might call to mind (or place greater importance on) attitudes consonant with her party identity to justify continued allegiance despite holding an attitude dissonant with her party identity. Alternatively, she could simply change her party identity to reflect the disagreement with her party, but this would be costly, just at it would be costly for the smoker to quit her habit. In short, justification via cognitive bolstering offers an ideal solution for the conflicted partisan, because it allows her to reduce her dissonance without changing her party identity or denying credible information (which would violate norms of civic duty).

If partisans engage in this type of behavior to justify maintenance of their party allegiance, evidence should not be difficult to find. I will therefore look for examples of party identity justification in instances in which individuals disagree with or negatively evaluate their party. If partisan motivation does not play a role in stabilizing party identification, no evidence of identity justification should be found. Partisans should simply update their identity to reflect their disagreement.

H1: Justification Hypothesis

When partisans disagree with their party, they will attempt to justify their existing party identity.

If evidence of party identity justification emerges, this will provide evidence that partisan motivation exists. However, the theory suggests not only that partisan motivation exists but that identity stability is contingent on one's motivation and ability to justify one's identity. When partisans disagree with their party, they devote their cognitive resources to justifying their existing party identity rather than updating their identity to reflect their disagreement. However, because some citizens are better equipped than others to perform these sorts of justifications, the probability of party identity change should be greater among those who have the fewest cognitive resources available to them. Political sophistication and experience serve as cognitive resources that make some individuals inherently better at justifying their identity, but variable factors such as political context and working memory availability should matter as well.

H2: Cognitive Resources Hypothesis

When cognitive resources are limited, partisans will be more likely to bring their identity into alignment with their attitudes.

These first two hypotheses pertain to partisan motivation, suggesting that party identity change occurs when individuals are unable to justify maintaining their identity. But what factors might increase responsiveness motivation such that individuals will update their party identity to reflect their evaluations? I hypothesize that responsiveness motivation should exert its most powerful influence on party identification when individuals' evaluations of parties are made salient to them *before* their party identification is considered—as is often the case in public opinion surveys. Under such circumstances, individuals may find it difficult to maintain a stable party identity, at least momentarily, as a result of their need for cognitive consistency. However, any changes in party identification should quickly dissipate as individuals justify returning to their original identity. In a survey context, evidence of justification should be evident in subsequent responses.

Although the existing literature on party identification is filled with conflicting findings, the dual motivations theory may help to illuminate the underlying source of this conflict. One important debate is between those who believe that partisans update their identity (Allsop & Weisberg, 1988; Brody & Rothenberg, 1988; Carsey & Layman, 2006; Dancey & Goren, 2010; Fiorina, 1981; Franklin, 1984, 1992; Franklin & Jackson, 1983; Jackson, 1975; Highton & Kam, 2011; Lavine et al., 2012; MacKuen et al., 1989; Markus & Converse, 1979; Page & Jones, 1979) and those who believe that most variation in party identification over time is attributable merely to measurement error (Green & Palmquist, 1990, 1994; Green et al., 2002; Green & Schickler, 1993). While these findings seem to be totally at odds with each another, there may be a good deal of truth to both.

If individuals adjust their party identity in the short term to reflect evaluations made salient to them in surveys, this constitutes important evidence of responsiveness motivation. Even if such effects are short-lived, these results suggest that partisans have a desire to appear pragmatic and a willingness to act on this desire. Yet, these individuals should also be motivated to maintain their party identity, so over the course of a survey, their efforts to return to their party identity should also be evident. Whereas responses provided before party identification measures are likely to drive partisan updating, responses provided after party identification should show evidence of identity justification and lead to subsequent identity reversion.

If party identification fluctuates within the context of a single survey, such variation may reasonably be characterized as measurement error. But doing so neglects the significance of this variation for understanding the nature of party identification. Examination of partisans' survey behavior may provide us with a window into the partisan mind and the process underlying party identification. If individuals are motivated to maintain consistency between their attitudes and their identity in the context of a survey, there is no reason why such motivations should not exert themselves in other situations as well. Of course, if identity justification allows individuals to return to their prior party identification, this is also likely to occur outside of the survey context.

H3: Saliency Hypothesis

Individuals will update their identity to reflect their attitudes when these attitudes are made salient prior to reporting their party identity. However, subsequent identity justification—observable in subjects' responses—will undo these changes in party identification.

If partisans feel pressure to update their identity when they are made conscious of their discrepant evaluations, the question remains whether this motivation is rooted in the incentive to identify with the party that offers the most favorable policies or the need to appear pragmatic and unbiased by partisanship. The dual motivations theory of party identification suggests that responsiveness motivation should be rooted much more in the latter than in the former. If there are psychological costs to updating one's party identity and the expected policy payoff of partisan updating approaches zero, consideration of policy stakes should have little impact on party identification. In other words, contrary to conventional wisdom, party identification should not be affected by consideration of the policies parties propose to enact upon taking power. Instead, partisan responsiveness is hypothesized to be a social norm associated with civic duty. Therefore, acting responsively and updating one's party identity to reflect evaluations is likely to provide expressive rewards in and of itself—independent of any effect partisan updating may have on policy benefits.

H4: Duty Hypothesis

Responsiveness motivation, and therefore partisan change, will be driven by the desire to appear unbiased and pragmatic, thereby conforming to norms of civic duty. Consequently, partisan identity updating will increase when norms of civic duty are made salient.

H5: Stakes Hypothesis

Party identification will *not* be affected by consideration of the policies the parties will attempt to enact upon taking power. Therefore, partisan identity updating will *not* increase when the policies at stake in an election are made salient.

These five hypotheses will be tested in the chapters that follow. Although alternative theories may explain the results of any one of these tests individually, each test is designed to build on the last, so that as the book progresses, alternative explanations may be ruled out until only the dual motivations theory remains plausible. Chapters 2 and 3 test the *justification hypothesis* using experiments and data from the American National Election Studies (ANES). Each focuses on a different justification method: the "lesser of two evils" defense and the issue reprioritization defense. Chapter 4 tests the *cognitive resources hypothesis* through a national experiment in which disagreement with one's party and cognitive resources are each manipulated. In Chapter 5, the *saliency hypothesis* is tested in another national experiment—this time focusing on Republican identifiers at a time when their attitudes and party identities were particularly likely to conflict with one another. Chapter 6 tests the *duty hypothesis* and the *stakes hypothesis* with data from the 2004 GSS and a third national experiment in which subjects were primed to consider either what it means to be a good citizen, the policies implications at stake in an upcoming election, or nothing at all. Chapter 7 summarizes all these results and considers both normative and empirical implications of the findings.

CHAPTER 2

Identity Justification

Identifying with the "Lesser of Two Evils"

Are partisans motivated to maintain stable party identities even when their party does something they disagree with? If so, how would we know? Given the stability of party identification, Campbell, Converse, Miller, and Stokes (1960) theorized that partisans screen out disagreeable information. Revisionist scholars disagree, suggesting instead that partisans are motivated to hold party identities that accurately reflect their issue positions and political evaluations (Achen, 1992, 2002; Fiorina, 1981; Franklin, 1984, 1992; Franklin & Jackson, 1983; Jackson, 1975; MacKuen, Erikson, & Stimson, 1989; Shively, 1979; Weinschenk, 2010). For revisionists, partisan stability arises, not from identity defense, but from the accumulation of information regarding party platforms (Achen, 1992, 2002; Franklin, 1984). In other words, people settle into stable party identities as they become better acquainted with the parties' positions.

Green and colleagues point out that much hinges on the assumption that party positions are stable. If party platforms change, the model no longer predicts stable party identification (Gerber & Green, 1998; Green, Palmquist, & Schickler, 2002). In their 2002 book, Green and colleagues propose a model in which partisan stability results from the persistence of party stereotypes (see Hilton & von Hippel, 1996). They stress that partisans evaluate parties quite objectively, but party identification does not rest on these evaluations. Instead, partisans determine their identity by asking themselves how well their self-image matches their image of each of the parties. As long as their stereotypes persist, their party identity persist. Identity defense plays no part in the equation.

In short, the party identification literature has begun to turn away from the notion that partisans are motivated to protect their identities, and many now embrace the revisionist assumption that partisans are *willing* to change their identities even if those identities tend to be stable. This places the onus on proponents of the classic Michigan model (see Chapter 1) to provide evidence, not only of partisan stability, but of actual identity defense. Although this may seem like a minor difference between theories, the significance of these assumptions should not be underestimated. As outlined in the previous chapter, the normative implications of partisan behavior diverge dramatically depending on whether partisans are motivated to update their identities or to defend them. On one hand, party identification serves as a highly efficient shortcut that guides individuals through the complexities of politics, but on the other hand, party identification causes individuals to disregard valuable information and leads them astray in the voting booth.

EXAMINING THE NATURE OF PARTISAN STABILITY

Cowden and McDermott (2000) took a novel approach to the party identification debate by attempting to test the Michigan and revisionist models of party identification against one another in an experimental context. In one experiment, the authors examined the claim by Markus and Converse (1979) that partisans update their identities to reflect their vote choices. In another experiment, they tested Page and Jones' (1979) assertion that partisans update their identities in light of their candidate evaluations. Both experiments yielded null results, which the authors took as support for the classic model.

However, as Cowden and McDermott (2000) acknowledge, null results do not provide conclusive evidence of null effects. Their experimental stimuli may simply have lacked sufficient "punch" to produce a change in party identification. Moreover, even if the stimuli were sufficiently strong, Bayesian learning models can account for stable party identification as long as party positions remain stable. Although these investigations contribute to the literature, the results illustrate the challenge of confirming the Michigan model of party identification.

To establish conclusively that partisan stability rests on partisan motivation, it must be shown not only that party identification remains stable but that this stability is accompanied by party identity defense. This approach uncouples the Michigan model from null predictions. Moreover, if partisan stability results from the accumulation of information regarding party positions, as Bayesian models suggest, then partisans have no reason to engage in identity defense. Therefore, by establishing evidence of party identity defense, we will be able to isolate the mechanism responsible for producing stable party identification.

A pair of experiments conducted by Pool, Wood, and Leck (1998) demonstrate individuals' motivation to defend group identities in general. Participants experienced lower self-esteem after discovering that they disagreed with a self-relevant valued majority group or that they agreed with a self-relevant disliked minority group. This effect emerged regardless of whether individuals expressed their attitudes in public or in private. When given the opportunity to reinterpret the groups' positions before reporting their self-esteem, subjects shifted their interpretations of those positions. In the favored majority group condition, they shifted their interpretation so that the group's position matched their own. But in the derogated minority group condition, they shifted their interpretation so that the group's position conflicted with their own. These reinterpretations helped subjects to maintain positive self-esteem.

Pool et al.'s (1998) findings have two important implications for the present study: First, people appear motivated to maintain consistency between their attitudes and group allegiances. Second, this motivation appears to be internal and not merely driven by concerns about social perceptions. These results contrast with Green and colleagues' (2002) claim that partisans maintain attitudes that conflict with their party identity and feel little internal pressure to bring them into alignment.

Green and colleagues (2002) also contend that durable party stereotypes allow partisans to maintain stable identities without engaging in motivated reasoning. However, motivated reasoning theory suggests that partisan biases play an important role in both the persistence of these stereotypes and the timing of their deployment. Studies show that stereotypes are maintained through biased retrieval in the face of counter-stereotypical information (Kunda, 1990; Kunda & Oleson, 1995; Kunda & Sanitioso, 1989). In other words, individuals retrieve stereotype-consistent memories to combat encounters with images that conflict with their existing stereotypes. They do this because negative stereotypes serve as a valuable tool for identity defense. In fact, stereotypes become automatically activated when individuals receive disagreeable information (Kunda, Davies, Adams, & Spencer, 2002) or information that threatens their self-concept (Spencer, Fein, Wolfe, Fong, & Dunn, 1998), because outgroup derogation allows individuals to reaffirm their identity (Fein & Spencer, 1997; Kunda & Spencer, 2003; Steele, 1988).

This identity defense mechanism seems to be particularly prevalent in politics. By derogating the opposition party after receiving information inconsistent with one's party identity, a partisan can "bolster" the consistency of her attitudes (see Abelson, 1959; Festinger, 1957) and reaffirm her sense of relative superiority (see Steele, 1988). In one particularly pertinent study, Cooper and Mackie (1983) evoked partisan dissonance by asking members of a pro-Reagan college group to write counter-attitudinal statements in favor of reelecting Jimmy Carter. Subjects who agreed to write these statements reacted by derogating Carter supporters.

In essence, people may avoid inconsistency between their party identity and evaluations of that party by calling to mind even more negative evaluations of the opposition party. This alleviates dissonance (Abelson, 1959; Festinger, 1957) and brings self-esteem back up to baseline (Fein & Spencer, 1997; Steele, 1988). As long as one has more negative attitudes toward the opposition party than toward one's own party, then one's own party remains the "lesser of two evils" and so continued identification is justified. All the while, those with a significantly large buffer between their attitudes toward the two parties may update their attitudes in the normal manner.

This chapter focuses on this notion of lesser of two evils identity justification, because it provides a clear and familiar example of identity defense. The point is to bring attention not just to this type of defense but to the notion of identity defense more generally. The methods by which an individual could potentially justify her identity are virtually limitless. However, if evidence of any kind of party identity justification is uncovered, it suggests a general motivation to defend one's identity. By focusing on lesser of two evils justification, I am simply attempting to "hunt where the ducks are."

Figure 2.1 diagrams how partisan attitudes are expected to move in two-dimensional space as individuals confront these inconsistencies. The x-axis and y-axis represent, respectively, attitudes toward one's favored party and toward the opposition party. The 45-degree line running from the bottom left to the top right represents indifference between parties. Crossing this threshold entails reporting more positive feelings toward the opposition party than toward one's own party. Under such circumstances, it would be very difficult to justify maintaining one's party identification. The first panel ("No Disagreement") represents a typical scenario in which two respondents express attitudes toward the parties. In general, these attitudes negatively reinforce one another, lining up on a dimension orthogonal to the indifference threshold.

The second panel in Figure 2.1 ("Disagreement") represents a scenario in which the same two respondents encounter a disagreement with their party.[1] Respondent 1 allows her attitudes toward the two parties to negatively

---

1. Although this chapter focuses on the lesser of two evils justification, the theory also accounts for the possibility of a "greater of two goods" justification. In other words, individuals may feel pressure to change their identity when they find themselves liking the opposition party. By rehearsing positive thoughts about their own party, individuals could maintain more positive attitudes toward their own party than toward the opposition party, thereby avoiding the indifference threshold. From an empirical standpoint, these individuals would appear

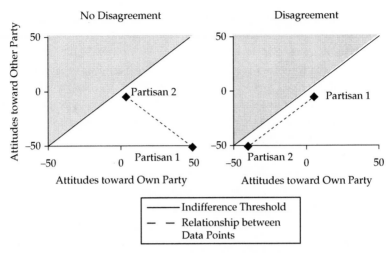

Figure 2.1 The figure represents attitudes toward parties in two-dimensional space. Conventionally, the more a person likes one party, the less that person likes the other party. However, partisans come up with justifications that allow them to avoid crossing over the indifference threshold—at which point they would be acknowledging that they like the other party more than their own party. When the indifference threshold is crossed, stable identification with one's party cannot be justified. The lesser of two evils justification is one common form of identity defense in which, as they approach the indifference threshold, partisans report disliking the other party more than they dislike their own party (a positive relationship).

reinforce one another, so she now reports a less positive attitude toward her own party and a somewhat more positive attitude toward the opposition party compared with the first panel. She reasons, "I now like my party less, so I suppose I must like the other party more." However, because her initial attitudes were farther from the indifference threshold to start with, her attitudes remain consistent with her party identity despite these changes. In other words, she continues to like her own party more than the opposition party. Respondent 2 began with attitudes much closer to the indifference threshold. Therefore, he risks crossing over the indifference threshold if he acknowledges the

---

in the upper right quadrant of Figure 2.1, lining up on the same orthogonal dimension as the lesser of two evils identifiers. However, both the data as and casual observation suggest that greater of two goods justifications are uncommon, and perhaps this is not surprising given the adversarial nature of politics. Therefore, attention is focused on the lesser of two evils justification.

disagreement with his party and allows his attitudes to negatively reinforce one another. To avoid this, he calls to mind negative images of the opposition party to offset the disagreement with his own party. This leads him into the lower left quadrant and prevents him from crossing over the indifference threshold.[2] He reasons, "I now like my party less, but I like the other party even less than that, so my party remains the lesser of two evils." Looking at respondents 1 and 2, notice that the relationship between attitudes toward the two parties is now positive.

In this hypothetical scenario, the magnitude of these shifts is exaggerated to illustrate the pattern more clearly, but it is easy to see how this process could cause otherwise negative correlations between attitudes toward parties to move toward zero and even become positive when a large number of partisans come to disagree with their party or disapprove of its performance. Also notice that the theory predicts a shift in the relationship between attitudes toward the parties rather than a shift in their mean values. Partisans are expected to engage in identity defense only as their attitudes approach the indifference threshold. Like respondent 1 in Figure 2.1, partisans will continue to allow their attitudes toward the parties to negatively reinforce one another up to the point at which these attitudes would otherwise conflict with their party identity. Therefore, the tests that follow examine the strength and direction of the relationship between these attitudes rather than comparing changes in their means.

MULTIDIMENSIONAL IDENTITY, MEASUREMENT ERROR, OR JUSTIFICATION?

Various authors have argued that party identification cannot be adequately measured on a single dimension (Alvarez, 1990; Greene, 2005; Kamieniecki, 1988; Katz, 1979; Valentine & Van Wingen, 1980; Weisberg, 1980).[3] Proponents

---

2. As partisans approach the indifference threshold, they face increasing levels of ambivalence. In other words, despite identifying with their party, they do not like that party much more than the other party. This can be seen as a model of "ambivalence avoidance." Also notice that lesser of two evils identifiers are not ambivalent according to the specifications outlined by Lavine, Johnston, and Steenbergen (2012). These partisans' attitudes are quite consistent with their party identities.
3. The works cited identify these dimensions somewhat differently, but the differences are largely a matter of factor rotation. In factor analysis, the difference between orthogonal "Republican" and "Democrat" dimensions versus

of such models often cite the small negative and sometimes positive correlations between "feeling thermometer" ratings of the Republican and Democratic parties (Alvarez, 1990; Weisberg, 1980).[4] However, I argue that what appears to some as evidence of multidimensional party identification may actually constitute evidence of party identity justification.

First, as explained in the previous chapter, attitudes are conceptually distinct from identities (Green et al., 2002; Groenendyk, 2012; Rosema, 2006). Whereas attitudes are evaluative in nature (Eagly & Chaiken, 1993), identities are rooted in self-conceptualization (Monroe, Hankin, & Van Vechten, 2000). Therefore, departure from the assumed one-dimensional negative relationship between attitudes toward the two parties does not necessarily constitute evidence of multidimensional party identification. Instead, it may result from party identity defense. As attitudes approach indifference between the two parties, a second attitude dimension should emerge as a result of individuals' attempts to justify continued identification with their party. Lesser of two evils identity justification entails a positive relationship between attitudes toward the two parties. Individuals who like their own party less will come to like the opposition party less as well.

In arguing against the claim that party identification is multidimensional, Green (1988) pointed out that deviation from the expected strong negative correlation between party feeling thermometer ratings may result simply from measurement error. Random measurement error drives correlation coefficients toward zero, whereas systematic error or "charitability bias" might actually lead to a positive correlation (Green, 1988; Green & Citrin, 1994). In other words, some individuals are likely to have a more charitable nature and therefore to rate both parties higher than average, whereas less charitable individuals will rate both parties lower than average. Because this charitability trait dimension is an omitted variable, it may bias correlation coefficients between

---

orthogonal "partisan direction" and "partisan intensity" dimensions are purely a matter of rotation. Weisberg (1980) found evidence of Democratic, Republican, and Independent dimensions.

4. Feeling thermometers are used extensively to measure attitudes. Although "feelings" are often defined as consciously experienced emotions (Damasio, 1994), these feeling thermometers contain no mention of any emotion such as anger, fear, or enthusiasm. Respondents merely rate how "warm" or "cold" they feel toward people and groups. Such simplistic measures cannot adequately capture emotions (Marcus, 2000; Marcus, MacKuen, Wolak, & Keele, 2006), but they do capture attitudes—which have a bipolar affect component (Eagly & Chaiken, 1993).

party feeling thermometer ratings in a positive direction. After accounting for measurement error, Green showed that Republican and Democratic Party feeling thermometer ratings were more negatively correlated.

Although Green (1988) offered a strong rebuttal to the multidimensional partisanship literature, there remains a third potential explanation for this pattern. The type of correlational dynamism hypothesized in the discussion of lesser of two evils identity justification is indistinguishable from measurement error in a survey context. Just as variation in respondent charitability may drive the correlation between party feeling thermometer ratings in a more positive direction, so might the motivation to justify one's party identity. Therefore, what first appeared to be evidence of multidimensional party identification, and then appeared to be measurement error, may actually be evidence of party identity justification.

I take a multimethod approach to understanding whether the relationship (or lack thereof) between party feeling thermometer ratings is best explained by a multidimensional model of party identification, measurement error, or identity justification. Experiments provide researchers with leverage over both random and systematic error through random assignment. This ensures that differences between groups can only be attributed to the treatment and not to measurement error. By pairing these tests with aggregate level analyses, it is possible to assess how these microlevel processes manifest themselves at the macro level. When making aggregate-level comparisons within a single population over time, the effects of measurement error should be greatly reduced. In large samples, random errors should cancel out. Moreover, if each cross-section is truly representative of the population of interest, then aggregate charitability biases cannot explain differences between samples.

Justification Hypothesis:
When partisans disagree with their party, they will attempt to justify their existing party identity.

LESSER OF TWO EVILS IDENTITY JUSTIFICATION AT THE INDIVIDUAL LEVEL

Previous studies have suggested that party identification is difficult to move in an experimental context (Cowden & McDermott, 2000). However, the question remains as to whether such stability is driven by partisan motivation. The following experiment built on knowledge gained from these previous experiments. Rather than focusing on whether subjects' party identities can be changed, I first concentrate on how partisans go about defending their identities when they are threatened—the implication being that partisan change

TABLE 2.1. *EXPERIMENTAL DESIGN*

Condition	Step 1	Step 2	Step 3
Disagreement	Viewed advertisement	Reported issue attitudes	Received partisan cues (via video format)
Party Cues	Viewed advertisement	Received partisan cues (embedded in ad)	Reported issue attitudes
Control	Reported issue attitudes (no advertisement)		

occurs when defenses break down. More specifically, this experiment induces conflict between individuals' party identities and the issue positions they espouse in order to understand how partisans go about reconciling this psychological inconsistency. The design is laid out in Table 2.1.

Methods

To induce identity conflict, subjects viewed an issue advocacy advertisement endorsing a fictitious bill. In one condition, subjects were provided with partisan cues telling them which party supported (or opposed) the bill. In another condition, subjects were not provided with party cues until after they had taken a position on the bill. Therefore, if they took the position advocated in the appeal, they discovered that this position conflicted with their party identity. In a control condition, subjects viewed no advertisement at all. Again, the idea here was to create pressure for partisan change in order to determine how partisans react to such pressure.

Participants

A total of 254 student participants were recruited during the fall of 2005 from the University of Michigan campus. Participants were offered 5 dollars to participate in a 30-minute public opinion study. No more than 12 subjects were allowed to participate at any one time, and usually only 1 to 4 were present in the laboratory. Results from seven subjects were excluded from analysis after it was discovered that they were not citizens of the United States. Given the political leanings of Michigan students, the stimuli were designed to target Democratic identifiers. Therefore, self-identified Republicans were excluded from analysis once it was determined that party identification had not been affected by treatment exposure.

Materials

The treatment was administered via a political advertisement created by the researcher. In an informal test, viewers were unable to distinguish the advertisement from an authentic political appeal. The advertisement appeared to be sponsored by the AFL-CIO and focused on a fictitious "Bankruptcy Abuse Bill." The Enron, Global Crossing, and WorldCom scandals had recently received considerable media attention, whereas legislation related to the issue had received much less attention. The appeal advocated passage of the Bankruptcy Abuse Bill and paired Enron, Global Crossing, and WorldCom job loss statistics with dramatic audio and visual effects to rouse the viewer. Clips borrowed from actual political advertisements showed an apparent corporate executive pleading his Fifth Amendment rights in front of the U.S. Senate. Another clip showed an apparently middle-class man rubbing his forehead as he looks over his bills at the kitchen table. A transcript of the advertisement with screen shots is included in the Appendix (see Appendix Figure 2.1).

Information about the parties' positions came in the form of three fictitious newspaper quotations. Each set of quotations commented on either Democratic opposition to the bill or Republican support for the bill. Because the stimuli were targeted toward Democrats, the quotes were attributed to sources Democrats would likely find credible.

> By *opposing* the bankruptcy abuse bill…
> "Democrats let corporate crooks off the hook"—The Washington Post
> "Democrats are simply wrong on bankruptcy abuse"—The Boston Globe
> "Democrats are playing politics with people's lives"—The New York Times
> OR
> By *supporting* the bankruptcy abuse bill…
> "Republicans are keeping the heat on corporate crooks"—The Washington Post
> "Republicans are right on bankruptcy abuse"—The Boston Globe
> "Republicans are putting people above politics"—The New York Times

Within each of the three experimental conditions, Democratic opposition and Republican support quotations were randomized to ensure that any effects would be attributable to inconsistency between issue attitudes and party identification and not to support versus opposition framing.

Procedure

Initially, subjects were randomly assigned to one of four treatment groups or the control group. As mentioned earlier, the *Republicans support* and

Democrats oppose groups were consolidated. This design yielded three experimental conditions: a *party cues* condition, a *disagreement* condition, and a *control* condition.[5] As described previously, those assigned to the *party cues* condition viewed a version of the advertisement in which the party cues were embedded. Those assigned to the *disagreement* condition viewed the same advertisement but with the partisan cues removed. Subjects in this condition received these cues only after viewing the advertisement and reporting their support or opposition for the Bankruptcy Abuse Bill. Cues were presented in onscreen text in exactly the same format and for the same amount of time in both conditions. The *control* group viewed no advertisement at all.

Those assigned to the *disagreement* condition (in which participants received no party cues until after taking a position on the bill) were expected to experience the greatest partisan dissonance. It was expected that subjects assigned to the *party cues* condition (in which participants received party cues during the advertisement) might also experience dissonance but that most would avoid it by following the available cues. The control group served as a baseline—no threat—condition against which the other groups were compared.

Measures

Opinions on the Bankruptcy Abuse Bill were assessed on a seven-point scale ranging from strongly oppose (–3) to strongly support (3) with a neutral point at zero. Party identification was measured using the standard ANES (American National Election Studies) branching question yielding a seven-point scale ranging from strong Republican (–3) to strong Democrat (3). Partisan feeling thermometers allowed subjects to rate how warm or cold they felt toward the Republican Party and the Democratic Party. Smaller values correspond to colder (more negative) feelings, and larger values correspond to warmer (more positive) feelings. Feeling thermometers were rescaled to run from –50 to 50.

Four additional questions were posed to each subject: "Regardless of who you tend to vote for, how often do you find yourself supporting [opposing] what the Democratic [Republican] party stands for?" Subjects were asked to

---

5. Comparisons between the *Republicans support* and *Democrats oppose* groups— both of which conflict with Democratic identity—showed that effects of both stimuli ran in the same direction, although *Democrats oppose* tends to produce larger effects, as one might expect.

answer by placing themselves on a seven-point scale ranging from "never" to "always." In contrast to the bipolarity of feeling thermometers, these questions allowed subjects to express occasional support and occasional opposition for the same party.

An open-ended question was administered near the end of the study to allow subjects a chance to explain, in their own words, why they identified with a particular party. This item read, "You have already indicated that you usually think of yourself as a Republican, Democrat, Independent, or something else. In a few sentences, please explain why you consider yourself a Republican, Democrat, Independent, or something else. The study is nearly complete, so feel free to take your time." Responses to this item ranged from 1 to 327 words and were blind-coded so that there would be no way to determine which subjects had been assigned to which condition. This simple coding scheme was meant to capture lesser of two evils identity justification. Subjects who flatly stated that they identified with the lesser of two evils or that their identity was primarily based on negative attitudes toward the opposition party were coded as lesser of two evils identifiers. Also included in this group were subjects who made less overt statements yet explained their identity largely in terms of their negative attitudes toward the opposition (rather than positive attitudes toward their favored party). All other subjects were coded as "0" to create a dummy variable for lesser of two evils identity justification. Dummy variables called *disagreement* and *party cues* were created to correspond to treatment conditions. Each of these variables was coded "1" for that particular treatement condition and "0" for either of the other conditions.

Results

Based on the standard seven-point measure of party identification, no partisan differences emerged between cells [$F(4, 244) = .03$].[6] Nor did any significant pairwise differences emerge. Group means ranged from .75 to .88 on a scale from −3 to 3. As previously mentioned, this study was designed for Democrats. Because party identification appears to be very stable across groups, Republicans could be excluded from further analyses without concern. More specifically, analyses were restricted to those who labeled themselves as a strong Democrat, weak Democrat, Independent-leaning Democrat, or Independent not leaning toward either political party.[7] This

---

6. The reported *F*-statistic comes from a one way analysis of variance (ANOVA).
7. Pure Independents were included in the analysis in order to avoid losing data on any subjects who might have been leaning toward the Democratic party before the treatment and shifted into the pure Independent category as a result of the

allowed me to focus on those subjects for whom the treatment was likely to be threatening.

Examination of the subjects' opinions on bankruptcy abuse indicated that the manipulation worked largely as expected. Of the 153 non-Republican subjects assigned to one of the two treatment conditions, 150 were able to correctly identify the Bankruptcy Abuse Bill as the issue on which the advertisement focused. Findings also indicate that subjects in the *disagreement* condition (mean (M) = 0.90, standard deviation (SD) = 1.53) and those in the control group ($M = 0.89$, $SD = 1.29$) expressed an almost identical amount of support for the bill. This suggests that, although subjects overall were supportive of the bill, the advertisement itself did not prove to be particularly persuasive. However, because subjects tended to support the bill anyway, this is of little consequence for the manipulation. Despite the weakness of the appeal, the vast majority of the subjects in the *disagreement* condition did express opinions inconsistent with those of their party. Moreover, those in the *partisan cues* condition seem to have followed those cues and avoided disagreement with their party—although they were apparently not able to avoid it completely because, on average, they still showed support for the bill. This means that we should expect to see some degree of party identity justification in this group, although probably not as much as in the *disagreement* condition. Finally, whereas those in the control group actually expressed support for the bill as well, they did not experience disagreement with their party because they were never provided with any partisan information (or other cueing information). In other words, the experimental manipulation appears to have operated as it was designed.

---

treatment. Although no differences in party identification emerged between cells, it is possible that changes may have occurred that were too small to detect statistically. By including pure Independents in the sample, I avoided improperly excluding these subjects. Inclusion simply made the test more conservative. In the chapters that follow, pretest measures of party identification were available, and therefore it was not necessary to include pure Independents in the analyses. It is also important to note that, in the sample used in this chapter, the pure Independent category appears to include closet Democrats—as one might expect in a college student sample. A look at the characteristics of pure Independents within this sample of college students shows that, on average, they look a good deal like Democrats. On a feeling thermometer scale from 50 to −50, pure Independents gave the Republican party an average rating of −11.11 and the Democratic party an average rating of 2.04. The chapters that follow make use of national samples.

Given that disagreement was successfully evoked between subjects and the Democratic Party, yet no change in party identification appears to have occurred, attention can now be directed toward the original question of interest: Is the observed partisan stability a result of motivated identity justification, or was the stimulus simply not powerful enough to produce party identification change? To answer this question, I first examined responses obtained through an open-ended measure in which subjects were asked to explain why they identified with their party.

Open-ended responses were also coded for whether or not they contained evidence of a lesser of two evils justification. When participants' attitudes approach the indifference threshold (see Figure 2.1), they are expected to avoid crossing over by calling to mind negative attitudes and stereotypes of the opposition party to offset negative attitudes toward their own party. Because the justification process is not necessarily expected to occur on the conscious level, this is an extremely blunt measure. Therefore, observations of such overt lesser of two evils identity justification are expected to be low across conditions. Nonetheless, Figure 2.2 shows that subjects in both the *disagreement* condition and the *party cues* condition were significantly more likely to use lesser of two evils justifications to explain their identity than those assigned to the control condition. In fact, not a single subject in the control group was coded as having used a lesser of two evils identity justification.

I next examined attitude correlations within each of the three experimental conditions. More positive (less negative) correlations between party feeling

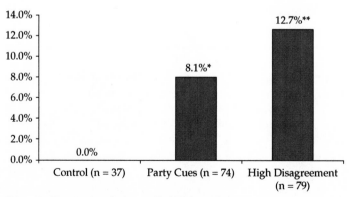

***p<.01, **p<.05, *p<.10 (one-tailed Fisher's Exact Test)

Figure 2.2 Cell entries represent percentage of responses coded "1" for lesser of two evils justification. Significance levels are based on Fisher's Exact Tests—a non-parametric test used when dealing with dichotomous dependent variables and very low positive outcome frequencies. Comparisons are made with respect to the control group.

thermometer ratings indicate reliance on lesser of two evils identity justification. Again, what may appear in cross-sectional snapshots to be multidimensional party identification (Alvarez, 1990; Valentine & Van Wingen, 1980; Weisberg 1980) may actually be party identity justification. I expected that in the absence of disagreement, attitudes toward parties would line up on a single dimension but when inconsistencies arose between issue attitudes and party identification, individuals would venture off of this dimension and begin to line up on a second lesser of two evils dimension. Again, this should be reflected in increasingly positive (less negative) feeling thermometer correlations from the control group to the *party cues* condition to the *disagreement* condition.

The results in Table 2.2 fit this prediction extremely well. In the control group, the standard expectation of a large negative relationship appears to hold, but this is not the case in the other two conditions. As party identity threat intensifies from the control group to the *party cues* condition to the *disagreement* condition, the negative relationship between attitudes toward the Republican and Democratic parties becomes smaller in magnitude and actually passes zero to become (nonsignificantly) positive.

Are these more positive (less negative) correlations arising because individuals venture out onto a new (lesser of two evils) attitude dimension in order to avoid crossing over the indifference threshold? Factor analysis was used to answer this question, because it makes it possible to determine whether these correlation differences arise as a result of partisans' attitudes splitting into two orthogonal dimensions. If this is the case, a new justification dimension should begin to emerge as party identity threat increases from condition to condition. On this new dimension, liking one's own party less should correlate with liking the other party less as well. Factor analyses were conducted separately for each experimental condition to facilitate comparisons between conditions.

TABLE 2.2. *CORRELATIONS BETWEEN ATTITUDES TOWARD REPUBLICAN AND DEMOCRATIC PARTIES BY CONDITION*

	Correlation Between Attitudes Toward Republicans and Democrats
Control (No Disagreement) (n = 35)	−.58
Party Cues (n = 71)	−.25*
Disagreement (n = 77)	.08***

Note: Significance levels are calculated relative to the control group. The control group itself is significantly different from zero ($p < .001$).

***$p < .01$, **$p < .05$, *$p < .10$

TABLE 2.3. *EXPLORATORY FACTOR ANALYSIS OF PARTISAN ATTITUDES BY CONDITION (UNROTATED)*

	Control (*n* = 34)	Party Cues (*n* = 68)	Disagreement (*n* = 75)	
	Component 1	Component 1	Component 1	Component 2
Support Democrats	.876	.731	.824	.362
Oppose Democrats	−.724	−.408	−.700	−.258
Support Republicans	−.829	−.478	−.697	.546
Oppose Republicans	.813	.781	.550	−.401
Democrats Thermometer	.824	.795	.609	.557
Republicans Thermometer	−.771	−.376	−.541	.607
Party Identity Strength	.594	.767	.652	.164
Eigenvalue	4.63	3.39	3.40	1.70
Variance Explained	66.20%	48.47%	48.60%	24.28%
Variance Explained by Extracted Factors	66.20%	48.46%	72.88%	

Note: Eigenvalue cutoffs are set to 1.0 (Kaiser's rule). Cattel's scree test yields the same number of factors, as indicated by the Eigenvalues. Extractions are based on principal axis factoring.

Included in these factor analyses were feeling thermometer measures, party support and opposition measures, and strength of party identification. Results are displayed in Table 2.3.

As hypothesized, a single factor emerged in the control group. On this dimension, liking Democrats more means liking Republicans less—just as conventional wisdom suggests. This factor explained slightly more than 66% of the total variance within the condition. A single-factor solution also emerged in the *party cues* condition. However, this factor accounted for only about 48% of the variance in this condition—suggesting that subjects' attitudes no longer lined up as well on a single dimension. Finally, as predicted, two orthogonal factors emerged in the *disagreement* condition.[8] Before rotation,

---

8. Eigenvalue cutoffs were set to 1.0 (Kaiser's rule), although the number of unique factors was very clear in each condition. Cattel's scree test yielded the same number of factors. In the control group, the first factor had an Eigenvalue of 4.624, compared with a value of .692 for the second factor. In the *party cues* condition, a second factor with an Eigenvalue of .953 approached the threshold of 1.0. However, this factor still explained relatively little variance compared to

the first of these two factors was identical to the factor extracted in each of the other two conditions. As in the *party cues* condition, this factor explained about 48% of the total variance. Looking across conditions, it appeared that this factor explainedless variance as partisan dissonance increased.[9] On the second factor, liking one party less corresponds to liking the other party less, and liking one's party more corresponds to liking the other party more. In a cross-sectional survey context, it is understandable how this dimension might be interpreted as a unique independence or ambivalence dimension (Alvarez, 1990; Dennis, 1988; Greene, 2000; Kamieniecki, 1988; Valentine & Van Wingen, 1980; Weisberg, 1980). However, given that this second factor arose only in the *disagreement* condition and that strength of party identification still loaded onto the first factor, this experiment suggests a very different interpretation: identity justification. In sum, as party identification came under threat, partisans departed from zero-sum attitude reinforcement. As they approached indifference between the two parties, they called to mind negative evaluations and stereotypes of the opposition party in order to justify maintaining their party identity.

LESSER OF TWO EVILS IDENTITY JUSTIFICATION AT THE AGGREGATE LEVEL

Results from the experiment just described suggest that motivated reasoning is triggered when inconsistencies arise between individuals' issue positions and their party identity. Under such conditions, people feel the need to justify their party identity in order to avoid changing it. As individuals approach indifference between the two parties, they engage in lesser of two evils identity justification. This entails a departure from the strong negative relationship between attitudes toward the Republican and Democratic parties that one might expect. In fact, in the *disagreement* condition, we saw the emergence of a second attitude dimension, on which liking one party less was associated with liking the other party less—consistent with lesser of two evils identity justification.

---

the first factor with its Eigenvalue of 3.93. In the *disagreement* condition, the first two factors had Eigenvalues of 3.390 and 1.692, respectively. The next factor had an Eigenvalue of only .630.

9. After rotating the matrix to maximize the variance of loadings for each factor, the two dimensions extracted in the *disagreement* conditions came to reflect attitudes toward the Democratic Party and attitudes toward the Republican Party, respectively. Strength of party identification was associated with both of these dimensions (negatively with the opposition party dimension), albeit more strongly with the favored party dimension.

In a number of the American National Election Studies (ANES) cross-sectional surveys, the correlation between attitudes toward the Republican Party and the Democratic Party appears to be weak and even positive in some cases. This pattern is often cited as evidence of multidimensional party identification (Alvarez, 1990; Weisberg, 1980). However, the results from the experiment described here imply that this interpretation may be inappropriate. It may be that these correlations become less negative and more positive as individuals attempt to justify their party identity. Of course, if this is the case, the relationship between attitudes toward the parties should vary systematically as a function of political circumstances. In other words, correlations between attitudes toward parties should become more positive when circumstances require identity justification. Despite the debate over the dimensionality of partisanship, little attention has been paid to variation over time in the correlation between these attitudes. As is evident in Figure 2.3, substantial temporal variation does occur in these correlations.[10] Multidimensional models of party identification clearly require a stable number of dimensions, so the observed pattern proves an awkward fit for such theories. Green (1988) points out, the negativity of the correlation between attitudes toward the two parties may be underestimated due to measurement error. However, both random and systematic measurement error should be relatively constant over time in aggregate-level analysis, so the temporal variation on display in Figure 2.3 suggests that measurement error cannot tell the whole story either.

Because neither of the dominant theories in the partisan dimensionality debate can explain this temporal variation, I examined the effect of economic performance on the correlation between attitudes toward the two parties. As in the previous study, I suspected that this variation occurs as partisans attempt to justify maintaining their party identity. When our ongoing evaluations of party performance are consistent with our party identity, attitudes toward the two parties are likely to reinforce one another, yielding a strong negative correlation, as conventional wisdom suggests. However, the state of the world may sometimes be such that partisan-consistent evaluations are difficult to maintain. For instance, objective economic indicators may suggest that one's preferred party has performed poorly while in power. Recalling Figure 2.1, this may strain party evaluations for some partisans to the point that they are in danger of crossing over the indifference threshold. Under such

---

10. The figure represents feelings toward one's "own" party and the "other" party, but Weisberg and Christenson (2007, 2010) also show that these correlations between Republican and Democratic feeling thermometer ratings have risen substantially since the 1970s.

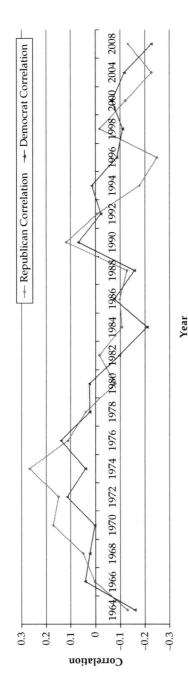

Year

Figure 2.3 Correlations were calculated separately for Republican identifiers and Democratic identifiers. The purpose was to determine whether the correlation within a group of partisans (Republicans or Democrats) decreased when their partisan expectations conflicted with actual political outcomes. This required separate correlation calculations, because a poor economy under a Republican president is inconsistent with Republicans' expectations but entirely consistent with Democrats' expectations. The weighted average of these within-party correlation coefficients are not necessarily equal to the correlation calculated for all partisans. Within-party correlations tend to be lower precisely because partisans with attitudes near the indifference threshold tend not to line up on the standard negative dimension. The attitudes of this very important group are somewhat obscured when Republicans and Democrats are analyzed together, because a large cluster of Republicans feel very warm toward their own party and very cold toward Democrats and a large cluster of Democrats feel just the opposite. For the purpose of analysis, those who leaned toward a party were included as members of that party. "Pure" Independents were excluded from analysis because they have no allegiance.

circumstances, these individuals are likely to turn to lesser of two evils identity justification in order to maintain loyalty to their party. From an empirical standpoint, this means that when economic performance threatens party identification, we should observe a less negative (more positive) correlation between attitudes toward the Republican Party and the Democratic Party than conventional wisdom suggests. Because economic performance is exogenous to attitudes toward the parties, we can be certain that economic performance is affecting the relationship between attitudes and not vice versa.

Methods

As discussed, the correlation between attitudes toward the Republican Party and Democratic Party serves as the primary dependent variable of interest. Because correlations are, by nature, aggregate-level assessments, aggregate-level analysis is required. These correlations were calculated separately for Republican and Democratic identifiers (including leaners) for each election year available over a 48-year period. I calculated these correlations separately for Republicans and Democrats so that I could distinguish between the effects of economic performance by one's own party and the effects of the opposition party's performance. Poor performance by one's own party threatens party identification, whereas poor performance by the other party reinforces party identification.

Economic performance was calculated by determining change from the previous year's unemployment level and change from the previous year's level of inflation and then adding these two values together.[11] However, to facilitate interpretation, the signs were flipped so that larger values would indicate better economic performance. This variable was scaled to run from −1 to 1. An incumbency dummy variable was used to signify which party controlled the White House in the year leading up to the election.

The ANES feeling thermometer questions were at one point altered to ask about the "Republican Party" and "Democratic Party" rather than "Republicans" and "Democrats." Therefore, a control for question wording was also included.

---

11. Unemployment plus inflation is often referred to as the "misery index." Therefore, this value is essentially a measure of change in economic misery, but it is reversed so that negative values correspond to greater misery. Unemployment and inflation were chosen over other measures of economic performance such as growth in the gross domestic product (GDP) because of their direct influence on voters. GDP growth is felt largely through its influence on the availability of jobs and inflation.

Finally, because the point of this exercise is to understand how stable party identities are maintained, I controlled for party identity polarization (across all subjects) in order to isolate the variation in attitude correlations that occurs independently from variation in the distribution of party identification. Clearly, the correlation between party feeling thermometer ratings should relate to the spread of party identification—as a cause, a consequence, or, more likely, both. However, I hypothesized that partisan threat would affect these attitude correlations even when identity polarization was controlled. The standard deviation of party identification in each year served as the measure of party identity polarization.[12] By controlling for polarization between parties, the pattern of variation in attitudes within parties became easier to identify.

Results

The theory was tested using an ordinary least squares (OLS) regression model with panel-corrected standard errors.[13] Results are presented in Table 2.4 and represented graphically in Figure 2.4. First, as one would expect, attitudes and identities appear to be powerfully related. The correlation between attitudes toward the parties becomes substantially more negative when partisan polarization increases. In other words, attitudes polarize when party identities polarize. However, as the theory predicts, this is not the whole story.

Economic performance, in interaction with *own party incumbency*, has a substantial effect on the correlation between attitudes toward the two parties. More specifically, Figure 2.4 shows that when one's own party is in power and the economy performs poorly, the correlation between attitudes toward the two parties becomes less negative (more positive). On the other hand, the correlation between partisan attitudes becomes more negative when one's own party is in power and the economy performs well or when the opposition

---

12. The standard deviation variable was mean deviated so that the constant would take on a more intuitive value. If this step had not been taken, the constant would have represented the predicted correlation between party feeling thermometer ratings when the standard deviation of party identification (as well as all the other variables in the model) equaled zero. Because a standard deviation of zero is clearly a nonsensical notion, this variable was rescaled so that the constant took on the value it would have when the standard deviation of party identification (partisan polarization) was at its average level. The variable is also rescaled to run from −1 to 1.
13. Similar models were run to check for robustness. Fixed and random effects models yielded similar results.

TABLE 2.4. *THE EFFECT OF INCUMBENT PARTY PERFORMANCE ON THE DIMENSIONALITY OF PARTISAN ATTITUDES*

	OLS Regression with Panel-corrected Standard Errors Dependent Variable: Correlation Between Attitudes Toward Democrats and Republicans (N = 42) B (SE)
Constant	.005 (.023)
Economic Performance	.087* (.008)
Own Party Incumbent	.045*** (.017)
Own Party Incumbent*Economic Performance	−.130** (.008)
Party Question	−.108*** (.028)
Partisan Polarization	−.156*** (.033)

Note: Correlations between party feeling thermometers were calculated for each year in which they were available from the American National Election Studies (ANES). These correlation coefficients were used as the dependent variable in this aggregate-level analysis. Correlations were calculated separately for Republican and Democratic respondents (includes leaners). The two partisan groups were pooled in this analysis.

Results were calculated using ordinary least squares (OLS) regression with panel corrected standard errors. Regression coefficients (B) and standard errors (SE) are reported.

***$p < .01$, **$p < .05$, *$p < .10$

party is in power and the economy performs poorly. In other words, negative attitude reinforcement occurs when the economy conforms to partisan expectations, but these attitudes cease to reinforce one another when economic realities threaten party identification. This pattern corresponds perfectly to the notion of a lesser of two evils identity justification. When their own party performs poorly (or the other party performs well), partisans with attitudes near the indifference threshold avoid crossing over by reporting more negative attitudes toward both parties—pushing the correlation in a more positive direction. However, when their own party performs well (or the other

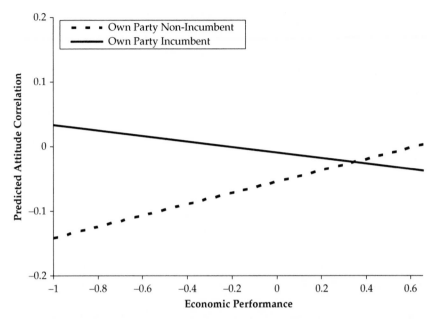

Figure 2.4 Findings come from OLS regression with panel-corrected standard errors. The dependent variable is the correlation between attitudes toward the two parties among Republicans and Democrats in a given year. The figure illustrates how these correlations systematically varies with political context. When politics conforms to partisan expectations (i.e., one's own party performed well or the other party performs poorly), the relationship is strongly negative. However, the correlation shifts in a positive direction when political events challenge partisan expectations (i.e., one's own party performs poorly or the other party performs well). This pattern fits with the theory that when party identification is challenged, individuals attempt to justify their identities, resulting in the emergence of a second partisan attitude dimension.

party performs poorly) and partisan expectations are confirmed, no identity justification is needed, so the expected negative relationship between attitude dimensions appears.

To illustrate the size of this effect, the predicted attitude correlations among incumbent party identifiers and non-incumbent party identifiers differed by .17 when economic performance was set to its lowest observed level. This suggests that although attitudes and identity are powerfully related to one another, the relationship between attitudes toward the two parties is not determined entirely by party identification, or vice versa. Attitudes and identity are distinct, and the relationship between attitude dimensions appears to vary systematically with at least one important exogenous source of identity threat: economic performance.[14] Consistent with the experimental findings, when economic performance conflicts with partisan expectations, the relationship between partisan attitudes becomes more complex. Individuals begin to venture off the single dimension presumed by conventional wisdom to explain attitudes toward parties. This finding, in conjunction with the experimental results, suggests that previously uncovered evidence of multidimensional party identification should be reconsidered in favor of a model in which independent attitude dimensions emerge as partisans attempt to justify their identity.

Discussion

What mechanism produces partisan stability? Results of a laboratory experiment and aggregate-level analysis of ANES data suggest that partisan motivation plays an important role. Therefore, models that downplay the role of motivated reasoning in party identification may offer misleading conclusions. When individuals become aware of inconsistencies between their attitudes and their party identity, they do not necessarily bring their identity into alignment with their attitudes; rather, they generate justifications for maintaining a stable party identity. Although there exist any number of ways to go about justifying one's party identity, one specific type of identity justification, referred to as identifying with the lesser of two evils, constituted the primary focus of this chapter. This method of justification has a specific empirical signature—a positive relationship between attitudes toward the two parties—and therefore serves as an ideal signal of identity justification.

An experiment was undertaken to intentionally evoke inconsistency between participants' issue positions and their party identity so that their responses could be compared with those of a control group in which such inconsistencies were not evoked. Both open-ended and closed-ended measures demonstrated that responses of subjects exposed to the treatment conditions were consistent with lesser of two evils identity justification. Participants appear to have evaluated the opposition more harshly as they approached

---

14. Negative inconsistency (i.e., poor performance by one's own party) appears to exert a larger influence than positive inconsistency (i.e., positive performance by the opposition party). In other words, the difference between incumbency and non-incumbency of one's own party is much larger when the economy is bad than when it is good. Recall the similar pattern in the experiment, wherein agreeing with the opposition party exerted less influence than disagreeing with one's own party.

indifference toward the two parties. In this way, they were able to ensure that their party remained the lesser of two evils even as their attitudes toward their party declined.

Aggregate-level analysis of national survey data suggests that these experimental results generalize to the population at large. At times when economic conditions are likely to threaten party identification (i.e., poor performance by one's own party or impressive performance by the opposition party), aggregate-level attitudes shift in a pattern that is consistent with lesser of two evils identity justification.[15] By engaging in identity justification, individuals are able to maintain partisan loyalty without appearing "irrational" or biased. These findings lend additional credence to the notion that attitudes toward opposition parties (Maggiotto & Piereson, 1977; Rose & Mishler, 1998) and toward opposition candidates (Gant & Davis, 1984; Gant & Sigelman, 1985; Lau, 1982, 1985; Sigelman & Gant, 1989) are important to consider independent of attitudes toward one's own party and its candidates.

These results also shed new light on the longstanding debate over the dimensionality of party identification. By simply maintaining the distinction between attitudes and identity, it becomes apparent that party identification is not itself multidimensional but rather justified in two-dimensional space. The results suggest that the small negative (and sometimes positive) correlations often observed between attitudes toward the Republican and Democratic parties result from individuals' efforts to defend their party identity. Experimental results showed that these correlations vary systematically as individuals experience disagreement with their party. This pattern was replicated in aggregate-level ANES survey analysis. When indicators of the incumbent party's economic performance do not match partisan expectations, the relationship between party feeling thermometer ratings becomes more positive (less negative).

Although debates about party identification have traditionally pitted the irrationally loyal partisan against the rationally updating partisan, the results presented here suggest that this is a false dichotomy. Partisans do not necessarily ignore relevant political information in order to preserve their identity, nor does party identification appear to constitute a perfect running tally of attitudes. Instead, individuals find ways to incorporate inconsistent attitudes into their existing identity without actually changing it. The next chapter continues this investigation by examining partisans' propensity to reprioritize issues in defense of their party identity.

---

15. In the case of impressive performance by the opposition party, this may entail a greater of two goods justification, as discussed in footnote 1.

Identity Justification

Issue Reprioritization

The previous chapter examined a method of party identity justification referred to as "identifying with the lesser of two evils." This chapter continues with the task of uncovering evidence of party identity defense but shifts focus to another mechanism: issue reprioritization. The issue importance literature suggests that priorities are shaped by a combination of citizens' own values and interests (Boninger, Krosnick, & Berent, 1995) and elite influence (for examples, see Behr & Iyengar, 1985; Cohen, 1995; Erbing, Goldenberg, & Miller, 1980; Iyengar & Kinder, 1987; Kingdon, 1995; McCombs & Shaw, 1972; Petrocik, 1996; Petrocik, Benoit, & Hansen, 2003–2004; West, 2010). However, largely absent from this discussion is consideration of whether individuals' own partisan motivations might bias their issue priorities.

Issue reprioritization has the potential to serve as a powerful method of party identity justification. When citizens hold issue positions or performance evaluations that conflict with their party identity, they can alleviate this inconsistency by placing less importance on these attitudes and reallocating the importance to attitudes consonant with their party identity. Like the lesser of two evils identity justification, this technique appears quite attractive in comparison to other methods of reducing cognitive inconsistency. Because changing one's party identity to reflect one's attitudes entails a psychological cost and changing one's attitudes to reflect one's party identity entails violation of social norms against overt partisan bias (Dalton, 2008; Schudson 1998), issue reprioritization serves as an ideal defense.

The drive to appear pragmatic creates an incentive for partisans to conceal their biases, and issue priorities are a natural place to hide them.[1] For

1. This raises questions about model specification (or at least interpretation) when issue importance is assumed to be unaffected by partisan bias. For instance, Krosnick (1988, 1990) contends that issue importance moderates the effect of issue positions on candidate evaluations. Similarly, Carsey and Layman (2006) argue that individuals update their party identity to reflect their positions on issues they consider to be important but not on issues they consider less

instance, a person who identifies with the president's party may argue, "Yes, unemployment is high right now, but our main priority needs to be global warming." This person is able to maintain the appearance of objectivity by acknowledging unemployment, yet she is able to maintain her party allegiance by simply reweighting her issue priorities. This notion meshes nicely with work showing that character weakness (Goren, 2002, 2007) and economic performance (Lebo & Cassino, 2007) influence evaluations of opposition party candidates more than candidates of one's own party. It is also consistent with recent research suggesting that partisan interpretations mediate the relationship between facts about weapons of mass destruction and opinions toward the Iraq War (Gaines, Kuklinski, Quirk, Peyton, & Verkuilen, 2007). In each case, citizens accept information that is potentially inconsistent with their party identity, yet they manage to avoid cognitive inconsistency by placing minimal weight on that information.

Two distinct methods were employed to test for issue reprioritization. First, I examined survey data from the American National Election Studies (ANES) conducted between 1960 and 2000 to determine what drives individuals' assessments of the nation's most important problem.[2] In accordance with previous research, I expected real-world economic circumstances (unemployment and inflation rates) to shape individuals' issue priorities (Hibbs, 1979). However, I predicted that partisans who identified with the incumbent party would downplay the importance of high unemployment and inflation rates in order to avoid cognitive inconsistency. In other words, partisan motivation should not completely obscure the real world, but it should distort the priorities of those willing to act on this source of motivation. Individuals who express no partisan leaning, and therefore have no source of partisan motivation, should not show evidence of bias. Likewise, I did not expect to observe this effect among individuals for whom the issue in question was likely to be particularly impactful.

Researchers have debated whether partisanship shapes economic perceptions (Bartels, 2002; Conover, Feldman, & Knight, 1987; Evans & Anderson,

---

important. Although some individuals may update their candidate evaluations and party identity to reflect their positions on issues they deem important, I suggest here that this group is composed of people who are unmotivated or unable to reprioritize the issues in defense of their party. This, of course, changes the implications markedly. Issue publics might be capable of holding their party accountable on important issues (Krosnick, 1990), but these efforts will likely be offset by their fellow partisans' efforts to downplay the importance of the same issues.

2. These are all the years for which ANES data are available.

2006; Gerber & Huber, 2010; Lewis-Beck, Nadeau, & Elias, 2008), but if partisan motivation affects the weights placed on economic perceptions, this debate becomes somewhat moot. Partisan bias may abound even in the presence of perfectly objective perceptions.

Given the objective nature of unemployment and inflation rates, we can be reasonably confident that causation runs in the predicted direction.[3] Still, the role of elite communication remains a concern. Certainly, one would expect political actors to tailor their messages to the political and economic context and attempt to shape issue priorities in their own favor (Petrocik, 1996; Petrocik et al., 2003–2004; West, 2010). Therefore, although survey analyses help determine whether party identification shapes issue priorities, such analyses do not allow us to establish whether individuals are simply more likely to accept agenda cueing messages from their own party or whether they engage in issue reprioritization all on their own.

To resolve this issue, I ran a national experiment designed to induce cognitive inconsistency between respondents' party identification and their attitude toward a particular bill. The primary purpose of this experiment was to determine whether issue reprioritization constitutes a psychological defense mechanism or whether it is merely elite driven. Of course, if partisans take weight off one issue, they must reallocate that weight to some other issue (or set of issues). Therefore, in addition to decreasing the importance placed on issues that threaten their party, I also expected partisans to place greater importance on issues that *favored* their party. Because parties are thought to "own" particular issue domains (see Petrocik, 1996; Petrocik et al., 2003–2004), partisans should shift their issue priorities away from issues upon which they disagree with their party and place greater importance on these "party owned" issues.

---

3. The use of objective measures as opposed to perceptions substantially reduces concerns about endogeneity, but unemployment and inflation have been shown to fluctuate with the party in power (conservatives versus liberals) (Hibbs, 1977). To alleviate this concern, I examined "own party incumbency" rather than "Democratic [Republican] incumbency," which allows the effects of Republican and Democratic incumbency to offset one another. To be safe, a Democratic incumbency dummy was included to control for any portion of this effect that did not cancel. Another potential concern is that citizens leave the incumbent's party during times of economic turmoil. However, given the tendency for partisans to maintain stable identities (Green, Palmquist, & Schickler, 2002), one would expect this effect to be negligible. An empirical check confirmed this expectation. Controlling for other variables in the model, unemployment and inflation were both found to be unrelated to own party incumbency.

A second factor—which will receive greater attention in the next chapter—manipulated the availability of cognitive resources. To actively defend one's party identity requires cognitive effort, but much of the literature suggests that citizens follow party cues to cut down on cognitive effort (Rahn, 1993; Shively, 1979). To determine whether issue reprioritization indeed constitutes a method of effortful party identity defense, cognitive resources were experimentally manipulated via a cognitive load induction. I reasoned that, if partisans ceased to engage in issue reprioritization once cognitive resources were inhibited, then it would be clear that party identification had not merely functioned as a heuristic but instead served as a source of directional motivation. Additionally, if participants changed their identity to reflect disagreements in the absence of sufficient cognitive resources, then it would be clear that identity stability was contingent on defense.

ECONOMIC CONDITIONS AND THE MOST IMPORTANT PROBLEM

I began by considering whether individuals respond to economic conditions in the same way when their own party is in power as they do when the opposition party is in power. To do this, I examined the impact of actual economic indicators (unemployment rate and inflation rate) on issue priorities using data from the ANES surveys conducted between 1960 and 2000. Yearly unemployment and inflation rates (based on the consumer price index) were acquired from the Bureau of Labor Statistics. These variables were recoded to run from 0 to 1, with 1 corresponding to the highest observed value.

A series of most important problem dummy variables were created based on the open-ended question administered in the ANES. The dummy variable corresponding to social welfare issues is based on the codes provided by the ANES.[4] This variable contains mentions of issues including, but certainly not limited to, unemployment, healthcare, poverty, housing, child care, and aid to education. Unemployment and inflation importance dummies were created using the more elaborate codes provided in the appendix to the ANES cumulative file. These two variables were coded much more narrowly to include only direct mentions of unemployment and inflation, respectively.

An additional dummy variable was created to denote own-party incumbency. Respondents were coded as "1" if their party controlled the presidency at the time of the election regardless of whether the president was running for reelection. Controls for income, education, age, gender, race, and union membership were also included, because these factors are likely to affect the degree to

---

4. For more information see the codebook and appendix for the ANES cumulative file, available at http://www.electionstudies.org/.

which high unemployment and inflation are felt by respondents. These variables were coded to run from 0 to 1. A Democratic president dummy variable was also included to ensure that the results were not party specific.[5] It should be noted, however, that the results remain robust even when all controls are excluded.

Results

To estimate the effect of motivated reasoning on the public agenda, I examined the impact of economic indicators on responses to the *most important problem* question. Because this question was open-ended and response options were therefore limitless, I conducted a series of probit analyses on dummy variables created to correspond to various issue domains. Because some variables varied by respondent and others varied by year, all models were estimated with standard errors clustered by year. I began by examining what caused respondents to mention social welfare as the most important problem facing the country. As explained earlier, this variable includes mentions of unemployment as well as various issues that one might expect to be of concern during periods of high unemployment (e.g., healthcare, poverty, housing). Table 3.1 presents the results of a probit regression in which the national unemployment rate, own-party incumbency, and the interaction between unemployment rate and own-party incumbency were used to predict mentions of social welfare issues.

Results are displayed in the first two columns of Table 3.1. As one would expect, among both Independents and partisans, higher levels of unemployment were positively associated with mentions of social welfare issues. However, consistent with the theory, this effect diminished substantially when the subject's own party was presiding over high unemployment. This effect is reflected in the large negative coefficient on the interaction term (*own-party president*unemployment rate*) in the second column from the left. To ensure that these findings cannot be attributed to perceptual bias in economic evaluations, the third column displays the results when the model was rerun with a control for economic perceptions. The economic perceptions item has been included in the ANES only since 1980, so the addition of this control variable cost a large number of cases. Nonetheless, the results appear remarkably robust.

---

5. Given the relative abundance of Democratic compared to Republican identifiers, one might be concerned that the own-party president variable would disproportionately pick up effects among Democrats during Democratic administrations. The model cannot be estimated when the Democratic president dummy variable and party identification are both included, so the choice was made to include the former rather than the latter. However, the results remained substantively very similar when party identification was substituted into the model.

TABLE 3.1. *IMPACT OF PARTISAN BIAS AND UNEMPLOYMENT RATE ON MENTIONS OF SOCIAL WELFARE ISSUES*

	Social Welfare (Independents) B (SE)	Social Welfare (Partisans) B (SE)	Social Welfare (Partisans) B (SE)
Own-Party President		.716*** (.173)	.912*** (.198)
Unemployment Rate	1.34*** (.508)	2.11*** (.447)	1.65*** (.531)
Own-Party President* Unemployment Rate		−1.22*** (.236)	−1.48*** (.263)
Economic Perception			.014 (.192)
Income	.020 (.103)	−.230*** (.056)	−.142*** (.052)
Education	−.071 (.123)	−.056 (.088)	−.211*** (.073)
Age	.001 (.181)	−.022 (.074)	−.108 (.104)
Female	.235*** (.057)	.141*** (.027)	.207*** (.024)
Black	.225** (.097)	.281*** (.068)	.209** (.091)
Union	.002 (.053)	.110*** (.039)	.076** (.031)
Democrat President	.154 (.235)	.166 (.193)	.178 (.222)
Constant	−1.85*** (.362)	−2.18*** (.303)	−1.70*** (.352)
N	3,209	25,167	13,803

Note: The coefficients (*B*) and standard errors (*SE*) reported in the table were obtained via probit models with clustered standard errors. Data are from the American National Elections Studies (1960–2000).

***$p < .01$, **$p < .05$, *$p < .10$

The predicted probabilities on display in Figure 3.1 provide a substantive indication of the effect.[6] When the opposition party was in power, the probability of mentioning an issue related to social welfare increased dramatically with the

6. All predicted probabilities were calculated with income, education, and age set to their means. Female was set to "1," and black, union, and Democratic president were set to "0."

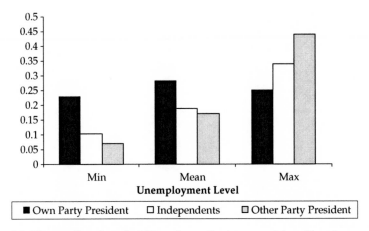

Figure 3.1 The predicted probability of mentioning a social welfare issue as the nation's most important problem.

unemployment rate, climbing from 8.1% at the minimum observed level of unemployment to 47.1% at the highest observed level of unemployment. However, when one's own party was in power, the probability of mentioning a social welfare issue remained quite steady—only increasing from 24.7% at the minimum observed unemployment level to 28.2% at the maximum observed level.

"Pure" Independents serve as a valuable baseline for comparison in Figure 3.1 (see Jessee, 2010). Relative to Independents, at high levels of unemployment, partisans who identified with the incumbent party were less likely to mention unemployment as the nation's most important problem. On the other hand, those identifying with the non-incumbent party moved in the opposite direction. In other words, these biases appear to be not only defensive reactions but offensive as well.

These findings are powerful because they suggest that, depending on the partisan context, the unemployment rate may have a large effect or only a small effect on the likelihood of mentioning a wide variety of problems. Still, given the breadth of issues captured by this variable, one might wonder whether these results hold up when the dependent variable is coded more narrowly to capture only mentions of unemployment. To test whether the pattern holds, the same models were run with mentions of unemployment as the dependent variable. Results are presented in Table 3.2.

Just as before, the actual unemployment rate had a sizeable effect on respondents' likelihood of mentioning unemployment as the country's most important problem. Again, however, the interaction term shows that this relationship was substantially smaller when one's own party was in power. Results are virtually identical even after including the measure of economic perceptions in

TABLE 3.2. *IMPACT OF PARTISAN BIAS AND UNEMPLOYMENT RATE ON MENTIONS OF UNEMPLOYMENT*

	Unemployment (Independents)	Unemployment (Partisans)	Unemployment (Partisans)
	B	*B*	*B*
	(SE)	*(SE)*	*(SE)*
Own-Party President		.388	.313*
		(.275)	(.186)
Unemployment Rate	4.32***	4.32***	2.90***
	(.683)	(.819)	(.257)
Own-Party President* Unemployment Rate		−.685*	−.548**
		(.390)	(.247)
Economic Perception			−.306***
			(.095)
Income	−.020	−.256***	−.282***
	(.102)	(.073)	(.058)
Education	−.071**	−.289***	−.389***
	(.181)	(.094)	(.073)
Age	−.001	−.200	−.119
	(.196)	(.138)	(.179)
Female	.235*	.107***	.100***
	(.061)	(.023)	(.026)
Black	.225*	.343***	.307***
	(.150)	(.056)	(.059)
Union	.002	.124***	.130***
	(.058)	(.037)	(.049)
Democrat President	.154	−.096	−.138
	(.142)	(.131)	(.106)
Constant	−1.85***	−4.06***	−2.84***
	(.441)	(.585)	(.234)
N	3,209	25,167	13,803

Note: The coefficients (*B*) and standard errors (*SE*) reported in the table were obtained via probit models with clustered standard errors. Data are from the American National Elections Studies ANES (1960–2000).

***$p < .01$, **$p < .05$, *$p < .10$

the model. The predicted probability of naming unemployment as the country's most important problem is displayed Figure 3.2. At the maximum observed level of unemployment, partisans who identified with the incumbent party were almost 12% less likely to mention unemployment than were partisans who identified with the non-incumbent party. Independents reacted more similarly

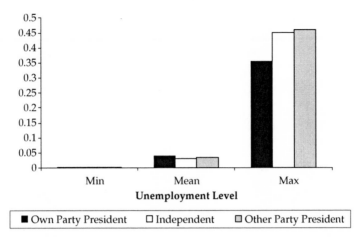

Figure 3.2 The predicted probability of mentioning unemployment as the nation's most important problem.

to non-incumbent partisans, showing an almost 10% greater likelihood of mentioning unemployment at the maximum observed level. As before, it appears that partisans reprioritized issues in favor of their own party.

Still, one might wonder whether these results were uniform across the electorate. Responsiveness motivation should increase relative to partisan motivation among individuals for whom the issue (in this case, unemployment) is more threatening. This means that the impact of partisan bias should be strongest among those who are least affected by unemployment and should disappear among those who are most affected. Table 3.3 and Figure 3.3 show the results among respondents whose incomes fall into the lower third of the distribution compared with those in the upper two-thirds of the distribution.[7]

Among those with higher incomes, the pattern was identical to the results described earlier, except that the effects were larger, as expected. At the highest observed level of unemployment, the predicted probability of mentioning unemployment as the nation's most important problem differed between members of the incumbent party and the opposition by almost 17%. On the other hand, partisan biases gave way to accuracy motivation among those in the lower third of the income distribution.

7. Income was measured on a five-point scale coded by income percentile: 0%–16%, 17%–33%, 34%–67%, 69%–95%, and 96%–100%. The variable mean fell between the second and third category, leaving the first 33% of the distribution below the mean and the upper 67% above the mean. In other words, because of the ordinal nature of the variable, dividing the sample at its mean equated to separating the lower third of the income distribution from the upper two-thirds.

TABLE 3.3. *IMPACT OF PARTISAN BIAS AND UNEMPLOYMENT RATE ON MENTIONS OF UNEMPLOYMENT BY INCOME*

	Unemployment (Low Income)	Unemployment (High Income)
	B	B
	(SE)	(SE)
Own-Party President	.090	.533**
	(.406)	(.232)
Unemployment Rate	3.85***	4.61***
	(.909)	(.773)
Own-Party President* Unemployment Rate	−.127	−.963***
	(.585)	(.322)
Income	.085	−.359***
	(.153)	(.094)
Education	−.126	−.372***
	(.117)	(.102)
Age	−.160	−.153
	(.145)	(.204)
Female	.080***	.122***
	(.027)	(.029)
Black	.349***	.368***
	(.063)	(.073)
Union	.056	.126***
	(.061)	(.037)
Democrat President	−.089	−.113
	(.143)	(.134)
Constant	−3.86***	−4.17***
	(.637)	(.559)
N	8,165	17,002

Note: The coefficients (*B*) and standard errors (*SE*) reported in the table were obtained via probit models with clustered standard errors. Data are from the American National Elections Studies ANES (1960–2000).

***$p < .01$, **$p < .05$, *$p < .10$

Given that partisan biases have such a powerful influence on the relationship between unemployment rates and issue priorities, one might wonder whether these results would hold up when looking at other types of economic problems. In Table 3.4, I replicated the previous analyses with a focus on inflation. Given the relative inattention to inflation compared with unemployment, this replication serves as a conservative test of the theory. Nonetheless, the pattern emerged

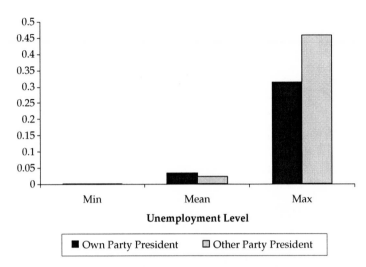

Figure 3.3 The predicted probability of mentioning unemployment as the nation's most important problem among those respondents in the upper two-thirds of the income distribution.

yet again. Among both partisans and Independents, higher inflation rates corresponded to a higher probability of naming inflation as the country's most important problem. And, as with unemployment, people became less likely to provide this response when their own party was in power. However, Figure 3.4 shows that the influence of partisan bias is relatively small from a substantive standpoint. The effect actually became slightly stronger when economic perceptions were included as a control, but it remained relatively small.

Recall, however, that in the analysis of unemployment, the effect of partisan bias varied with income. Given the natural tradeoff between unemployment and inflation, those with lower incomes are likely to be more tolerant of inflation, whereas those with higher incomes are likely to be more tolerant of higher unemployment. Therefore, the effect of partisan bias should be strongest among those with lower levels of income, and accuracy motivation should reduce the impact of partisan bias among those with higher levels of income. Results are displayed in Table 3.5 and Figure 3.5.

As predicted, substantively significant effects of partisan bias emerged among those on the lower end of the income distribution. More specifically, at the highest observed level of inflation, opposition party identifiers were about 16% more likely than those who identified with the president's party to mention inflation as the nation's most important problem. Also as predicted, these biases disappeared among those at the higher end of the income distribution.

TABLE 3.4. *IMPACT OF PARTISAN BIAS AND INFLATION RATE ON MENTIONS OF INFLATION*

	Inflation (Independents)	Inflation (Partisans)	Inflation (Partisans)
	B	*B*	*B*
	(SE)	*(SE)*	*(SE)*
Own-Party President		.161	.126
		(.112)	(.077)
Inflation Rate	2.38***	3.01***	2.75***
	(.489)	(.500)	(.242)
Own-PartyPresident*		−.245	−.289***
Inflation Rate		(.249)	(.074)
Economic Perception			.011
			(.220)
Income	.177	.188***	.145
	(.155)	(.067)	(.171)
Education	.073	.027	.083
	(.097)	(.088)	(.158)
Age	−.289	−.115	−.586***
	(.179)	(.130)	(.149)
Female	.123**	.012	.036
	(.057)	(.024)	(.088)
Black	−.463***	−.227***	−.198***
	(.176)	(.040)	(.069)
Union	−.007	−.050	−.053
	(.062)	(.040)	(.079)
Democrat President	.144	.104	−.255^
	(.427)	(.470)	(.152)
Constant	−2.42***	−2.73***	−2.74***
	(.276)	(.321)	(.232)
N	3,209	25,167	13,803

Note: The coefficients (*B*) and standard errors (*SE*) reported in the table were obtained via probit models with clustered standard errors. Data are from the American National Elections Studies ANES (1960–2000).

***$p < .01$, **$p < .05$, *$p < .10$

TABLE 3.5. *IMPACT OF PARTISAN BIAS AND INFLATION RATE ON MENTIONS OF INFLATION BY INCOME*

	Inflation (Low Income)	Inflation (High Income)
	B	B
	(SE)	(SE)
Own-Party President	.213	.137
	(.160)	(.111)
Inflation Rate	2.98***	3.04***
	(.533)	(.493)
Own-Party President* Inflation Rate	−.615**	−.055
	(.248)	(.257)
Income	.446	.251***
	(.299)	(.084)
Education	.098	.002
	(.132)	(.112)
Age	−.012	−.188*
	(.197)	(.108)
Female	.014	.007
	(.036)	(.025)
Black	−.191***	−.266***
	(.063)	(.056)
Union	.027	−.066
	(.048)	(.046)
Democrat President	.017	.157
	(.467)	(.473)
Constant	−2.72***	−2.80***
	(.346)	(.306)
N	8,165	17,002

Note: The coefficients (*B*) and standard errors (*SE*) reported in the table were obtained via probit models with clustered standard errors. Data are from the American National Elections Studies ANES (1960–2000).

***$p < .01$, **$p < .05$, *$p < .10$

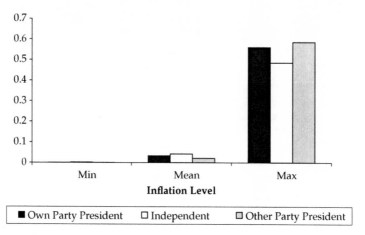

Figure 3.4 The predicted probability of mentioning inflation as the nation's most important problem.

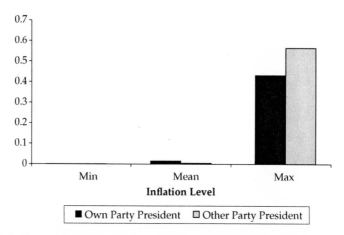

Figure 3.5 The predicted probability of mentioning inflation as the nation's most important problem among those respondents in the lower one-third of the income distribution.

ISSUE REPRIORITIZATION AS PARTY IDENTITY JUSTIFICATION

The survey-based results presented thus far demonstrate that party identity shapes partisans' issue priorities. However, additional evidence is needed to determine whether these results are indeed driven by individual motivation and not wholly attributable to elite influence. Although elites almost certainly play a role in shaping the public's agenda, I suspect that partisans also shift their issue priorities in an effort to insulate their individual party identities. If their party performs poorly while in office or they discover that they disagree with their party on a particular issue, partisans are able to reduce this cognitive inconsistency by lowering the importance they place on this issue and placing greater weight on other more consonant issues.

A national matched survey experiment of 400 participants was run through YouGov/Polimetrix during May 2007 to test the theory. YouGov/Polimetrix conducts surveys through their website (http://today.yougov.com). Based on demographics, they match respondents to a target matrix they have developed using voter lists and consumer databases. This regularly updated target matrix is what they use to define a representative sample. By modeling response and participation rates, they are able to avoid selection effects. YouGov/Polimetrix samples have been found to perform at least as well as other polling methods in predicting election outcomes.[8] For this study, 961 respondents were interviewed and matched down to a sample of 400 to produce the final data set. Subjects were matched on gender, age, race, education, party identification, and ideology.[9] Sample matching occurred completely independent of experimental randomization.

Methods

The experiment employed a 2×2 (disagreement $\times$ cognitive load) factorial design to determine how partisans allocate their cognitive resources after discovering a disagreement with their party. In order to evoke disagreement between subjects and their party, all respondents were asked to read a persuasive newspaper article about a fictitious bill, entitled the "Common Sense in Outsourcing Bill," soon to be introduced in Congress (see the Appendix for Chapter 3). The bill proposed to reduce outsourcing through tax incentives and to outlaw the outsourcing of federal government contracts. Importantly, no partisan cues whatsoever were provided in the article. The issue of outsourcing was chosen because it was quite prevalent in the news at the time of the study, yet neither party had taken a united and unambiguous stance on the subject. The argument made in the article was carefully crafted to avoid partisan or ideological flavoring that might substitute as a partisan cue for readers.

---

8. Information available at http://research.yougov.com.
9. Originally, I intended to sample only 200 respondents. However, YouGov/Polimetrix offered to rerun my entire study free of charge after discovering that they had neglected to match down the initial sample with sufficient precision. All 400 respondents were included in these analyses.

This meant that participants would be unaware of where the parties stood on the Common Sense in Outsourcing Bill while reading the article. After reading the article, respondents were asked whether they supported or opposed passage of the bill. Because no cues were provided and the article was written to make a strong case for the bill, subjects were expected to express support for the it.

Next, all participants were randomly assigned to either the *disagreement* condition or the *neutral* condition. Those assigned to the *neutral* condition were asked to read a second newspaper article stressing the potential electoral significance of the Common Sense in Outsourcing Bill and the fact that the bill had a *mixture of support and opposition* within both parties. The article also added that none of the leading contenders for the 2008 presidential race had yet taken a stance on the bill. Those assigned to the *disagreement* condition read an article that was virtually identical except for the fact that it stressed that the parties and candidates had taken *clear and opposite stances* on the outsourcing bill. Because YouGov/Polimetrix maintains records on their subject pool, I was able to cue the stimulus to respondents' pretest party identification. In other words, without jeopardizing randomization between groups, I was able to ensure that those in the treatment (*disagreement*) group would, in fact, read an article that indicated their own party opposed the Common Sense in Outsourcing Bill and the opposition party supported the bill, regardless of the subject's party identification.[10] This ensured that, assuming they were persuaded by the first article, subjects would face inconsistency between their own stated position on the outsourcing bill and the position taken by their party and its leading presidential contenders.

The second factor—cognitive load—was manipulated via a memory task in which respondents were asked to recall either a single-digit number (in the low cognitive load condition) or a six-digit number (in the high cognitive load condition). Subjects were told that they were participating in a memory study designed to understand how well people remember information they read in the newspaper. They were also told that they would be asked to recall their single-digit or six-digit number later in the study. The idea behind this cover story was to ensure that subjects made every effort to remember their number while still reading the newspaper article carefully. Just after reporting their position on the Common Sense in Outsourcing Bill, subjects were provided with the number that they would later be asked to recall. This meant that they had to hold the number in their mind as they read the second article (which, in

10. Independents who identified as leaning toward a particular party were considered partisan identifiers. Pure Independents are excluded from analysis.

the *disagreement* condition, revealed to them that they had just taken a position at odds with their own party and consistent with the opposition party) and as they answered the subsequent questions regarding party identification.

By manipulating cognitive load, it is possible to determine how individuals allocate their cognitive resources. The proposed theory suggests that partisans devote their cognitive resources to identity defense—in this case, issue reprioritization. Therefore, although I expected to observe evidence of issue reprioritization in response to disagreement, I expected this effect to disappear among subjects placed under cognitive load.

Measures

Rather than obtaining issue importance via open-ended measures and creating issue dummy variables (as in the previous analysis), issue importance was measured with the use of a seven-point scale ranging from "not that important" to "extremely important." For ease of interpretation, issue importance measures were rescaled to run from 0 to 1 in the analyses. Building on the work of Petrocik and colleagues (Petrocik, 1996; Petrocik, Benoit, & Hansen, 2003–2004), a Democrat owned issues variable was constructed from items measuring the importance of the Iraq War, healthcare, and global warming. A Republican owned issues variable was constructed from items measuring the importance of terrorism, taxes, and the budget.

As indicated, I relied on two measures of party identification. The first was obtained at the time subjects joined the YouGov/Polimetrix participant pool. The second was obtained shortly after subjects read the second stimulus article and before they were asked to recall their assigned number. The standard seven-point measure was used in both cases.

Dummy variables were created for each of the two factors: *disagreement* and *cognitive load*. Subjects assigned to treatment conditions received a value of "1," and those assigned to nontreatment conditions received a value of "0."

Results

I began by examining whether the first article actually persuaded subjects to support the Common Sense in Outsourcing Bill. Because the theory pertains to partisans, the 52 subjects who identified as "pure" Independents in the pre-test were excluded from this analysis. The results suggest that the article produced the anticipated outcome. On the seven-point scale ranging from "strongly oppose" to "strongly support," the mean was 5.39 and the standard deviation was 1.67. In all, more than 75% of the sample expressed support for the bill, with approximately 33% reporting the maximum level of support (i.e., 7—"strongly support").

The *cognitive load* manipulation appears to have been quite successful given that just under 93% of partisan subjects were able to successfully recall their assigned number. In order to ensure that the *cognitive load* manipulation did not undercut the power of the *disagreement* manipulation, I also examined partisans' ability to correctly recall which party supported and which party opposed the bill in the minimal cognitive load versus high cognitive load conditions. No significant differences in recall were found between partisans in the minimal cognitive load condition ($M = .76$, $SD = .43$) and in the high cognitive load condition (mean (M) = .80), standard deviation ((SD) = .40); t(df = 342) = 1.08).[11] Nor were differences found between the no disagreement condition ($M = .78$, $SD = .42$) and the disagreement condition (($M = .79$, $SD = .41$); t(df = 342) = 0.16).

Given that the treatment appears to have been successful, I now turn to analysis of the experiment's substantive effects. The first issue to consider is whether partisans engaged in identity defense (via issue reprioritization) or whether they simply brought their party identity into alignment with the position they took on the outsourcing bill. Results in the first column of Table 3.6 show that Republicans and Democrats reacted differently to the stimulus. Among Republicans, exposure to disagreement actually led to a significant

TABLE 3.6. *EFFECT OF DISAGREEMENT ON PARTY IDENTIFICATION*

	Party Identification (Republicans) Ordered Probit B (SE)	Party Identification (Democrats) Ordered Probit B (SE)
Disagreement	−.456**	−.039
	(.187)	(.182)
Party Identification ($t-1$)	1.25***	1.54***
	(.130)	(.141)
Cut 1	−.788 (.403)	−3.75 (.365)
Cut 2	−.558 (.344)	−2.11 (.297)
Cut 3	.065 (.270)	−.761 (.279)
Cut 4	1.48 (.263)	.231 (.404)
Cut 5	2.72 (.316)	NA
N	166	182

Note: The coefficients (B) and standard errors (SE) reported in the table were obtained via ordered probit models.

***$p < .01$, **$p < .05$, *$p < .10$

11. The t-test statistic (t) indicates that the difference between means was not significant with 342 degrees of freedom (df).

weakening of party identification (Figure 3.6). However, Democrats appear to have been able to resist changing their party identity.

Although this pattern of effects was not predicted, it is not entirely surprising given the political context at the time of the study. The experiment was conducted in May 2007, a tumultuous time for the Republican Party. According to a report released by The Pew Research Center, Republican Party identification dropped from 29% in 2005 to 25% by 2007 (Kohut, Doherty, Dimock, & Keeter, 2007) as President Bush's approval ratings dipped below 30% for the first time (Gallup, 2008). Moreover, waning enthusiasm for the Republican Party and its administration was not confined to Democrats. Between September 2006 and July 2007, *Republicans'* approval of the Bush administration dropped from 86% to 65% (Gallup). In short, it appears that the study was conducted at a time when Republicans were running low on motivation and/or ability to continue to defend their party.[12] Of course, all of this bad news for Republicans just insulated Democratic identifiers from identity change even more.

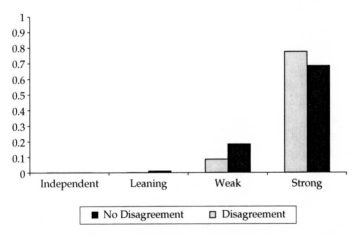

Figure 3.6 The predicted probability of party identification (post-treatment) given strong identification with the Republican Party (pre-treatment).

12. Alternatively, one might wonder whether these results reflect stable underlying differences in the way conservatives and liberals process information (see Jost, Glaser, Kruglanski, & Sulloway, 2003). However, if anything, motivational asymmetries appear to operate in the opposite direction, with conservatives (Jost, et al., 2003), authoritarians (Lavine, Lodge, & Freitas, 2005), and dogmatics (Rokeach, 1960) exhibiting more bias, close-mindedness, and willingness to deny logical contradictions (Jost, Hennes, & Lavine, in press). Group-based biases (more akin to the type observed here) occur among both liberals and conservatives (Jost, Hennes, & Lavine).

In addition to being interesting in its own right, this partisan asymmetry provides a valuable opportunity for comparison. Given that Democrats resisted identity change, they should show evidence of party identity defense. However, because Republicans appear to have simply given in and changed their identity, they should not have engaged in issue reprioritization. The findings displayed in Table 3.7 bear out this prediction. The data shown in the first four columns of the table suggest that Republicans did not decrease the weight they placed on outsourcing nor increase the weight they placed on issues owned by their party. These null effects were robust to dichotomization of the dependent variable.

On the other hand, as expected, Democrats did engage in issue reprioritization after being made to experience inconsistency between their party identity and their position on the outsourcing bill. First, Democrats deprioritized outsourcing as a political issue (see columns 5 and 6 of Table 3.7). When the dependent variable consisted of the full outsourcing importance scale, disagreement had a negative but nonsignificant effect. However, when the variable was dichotomized at its mean, a more sizeable and statistically significant effect emerged. This suggests that most of the action occurred around the scale's mean. Those who considered outsourcing to be extremely important or not at all important were less likely to shift their opinion in service to their party identity. Perhaps, as we saw in the survey analyses, these were people who had a personal stake in the outsourcing debate.[13] The positive coefficient on the interaction term shows that this effect disappeared when disagreement occurred in the presence of cognitive load. In other words, Democrats appear to have shifted their issue priorities to avoid partisan inconsistency as long as they possessed the cognitive resources necessary to engage in issue reprioritization.

The predicted pattern also appeared when party owned issues were examined (see columns 7 and 8 of Table 3.7). Democrats exposed to the *disagreement* treatment allocated greater importance to these issues. Again, this effect disappeared when cognitive resources were inhibited. As with the importance of outsourcing, this effect showed up more clearly after dichotomization of the dependent variable. Predicted probabilities associated with the two probit models are displayed in Figure 3.7.

Given the conservative nature of the experimental manipulation, the consistency of these results is striking. It appears that Democrats were able to reprioritize away cognitive inconsistency when they had sufficient cognitive resources available to them, decreasing the importance they placed

---

13. Unfortunately, the sample size was not sufficient to pursue this hypothesis with the experimental data obtained.

TABLE 3.7. *DISAGREEMENT AND COGNITIVE LOAD EXPERIMENT*

	Outsourcing OLS (Republicans)	Outsourcing Probit (Republicans)	Owned Issue OLS (Republicans)	Owned Issue Probit (Republicans)	Outsourcing OLS (Democrats)	Outsourcing Probit (Democrats)	Owned Issue OLS (Democrats)	Owned Issue Probit (Democrats)
	B (SE)	B (SE)	B (SE)	B (SE)	B (SE)	B (SE)	B (SE)	B (SE)
Disagreement	.044 (.071)	.206 (.359)	-.025 (.027)	-.106 (.294)	-.034 (.053)	-.882* (.478)	.061** (.031)	.660** (.312)
Cognitive Load	.043 (.068)	-.102 (.323)	-.021 (.025)	-.099 (.280)	-.006 (.052)	-.604 (.485)	.028 (.030)	.352 (.284)
Disagreement* Cognitive Load	-.070 (.095)	-.208 (.465)	.048 (.035)	.303 (.393)	.038 (.075)	1.16* (.631)	-.058 (.044)	-.881** (.427)
Constant	.593*** (.052)	.929*** (.252)	.835*** (.019)	.074 (.215)	.765*** (.040)	1.95*** (.424)	.840*** (.023)	.502** (.210)
N	166	166	166	166	182	182	182	182

***$p < .01$, **$p < .05$, *$p < .10$

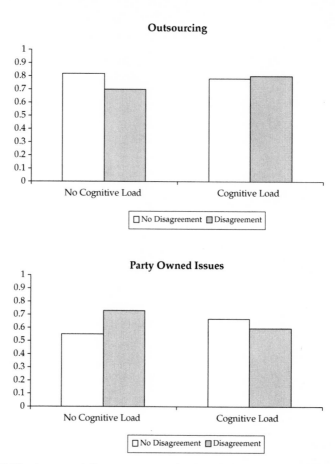

Figure 3.7 The impact of disagreement and cognitive load on issue of importance among Democrats.

on the disagreed-upon issue and increasing the importance they placed on party-owned issues. However, when their cognitive resources were inhibited, efforts to defend their identity via issue reprioritization were obstructed. Republicans, who appear as a group not to have engaged in issue reprioritization, reported weaker party identities in response to the disagreement induction even in the absence of cognitive load.

Discussion

Over the years, a number of scholars have examined the ability of elites to manipulate the public agenda. Often overlooked is the fact that individuals themselves have a strong incentive to reweight their issue priorities to favor their preferred party. Not only is this an effective way to reduce inconsistency between one's party identity and political attitudes, but this method of inconsistency reduction also prevents the appearance of bias. Social norms of independent thinking and objectivity have reshaped American political culture since the Progressive Era (Dalton, 2008; Schudson, 1998), and these norms undoubtedly reduce the amount of overt partisan bias citizens are willing to display.

Results from two studies demonstrated that partisans reprioritize issues to favor their party. Analysis of 40 years of ANES survey data showed that respondents downplayed the importance of economic issues when their party was presiding over a poor economy. Additionally, experimental results showed that Democrats devoted their cognitive resources to issue reprioritization in order to reduce inconsistency between their party identification and their issue positions. This allowed them to maintain a stable identity. Republicans, on the other hand, appeared not to have engaged in identity defense and instead showed evidence of party identification change (presumably as a result of the political climate in May 2007). Of course, an important question remains: Given that Democrats were unable to defend their identity once their cognitive resources were inhibited, did they then change their identity to reflect disagreement with their party? This question is taken up in Chapter 4.

CHAPTER 4

Cognitive Resources and Resistance to Identity Change

Chapters 2 and 3 showed that partisans generate justifications in order to defend their party identity, and in Chapter 3 we saw that this requires cognitive resources. Democrats were able to successfully reprioritize their issue positions only in the absence of cognitive load. This chapter examines whether partisan stability is contingent on the availability of cognitive resources. If partisans are unable to defend their identity, they should feel compelled to change their party identification in response to disagreement with their party. In short, partisans who appear to be acting as good citizens may, in fact, just be exhausted fans.

The dual motivations theory is unique in making this prediction. The notion that individuals devote their cognitive resources to justification of their exiting identity runs directly counter to the two dominant theories in the contemporary debate over party identification. Revisionist models assume that citizens are motivated to identify with whichever party best represents their policy interests. Therefore, partisans should allocate their cognitive resources to updating their identity to reflect their issue positions and not to engaging in identity defense. Critics of the revisionist model suggest that party identification should remain stable regardless of whether cognitive resources are available (Green, Palmquist, & Schickler, 2002). According to this camp, partisans are unmotivated to resolve inconsistency between their party identity and their political evaluations, so identity defense is not necessary for the maintenance of stable party attachments.

The dual motivations theory argues that citizens want to *believe* that their party identity is rooted in objective political evaluations in order to conform to norms of good citizenship. Therefore, contrary to the claims of Green et al. (2002), partisans feel psychological pressure to bring their party identity into alignment with their political evaluations. However, updating their party identity to reflect disagreements with their party, as revisionist theory suggests, would mean acting against their partisan motivation. Therefore, the optimal strategy is to generate a justification for maintaining their existing identity despite their disagreements. This, however, requires cognitive resources. Consequently, party identification change should be most likely when an individual disagrees with her party but lacks cognitive resources.

RESOURCE ALLOCATION IN SOCIAL COGNITION

Stereotypes and prejudices were once thought to be causally linked (Allport, 1954), but scholars have come to view them as independent constructs (Duckitt, 2003; Amodio & Devine, 2006). Prejudices are affective orientations toward groups, whereas stereotypes are cognitive representations of groups (Amodio & Devine) that allow information to be processed more quickly (Macrae, Milne, & Bodenhausen, 1994) and potentially more efficiently (Sherman, Lee, Bessenoff, & Frost, 1998). However, for stereotypes to facilitate processing efficiency, they must be updated to reflect counter-stereotypical information when it is encountered. Of course, the idea of updating stereotypes conflicts with their well-known resistance to change (Hilton & Von Hippel, 1996). Even in the face of counter-stereotypical information, individuals are able to maintain their stereotypes through biased retrieval (Kunda, 1990; Kunda & Oleson, 1995; Kunda & Sanitioso, 1989), and this makes it possible to deploy stereotypes again and again for the purpose of identity reaffirmation (Fein & Spencer, 1997; Kunda & Spencer, 2003; Steele, 1988).

When the literature on party identification and the literature on stereotyping are placed side-by-side, the parallels are hard to miss. Although party identification was originally seen as an affective orientation that colors political perceptions (Campbell, Converse, Miller, & Stokes, 1960), it is now viewed by many as an efficient heuristic for simplifying politics (Brady & Sniderman, 1985; Huckfeldt, Levine, Morgan, & Sprague, 1999; Kam, 2005; Popkin, 1991; Schaffner & Streb, 2002; Shively, 1979; Tomz & Sniderman, 2005). However, this efficiency depends on partisans' willingness to bring their identity into alignment with their evaluations, as revisionist theories suggest. Critics of the revisionist model argue that party identification is highly stable and resistant to change even when partisans disagree with their party (Green et al., 2002).

Noticing the parallels between these literatures, the dual motivations theory of party identification builds on research into stereotype maintenance. In a series of experiments, Yzerbyt, Coull, and Rocher (1999) manipulated cognitive resources during an encounter with a member of a stereotyped group who deviated from that stereotype. They found that participants devoted their cognitive resources to stereotype maintenance rather than updating their preconceptions to reflect new information. Most stereotype change occurred when subjects encountered deviant individuals but lacked the cognitive resources necessary to preserve their stereotypes. In a separate set of experiments, Sherman, Stroessner, Conrey, and Azam (2005) found that participants who were high in prejudice attended more closely to stereotype-inconsistent information as long as they had sufficient cognitive resources. Participants then attributed this stereotype-inconsistent information to external factors while attributing stereotype-consistent information to internal factors. In short, prejudice motivated participants to devote whatever resources they had to explaining away inconsistencies in order to maintain their existing stereotype.

According to Sherif (1966), "Whenever individuals belonging to one group interact, collectively or individually, with another group or its members in terms of their group identification, we have an instance of intergroup behavior" (p. 12). Therefore, theories of intergroup stereotyping and prejudice should apply just as readily to the partisan context as they do to domains such as race, ethnicity, and gender. Moreover, if we take seriously the notion that partisan orientations truly constitute identities (Campbell et al., 1960; Campbell, Gurin, & Miller, 1954; Green et al., 2002; Greene, 1999), then a threat to one's party identity amounts to a threat to one's self-concept and, by extension, to one's self-esteem. Therefore, partisans should be expected to utilize their cognitive resources for the purpose of identity defense.

Cognitive Resources Hypothesis:
When cognitive resources are limited, partisans will be more likely to bring their identities into alignment with dissonant attitudes.

COGNITIVE RESOURCES AND IDENTITY CHANGE

As explained in the preceding chapter, I conducted an experiment during May 2007 in which I manipulated disagreement with one's party as well as the cognitive resources available at the time of that disagreement. Partisan motivation was expected to drive identity justification, enabling partisans to reconcile the inconsistency between their party identity and their issue positions without changing their identity to reflect the disagreement. However, when cognitive resources were inhibited through the induction of cognitive load, participants were expected to have a more difficult time constructing a justification for continued identification with their party. The findings reported in Chapter 3 confirmed these expectations. This chapter investigates whether participants' inability to construct an identity justification resulted in party identification change.

In addition to the experimentally manipulated factors, I examined three additional variables likely to be associated with one's ability to justify maintaining one's party identity: age, political sophistication, and Democratic identity. Age is a well-known correlate of partisan stability, but several competing theories have been proposed to explain this empirical phenomenon (see Sears & Levy, 2003). The dual motivations theory suggests that older, more experienced partisans will exhibit greater identity stability because they are better equipped to justify their identity. Therefore, older partisans should be more resistant to identity change even in the face of disagreement with their party.

Likewise, individuals with higher levels of political sophistication are expected to have an easier time developing justifications for their identity. Therefore, they should also show greater identity resilience. Finally, as seen in the previous chapter, the political climate in May 2007 seems to have made it easier for Democratic identifiers than for Republican identifiers to justify their identity. Therefore, Democrats should also show more resistance to identity change even after disagreeing with their party.

Still, no one's cognitive resources are limitless, so the addition of cognitive load would be expected to challenge the resistance of even the most resourceful partisans. Figure 4.1 outlines the expected pattern of interactions.

This investigation assumed that the ability to justify one's identity exists on a continuum. Although cognitive load, age, political sophistication, and Democratic identity should all affect where an individual falls on this continuum, it is difficult to know at what point justification will give way to partisan change. For instance, partisans of all ages may be able to avoid updating their identity in response to disagreement as long they have sufficient cognitive resources (see Figure 4.1, Panel A). However, once cognitive load is induced, partisan updating may occur among younger partisans, whereas older partisans may show continued stability (see Figure 4.1, Panel B). On the other hand, disagreement may lead the least politically sophisticated partisans to change their identity even if their cognitive resources are unencumbered, while their more sophisticated counterparts may avoid identity change as long as they are not placed under cognitive load (see Figure 4.1, Panel B). After being placed under cognitive load, however, even the most sophisticated partisans may begin to update their identity in response to disagreement (see Figure 4.1, Panel C). In short, partisan stability should first give way among the most vulnerable. Those with greater defensive capacity should hold out longer until their defenses are eventually overtaken as well. Vulnerability may stem from youth, low political sophistication, an unaccommodating political environment, or a lack of cognitive resources. If all four variables converge on the expected pattern, the likelihood is reduced that any one alternative explanation will remain plausible.

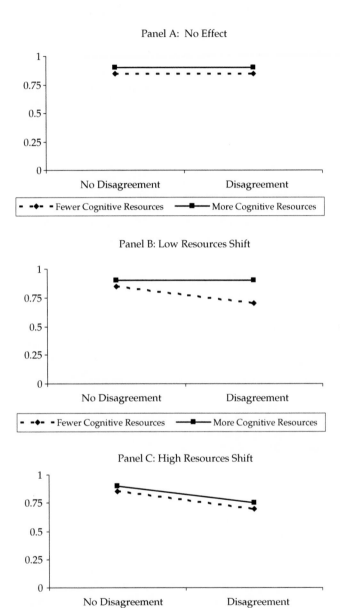

Figure 4.1 Each panel represents a stage in the hypothesized progression of party identification change. Those with the fewest cognitive resources are the first to change their party identity in response to disagreement, but they are eventually matched by those with more cognitive resources. The panels are not meant to reflect actual patterns in the data but merely predictions about what these patterns will look like.

All analyses were conducted using ordered probit regression to account for potential variation in the size of intervals between levels of party identification strength.[1] To facilitate interpretation, results are reported as predicted probabilities. More specifically, I present the probability of starting out as a strong identifier at time t–1 and remaining a strong identifier at time t. Ordered probit regression tables with cut points are included in the Appendix for Chapter 4.

Measures

A variable measuring party identification strength prior to the stimulus was created by simply folding the standard seven-point party identification measure in half. The new scale runs from 0 to 3. Strong Democrats as well as strong Republicans were coded as 3; weak partisans were coded as 2; leaners were coded as 1; and pure Independents were excluded from analysis because they had no party with which to disagree. As described in Chapter 3, YouGov/ Polimetrix uses sample matching to obtain nationally representative samples and maintains a party identification on record for everyone in their respondent pool. Using these data, it is possible to avoid the inevitable biases that would result if party identification were obtained immediately before the treatment.

Current party identification strength served as the primary dependent variable of interest in this study and therefore was measured after exposure to the stimulus. It was coded identically to past party identification strength except that those partisans who crossed over from one party to the other between time t–1 and time t were coded as having zero strength.[2]

I measured political sophistication with the use of a seven-item battery. Therefore, the political sophistication variable runs from 0 (none correct) to

---

1. As explained in more detail later, party identification strength serves as the dependent variable, rather than the standard seven-point measure of party identification. The reason for using this measure is that I was interested in determining what weakens party identification, not in what makes a person a Republican or a Democrat. Therefore, a valence scale (strong identity to no identity) is appropriate, rather than a bipolar scale (strong Republican to strong Democrat). It is important to note that this is not the standard measure of party identification strength, because partisans who crossover from one party to the other are coded as having zero strength.

2. Tests were also run using a measure in which crossover partisans were coded as having negative identity strength; for example, a subject who identified as a Republican at t–1 and as a strong Democrat at time t was coded –3 to indicate strong identification with the *other* party. The results did not substantively differ.

7 (all correct). This battery contains a variety of multiple-choice questions about political figures and institutions. More specifically, respondents were asked to identify the jobs filled by Nancy Pelosi, John Roberts, Tony Snow, and Tony Blair at the time of the study. Participants were also asked how many votes it takes to override a veto, which branch has the power to determine whether a law is constitutional, and which branch has the power of the purse. Surprisingly, the mean level of political sophistication was quite high (mean (M) = 5.43, standard deviation (SD) = 1.91), but there is substantial variation across the scale.[3]

Results

Findings presented in Table 4.1 indicate that at least some partisans did change their party identity from pre-treatment to post-treatement. However, the question remains as to whether treatment exposure caused this variation (or at least some of it). I began by examining the effects of disagreement on

TABLE 4.1. *CROSS-TABULATION OF PAST PARTY IDENTITY AND CURRENT PARTY IDENTITY*

Past Party Identification	Current Party Identification						
	Strong Dem	Weak Dem	Lean Dem	Indep	Lean Rep	Weak Rep	Strong Rep
Strong Dem	**85.0%**	12.5%	2.5%	0.0%	0.0%	0.0%	0.0%
Weak Dem	12.1%	**82.8%**	0.0%	3.4%	0.0%	1.7%	0.0%
Lean Dem	9.1%	9.1%	**65.9%**	15.9%	0.0%	0.0%	0.0%
Indep	5.8%	7.7%	17.3%	**57.7%**	5.8%	3.8%	1.9%
Lean Rep	0.0%	0.0%	0.0%	7.5%	**66.0%**	15.1%	11.3%
Weak Rep	0.0%	2.3%	2.3%	4.5%	11.4%	**68.2%**	11.4%
Strong Rep	0.0%	0.0%	0.0%	1.4%	0.0%	13.0%	**85.5%**

Note: Percentages are calculated so that rows sum to 100%.

---

3. Prior and Lupia (2008) found that subjects scored substantially higher on political knowledge questions when given more time or monetary incentives for correct answers. This means that online studies such as those administered by YouGov/Polimetrix should yield substantially higher knowledge scores than traditional telephone surveys or even face-to-face surveys in which interviewers wait for participants to respond. Prior and Lupia argue that such measures are superior because they capture the relevant skills necessary to acquire political information.

party identification strength while controlling for past party identification strength (see Appendix Table 4.1). The results indicate that when cognitive resources were unencumbered, disagreement had no effect on party identification strength. Thus, the results appear at first to be consistent with the Michigan model, which portrays party identification as a stable socialized identity. However, when subjects were placed under cognitive load, the results appear more intriguing. In this group, a reasonably large coefficient ($B = -.268$; $SE = .174$) emerged for disagreement, but this effect narrowly missed the standard threshold for statistical significance ($p = .12$).[4]

As discussed earlier, factors such as age, political sophistication, and Democratic identity were also expected to affect the ability to justify one's identity. When these sources of variation were included in the model, the effect of disagreement on party identification strength reached marginal significance among participants placed under cognitive load ($p < .10$). When cognitive resources were unencumbered, the coefficient on disagreement remained small and nonsignificant, as predicted. The predicted probability of maintaining a strong party identity is displayed in Figure 4.2. In the absence of disagreement, those placed under cognitive load had a 79% chance of maintaining a strong identity from pre-treatment to post-treatment. However,

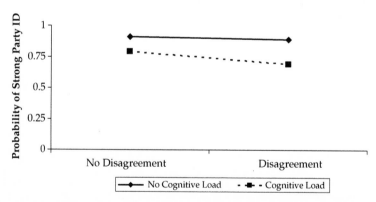

Figure 4.2 The figure illustrates predicted probabilities obtained from the ordered probit regressions with controls reported in Appendix Table 4.1. For the purpose of prediction, pre-test party identification strength was set to 3, age over 35 years to 1, knowledge to the mean, and Democrat identification to 1. The results represent the probability of maintaining a strong party identity from pre-treatment to post-treatment.

---

4. The coefficient (B) and standard error (SE) reported in the text come from an ordered probit model.

when disagreement was experienced under cognitive load, this probability dropped to 69%.

Although the effect of disagreement under cognitive load is not enormous, it is noteworthy given the reputation of party identification as the "unmoved mover" in political behavior research. Consistent with the dual motivations theory, significant partisan weakening occurred only when cognitive resources were scarce (see Figure 4.1, Panel B). Still, the result is only suggestive, because the moderating influence of cognitive load was not statistically significant. In other words, party identification change was established in the cognitive load condition, but the possibility of an equally large change in the absence of cognitive load cannot be ruled out.

As explained previously, the theory implies that the effect of disagreement should be larger among groups who are less equipped to defend their identity, such as young people, those who lack political sophistication, and those whose justification abilities are impeded by the political environment (i.e., Republicans). We now turn to an examination of these potential moderating variables.

Age

Age is a well-known correlate of party identification stability, but this empirical regularity has been surrounded by theoretical controversy. Whereas some favor an "impressionable years" model, others favor a "lifelong openness" model (Sears & Levy, 2003). The former suggest that party identification is susceptible to change during an individual's impressionable years but crystallizes with age and exposure to successive campaigns (Alwin & Krosnick, 1991; Campbell et al., 1960; Sears & Valentino, 1997; Stoker & Jennings, 2009; Valentino & Sears, 1998). Once partisans reach their 30s, party identification becomes fully crystallized and is unlikely to change thereafter. However, revisionist scholars interpret the relationship between age and stability quite differently, arguing that as individuals gain experience, they become more confident in their assessments of where they stand relative to the parties. Thus, the need for partisan adjustment is reduced, and this is reflected in an increasingly stable party identity (Achen, 1992, 2002; Franklin, 1984). In other words, partisans may have a "lifelong openness" to identity change even though their party identity becomes more stable over time.

The dual motivations model suggests a third possibility. Age and experience may facilitate an individual's ability to justify his or her party identity. Therefore, stability increases with age, at least in part, because partisans get better at defending their identity against conflicting information as they gain experience.[5] From this perspective, partisans are most susceptible to change during their impressionable years, yet they also possess a lifelong openness to change if their defenses give way.

To test this proposition, I analyzed the effects of age and disagreement in the presence and absence of cognitive load. For the purpose of this analysis, age was coded as a dummy variable in which those who were 35 years of age or younger were coded as a "0," and those older than 35 were coded as "1." Age 35 serves as a rough cutoff for the end of the impressionable years life stage.

When the dummy variable "Over 35" was interacted with disagreement, no disagreement effects emerged among those whose cognitive abilities were unencumbered—even those younger than 35 years of age (see Appendix Table 4.2). However, among those placed under cognitive load, the story was much different. Partisans younger than 35 showed substantial partisan updating in response to disagreement, whereas their older counterparts remained significantly more steadfast in their identity. In other words, partisans younger than 35 are more vulnerable to disagreement but are able to resist updating as long as they have the cognitive resources to do so. It is also noteworthy that this effect seems to occur at the expense of past party identification, because the effect of past party identification on current party identification dropped off dramatically in the cognitive load condition, particularly among those who were age 35 or younger ($p < .01$) (see Appendix Table 4.3).

Looking back at the predictions made in Figure 4.1 (Panels A and B), the observed pattern appears to fit expectations extremely well. Disagreement had a much larger and more significant effect on younger partisans than on older partisans, but only in the presence of cognitive load ($p < .05$). In other words, cognitive load appears to be particularly disruptive to the justification process among those with the least political experience. This contrasts with existing models that portray age as a proxy for either life stage or information acquisition. These theories cannot account for different effects in the "cognitive load" versus "no cognitive load" conditions. The results presented suggest that partisans devote their cognitive resources to identity defense, and

---

5. I acknowledge that this relationship is true only up to the point at which the experience that comes with age is outweighed by the cognitive deterioration that comes with age. To avoid overcomplicating the model, age is simply dichotomized at 35 years in order to focus the comparison between those who lack political experience and those who do not, thereby avoiding the nonlinearity associated with cognitive deterioration in advanced age. When the model was run with age as a continuous variable and all respondents over the age of 60 were excluded, the effects were almost identical.

these resources are particularly critical for those still honing their defenses. The predicted probability of maintaining a strong party identity is categorized by age and displayed in Figure 4.3.

Once again, however, while the disagreement effects that emerged under cognitive load were significantly different from zero, the results were not significantly different from the null results obtained in the absence of cognitive load—although they were in the expected direction. This is indicated by the interaction between cognitive load and disagreement in the full triple interactive model ($p = .23$) (see Appendix Table 4.3). Again, we are left with results that are suggestive but not incontrovertible.

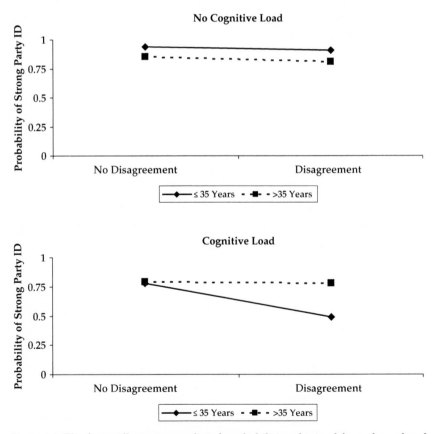

Figure 4.3 The figure illustrates predicted probabilities obtained from the ordered probit regressions reported in Appendix Tables 4.2 and 4.3. For the purpose of prediction, pre-test party identification strength was set to 3. Therefore, the results represent the probability of maintaining a strong party identity from pre-treatment to post-treatment.

Political Sophistication

The correlation between party identification and issue attitudes is known to increase with political sophistication (Delli Carpini & Keeter, 1996). But do these more knowledgeable citizens bring their party identity into line with their issue attitudes, or do they bring their issue attitudes into line with their party identity? Zaller (1992) argued that individuals with higher levels of political sophistication are able to avoid *accepting* information that runs counter to their party identity—but what happens when acceptance cannot be avoided or when acceptance occurs before one finds out where the parties stand? This is the central question in the debate over the relationship between attitudes and party identification. Building on the work of Taber and Lodge (2006) and Gaines, Kuklinski, Quirk, Peyton & Verkuilen (2007), I expected sophisticated partisans to be more adept at reconciling cognitive inconsistencies in favor of their party. Political sophistication was therefore interacted with disagreement to determine whether it moderated the relationship between disagreement and party identification.

The predicted probabilities in Figure 4.4 show that political sophistication did indeed have a substantial moderating effect on the relationship between disagreement and party identification strength even in the absence of cognitive load. Those at the lowest end of the political sophistication scale dropped from a 68% probability of continuing to report a strong party identity to a 17% probability of reporting a strong party identity when exposed to disagreement. In comparison, there was an increase from 92% to 96% probability of continuing to report strong party identification among the most sophisticated members of the sample. This extremely large effect among the least sophisticated partisans again suggests that partisan updating occurs predominantly among the most vulnerable members of the electorate. However, because the effect emerges without inducing cognitive load, proponents of the revisionist model of partisanship might argue in favor of an alternative explanation. Instead of defending their identity, highly sophisticated partisans may simply not be swayed by disagreement with their party over a single issue when there are many other issues on which they agree.

When subjects were placed under cognitive load, the enormous effect of disagreement on the least sophisticated appears to drop off. Although the coefficient remains negative, the effect of disagreement on the least knowledgeable is no longer statistically distinguishable from zero (see Appendix Tables 4.4 and 4.5). From this result, it might appear as if cognitive load undermined reception of the disagreement stimulus, but this possibility was ruled out in the manipulation check. Therefore, this pattern, although nonsignificant, seems to support the revisionist model of party identification

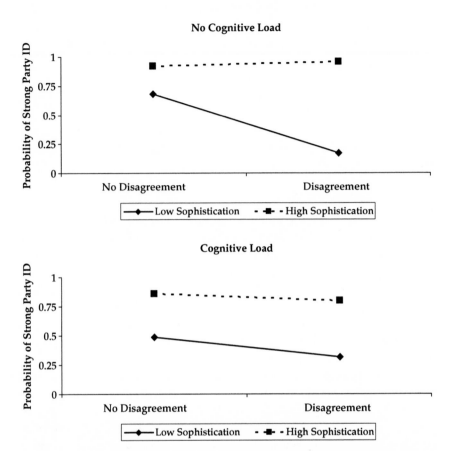

Figure 4.4 The figure illustrates predicted probabilities obtained from the ordered probit regressions reported in Appendix Tables 4.4 and 4.5. For the purpose of prediction, pretest party identification strength was set to 3. Therefore, results represent the probability of maintaining a strong party identity from pre-treatment to post-treatment. "High sophistication" means that predicted values are calculated with political sophistication set to 7; "low sophistication means" that predictions were calculated with political sophistication set to 0.

rather than the dual motivations theory. It appears that cognitive load may have inhibited the ability of the least sophisticated individuals to adjust their party identification in response to disagreement. It is noteworthy, however, that more sophisticated partisans appear to have moved in the opposite direction, becoming slightly more susceptible to identity change in response to disagreement. Although this slope shift does not reach statistical significance either ($p = .19$) (see Appendix Table 4.5), this pattern favors the dual motivations theory over the revisionist model (see Figure 4.1, Panels B and C).

The probability of maintaining a strong identity in response to the disagreement treatment is displayed for those highest and lowest in political sophistication in Figure 4.4.

In sum, although cognitive load may inhibit updating among the least sophisticated partisans, it may also increase partisan updating among the most sophisticated partisans. This suggests that cognitive load may at first reduce defensive abilities, but once cognitive resources drop below a certain threshold, partisans are no longer able to defend *or* update their party identity. This conclusion is, of course, merely speculative.

Democratic Identity

As discussed in Chapter 3, Republicans appear to have had a difficult time defending their identities during May 2007, whereas Democrats showed evidence of identity defense as long as their cognitive resources were uninhibited. The dual motivations theory goes a step farther by predicting that, absent the ability to defend one's identity, disagreement should lead to party identification change. Therefore, Democrats were expected to change their identities to reflect disagreement once they were placed under cognitive load.

Neither the Michigan model of party identification nor the revisionist model can explain this type of partisan asymmetry in a controlled experiment. Although proponents of the revisionist model would certainly expect to see more identity change among Republicans than Democrats in the context of a May 2007 survey, they would not predict this in an experiment in which all partisans received either the same disagreement stimulus or no disagreement stimulus. Critics of the revisionist model would not expect change in either partisan group. The dual motivations model is the only model of the three that can account for these types of asymmetries in an experimental context, because the political context should affect the ability to justify one's identity.

Results confirm the prediction derived from the dual motivations theory. When cognitive resources were uninhibited, a large and significant disagreement effect emerged among Republicans ($p < .05$) (see Appendix Table 4.6). Democrats were significantly less likely than Republicans to change their identity in response to disagreement ($p < .05$). However, when placed under cognitive load, Democrats joined Republicans in updating their identity in response to disagreement and became more likely to report a weaker party identity ($p < .10$). The predicted probability of maintaining a strong party identity is displayed in Figure 4.5. The pattern displayed matches almost perfectly with the predictions in Figure 4.1 (Panels B and C), and the moderating effect of cognitive load is statistically significant ($p < .10$) (see the triple interaction term in Appendix Table 4.7).

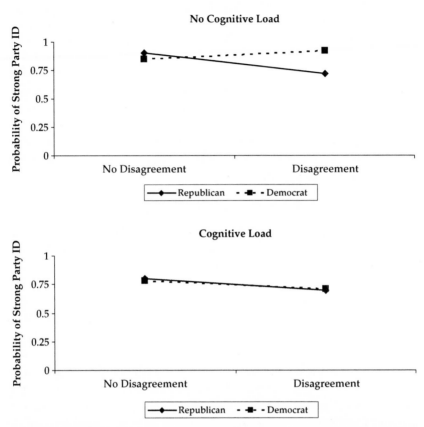

Figure 4.5 The figure illustrates predicted probabilities obtained from the ordered probit regressions reported in Appendix Tables 4.6 and 4.7. For the purpose of prediction, pre-test party identification strength was set to 3. Therefore, the results represent the probability of maintaining a strong party identity from pre-treatment to post-treatment. Party affiliation connotes identifying with or leaning toward a particular party in the pre-test.

In light of recent research on ideology as motivated social cognition (Jost, Glaser, Kruglanski, & Sulloway, 2003; Jost, Hennes, & Lavine, in press), one might wonder whether this partisan asymmetry is attributable to stable trait-based differences between liberals and conservatives rather than the political context of May 2007. However, this literature finds that both liberals and conservatives exhibit the type of group bias shown here,[6] and

6. See Nyhan and Reifler (2010) for examples of bias among conservatives.

conservatives actually demonstrate *more* bias than liberals when it comes to system justification. Moreover, if Republicans were predisposed to change their identity and Democrats were predisposed to defend their identity in light of disagreement with their party, this pattern would be clearly evident in trend data, but no such historical trend is apparent. In short, the existing literature provides no basis for attributing the observed effects to inherent differences between Republicans and Democrats. If anything, partisan trait distinctions make this a conservative test. Therefore, its seems that these results can be attributed only to differences between Republicans' and Democrats' state of mind at the time of the study.

Discussion

Although some findings appear to support the *cognitive resources hypothesis* more strongly than others, the overall pattern of findings conforms quite well to predictions. Considering the reputation of party identification as the "unmoved mover" in behavior research, to produce variation at all in an experimental context is striking. In the rare instances in which researchers have attempted to produce partisan change in controlled environments, party identification has appeared very stable (see Cowden & McDermott, 2000).[7] The inevitable question in response to such findings is, of course, whether they constitute evidence of partisan stability or merely amount to a null result stemming from insufficient stimulus power. The experiment presented here represents an attempt to move beyond dichotomous predictions in which party identification must be either responsive or highly stable. The results suggest that partisan stability is conditional, and given the convergence of patterns across a number of tests, partisan stability seems to be conditional on the ability to justify one's identity in the face of disagreement.

---

7. It should be noted that Hutchings, Walton, and Benjamin (2010) did find evidence of party identification change in response to explicit racial messages in their experiment investigating the controversy over the Georgia state flag. Their experiment was not designed to persuade partisans to change their identity but rather to evoke racial symbolism associated with parties. Their results reinforce the notion that partisan stability is rooted in the motivation to maintain one's identity. When party symbolism changes, the motivation to maintain one's identity may fade. Gerber, Huber, and Washington (2010) produced party identity *acquisition* in a field experiment (i.e., Independents becoming partisans), but their study did not examine whether partisans ever weaken existing attachments.

Rather than devoting cognitive resources to updating their party identity so as to reflect their attitudes, partisan identifiers devote their resources to identity defense. Cognitive resources were directly manipulated in the experiment through cognitive load induction in order to demonstrate their causal importance. However, these resources also appeared to vary within the population. Youth, lack of sophistication, and political context all appeared to function like cognitive load—making it more difficult to justify maintaining a stable party identity after experiencing disagreement with one's party. Partisans over the age of 35 years, those with higher levels of political sophistication, and Democratic identifiers all appear to have had an easier time maintaining their identity after experiencing disagreement with their party. However, individuals who were rich in cognitive resources were immune to the effects of the cognitive load manipulation. Once their resource advantage was taken away, they appeared to react to disagreement by updating their party identity, just like those who had fewer cognitive resources to begin with. In short, even the most loyal fans seem to have a breaking point. They must, in the end, maintain the belief that they are not merely acting as fans but as good citizens, and this requires justification of their team allegiance.

CHAPTER 5

Motivation and Measurement Error

In the 1950s, Angus Campbell and his colleagues developed the concept of party identification because they believed that partisanship was rooted in self-classification and not merely evaluation (Campbell, Converse, Miller, & Stokes, 1960; Campbell, Gurin, & Miller, 1954). Although they acknowledged that partisanship could change, they observed that such change was infrequent. From their point of view, party identification arises as individuals develop affective attachments to political parties during socialization. In arguing that partisanship constitutes an identity, they assumed that self-categorization has more to do with a person's self-image and less to do with how that person evaluates political parties. Although they expected individuals to feel pressure to bring their party identity into alignment with their attitudes, they believed the reverse influence of party identification on attitudes to be much stronger. In short, they were the first to see partisans as fans with durable affect-laden team allegiances.

In the half-century since this seminal work was published, the concept of party identification has been revised to place much greater emphasis on evaluation and change over time. Although party identification is quite stable relative to other concepts, revisionist works have shown that partisans do update their identity to reflect various types of attitudes. Some have gone so far as to argue that party identification approximates a "running tally" of evaluations (Fiorina, 1981) and that partisan stability results from the accumulation of information regarding party positions (Achen, 1992, 2002; Franklin, 1984). Thus, partisans have regained their reputations as good citizens.

Recently, however, revisionist scholarship has come under question for failing to account for measurement error (Green & Palmquist, 1990, 1994; Green, Palmquist, & Schickler, 2002). Party identification, like many other variables in public opinion research, is a latent construct that researchers can never directly observe. We attempt to measure party identification as accurately as possible using the famous seven-point scale developed by Campbell and colleagues, but no concept can be measured perfectly. Therefore, observed variation in party identification over time might result from actual change or from mere measurement error. When measurement error is corrected by using multiple measures of party identification over time or multiple indicators at a single point in time, party identification appears to be quite stable. Moreover, when measurement error is explicitly accounted for in revisionist models, short-term forces appear to have a much smaller impact on party identification than revisionist accounts suggest (Green & Palmquist, 1990, 1994; Green et al., 2002; Green & Schickler, 1993).

Of course, these researchers have made it a point to note that party identification is not necessarily perfectly stable. For instance, in their original work on the subject, Green and Palmquist (1990) explained, "[Our results] do not rule out the possibility of finding short-term change under certain circumstances and among certain individuals (p. 897)." They went on to discuss how certain subgroups within the population may respond to short-term forces even though the sample as a whole appears quite stable. In this respect, their model is entirely compatible with the dual motivations theory of party identification.

Additionally, variation characterized by Green and colleagues as measurement error may actually have a good deal to tell us about how people process information. They explain that much of the variation we see in party identification results from the inherent difficulty of measuring this latent construct. However, their measurement error estimates also capture variation due to question order effects. Such effects may reasonably be characterized as a source of measurement error because they are likely to be fleeting. Nonetheless, they offer a window into the mind of the voter. A large literature demonstrates that survey responses are affected by considerations brought to mind by the questions that precede them (see Schuman & Presser, 1981; Schwarz 1999). For instance, party identification might be influenced by political attitudes measured immediately prior. Of course, if partisans update their identity to reflect salient considerations even for a short time, this suggests that they are motivated to resolve inconsistency between their party identity and political evaluations. In short, they possess responsiveness motivation.[1]

---

1. Alternatively, one might argue that salient considerations enter into party identification as survey respondents average across salient attitudes to determine their party identity each time they are asked (see Zaller, 1992; Zaller & Feldman, 1992). However, because partisanship constitutes an identity and not an attitude, it is not expected to be constructed anew each time it is reported (Green & Palmquist, 1990). This type of memory-based processing is thought to occur in instances when people are asked to make surprise judgments on matters they had previously thought little about (Hastie & Park, 1986). Therefore, even if partisanship were considered a strongly held attitude rather than an identity, such a model would provide a poor fit.

In addition to capturing question order effects, survey questions also capture respondents' attempts to justify their preferences (Rahn, Krosnick, & Breuning, 1994). For example, a person may identify as a Democrat largely because her parents identified as Democrats and she has felt a strong affective attachment to the party since childhood. However, norms of good citizenship suggest that party identification should be grounded in reason and not mere affect. Thus, her partisan motivation drives her to justify her party identity through the answers she provides in the survey.

By evoking both responsiveness motivation and partisan motivation, surveys (and survey experiments) provide an excellent opportunity to examine the motivational struggle between the fan and the good citizens within the mind of the voter. For example, survey respondents might be disinclined to acknowledge strong identification with the Republican Party immediately after reflecting on their own lukewarm evaluations of the Republican Party's performance (or their positive evaluations of the Democratic Party's performance). However, the act of reconsidering partisan ties should trigger partisan motivation.[2] Therefore, we should expect to see evidence of identity justification after survey questions bring attitudes to mind that are inconsistent with party identification. And if party identification change occurs as a result of evoking these inconsistent attitudes, justification should lead individuals back to their identity. In short, subtle variation that might otherwise be dismissed as measurement error may provide insight into the empirical controversy surrounding party identification. And even more importantly, it may prove helpful in clarifying the motivational dynamics governing the content of party identification.

Saliency Hypothesis:
Individuals will update their identity to reflect their attitudes when these attitudes are made salient prior to reporting their party identity. However, subsequent identity justification—observable in subjects' responses—will undo these changes in party identification.

PARTY IDENTITY JUSTIFICATION AND CHANGE WITHIN A SURVEY

Through a national survey experiment, I examined how partisans reacted when asked about their attitudes toward parties before reporting their party identification. This study took advantage of political context by examining Republican identifiers during a time of declining attitudes toward, and identification with, the Republican Party. Employing a simple question

---

2. This should occur regardless of whether the act of reconsideration weakens party identification.

order manipulation, I viewed the survey as a microcosm of political life. As individuals experience politics, various attitudes become salient, just as they do in surveys, and undoubtedly some of these attitudes conflict with party identity. Since the 1950s, researchers have wrestled with the question of whether citizens update their identity to reflect their attitudes. However, while there is disagreement in the literature with regard to the amount of party identification change, even the most ardent proponents of a stable party identification model acknowledge the possibility of variation over time. Still, they believe that most of this variation is the result of measurement error and not substantive change (Green & Palmquist, 1990, 1994; Green et al., 2002).

But, if the psychological pressures at work in a survey are analogous to the psychological pressures partisans experience in their daily lives, this variation may tell us a great deal about the inner workings of the partisan mind—even if the changes are fleeting. It also means that systematic variation in party identity can be induced by manipulating question order. If partisans then revert back to their original identity by the end of the survey, the questions obtained between the two measures of party identification may be examined for evidence of identity justification. Presumably, if partisans are motivated to return to their identity, the identity justification process should be evident in their responses. Finally, if such evidence is uncovered, mediation tests can be run to determine whether justification is necessary for identity reversion. In other words, it may be possible to document the full dual motivations theory in action.

Methods

The *salience hypothesis* was tested through a national survey experiment administered by YouGov/Polimetrix to 300 adults on February 18–19, 2008.[3] The 118 respondents who identified as Republicans or Independents leaning toward

---

3. This experiment was originally a 600-subject study with a 3×2 design. The second experimental factor induced disagreement between individuals and their party using the same method as in the previous chapters. Subjects read two mock newspaper articles. The first article was an editorial arguing in favor of a fictitious balanced budget amendment. Subjects were then asked to take a position on the bill. In the disagreement condition, the second article informed subjects that their party (as determined by their pre-test party identity) had opposed the bill. In the no disagreement condition, the second article discussed

the Republican Party are the focus of the analysis. At the time the study was in the field, vigorous primary battles were going on in both the Democratic and Republican parties. On the Democratic side, Hillary Clinton was up against Barack Obama, and on the Republican side, Mike Huckabee was pitted against John McCain. Whereas Democratic identifiers viewed theirs as a choice between two excellent candidates, many Republicans were less enthusiastic about their options.[4] At the same time, Republican president George W. Bush faced a 31% approval rating due in large part to dissatisfaction over the Iraq War and a slowing economy.[5] Therefore, this moment in time provided an excellent opportunity to examine party identification under threat.

---

the potential political importance of the amendment and the fact that there was no clear partisan divide over it (remember that Democrats were criticizing the Bush administration for running up large budget deficits at this time). The question order primes were originally meant to provide partisans with an opportunity to justify their party identity after exposure to disagreement and before reporting their party identity. However, the primes themselves turned out to stimulate party identification change (for reasons explained earlier), and justification did not occur as a result of the disagreement manipulation. Interaction effects between the two experimental factors offered little additional insight. Therefore, the decision was made to exclude the disagreement treatment groups and to focus on the question primes, because they actually turned out to be a more effective stimulus to party identification change than the disagreement treatment in this case. In the excluded portion of the experiment, Republicans did report significantly weaker party identities after exposure to the disagreement stimulus ($p < .05$), whereas disagreement had no significant effect on Democrats. Consistent with the results reported in previous chapters, results from ordered probit regression show that the predicted probability of maintaining a strong Republican identity from t1 to t2 dropped from .96 to .84 after exposure to disagreement. This study was entirely distinct from those discussed in other chapters. YouGov/Polimetrix interviewed 759 respondents in order to match down to a sample of 600. Respondents were matched on gender, age, race, education, party identification, and political interest.
4. A Gallup poll conducted on February 8–10, 2008, asked, "Compared to previous elections, are you more enthusiastic than usual about voting, or less enthusiastic?" Among Democrats, 80% answered "more enthusiastic," compared with only 42% of Republicans. On the other hand, 50% of Republicans responded that they were "less enthusiastic," compared with only 30% of Democrats (Gallup & Newport, 2009).
5. Approval ratings were taken from a Gallup poll conducted on February 11–14, 2008 (Gallup & Newport, 2009).

How would Republicans react when primed to consider their party evaluations immediately before reporting their party identification?

Procedure

The *salience hypothesis* suggests that when attitudes are primed prior to
the reporting of party identity, subjects will feel psychological pressure
to update their party identity to reflect these attitudes. To test this hypothesis, a three-celled experiment was designed to prime attitudes toward the
Republican Party, Democratic Party, or neither (control) as subjects considered
how to answer the party identification questions. The study design is laid out
in Table 5.1. The treatment was delivered via a straightforward question order
manipulation. Attitude primes consisted of a series of three questions about the
Republican or the Democratic Party. The first of these questions asked about
the party's performance in Congress. The second question asked subjects how
much they trusted the party to handle the nation's problems. The third question asked subjects for their feelings toward the party in general. Those who
received the Republican Party attitude prime were asked about their attitudes
toward the Democratic Party immediately after the party identification question, and those who received the Democratic Party attitude prime were likewise asked about their attitudes toward the Republican Party after the party
identification question. Those assigned to the control condition were asked all
of these questions after reporting their party identification. In this condition,
the order of the question batteries was randomized so that half of the subjects were asked about the Republican Party before they were asked about the
Democratic Party, and the other half were asked about the Democratic Party
before being asked about the Republican Party.

TABLE 5.1. *QUESTION ORDER*

Control	Democratic Prime	Republican Prime
Party Identification (t1)	**Party Identification (t1)**	**Party Identification (t1)**
	Attitudes Toward Democratic Party	Attitudes Toward Republican Party
Party Identification (t2)	**Party Identification (t2)**	**Party Identification (t2)**
Attitudes Toward Both Parties (Randomized)	Attitudes Toward Republican Party	Attitudes Toward Democratic Party
Emotions Toward	Emotions Toward	Emotions Toward
Both Parties	Both Parties	Both Parties
Party Identification (t3)	**Party Identification (t3)**	**Party Identification (t3)**

Note: The dotted line represents the start of the study. Party identification at t1 were obtained from
YouGov/Polimetrix records.

Measures

Treatment groups were coded as dummy variables (i.e., *Republican Party prime* and *Democratic Party prime*). Three measures of party identification were obtained, including a pre-test measure of party identification acquired from YouGov/Polimetrix. As in the previous study, the pre-test measure was not obtained during the survey, because this would likely have skewed the results. Instead, it was attained from the YouGov/Polimetrix records. Because YouGov/Polimetrix uses a sample matching procedure, they have party identification on record for all of the respondents in their pool. The second party identification measure was obtained after exposure to the treatment. Both of these measures made use of the standard branching question from the American National Election Studies (ANES), which yields a seven-point scale running from strong Democrat to strong Republican. A third and final party identification question was asked near the end of the study. In order to reduce consistency bias, the seven-point self-placement measure of party identification was used. This item has been found to be similarly reliable when compared to the standard ANES party identification measure (Green & Schickler, 1993). The seven-point self-placement measure is a Likert-type scale rather than a branching question. Each of the seven points is labeled so that the scale runs from strong Democrat to strong Republican.

Responses to all three of the party identification questions were rescaled to run from strong Republican (3) to strong Democrat (–3). In the previous chapter, Republicans and Democrats were examined together in all analyses. Because this book examines the forces that weaken party identification (as opposed to forces that move the electorate toward a particular party), it was necessary to rescale the party identification items into measures of party identification strength. In this chapter, however, all analyses were conducted separately for Republicans and for Democrats. Therefore, rescaling was not necessary, and I simply used the full party identification measure.

As mentioned earlier, attitudes toward parties were measured with the use of an index composed of three questions regarding each of the two major parties. These questions were taken from the ANES. Factor analysis of these six items shows that they line up on two distinct dimensions: attitudes toward the Republican Party and attitudes toward the Democratic Party (see Appendix Table 5.1). Indices called *attitudes toward Republican Party* and *attitudes toward Democratic Party* were created by recoding each of the three items to run from –1 to 1 and then averaging across the three items. The end result was two indices, each running from –1 (negative attitudes) to 1 (positive attitudes). The first item read, "Do you approve or disapprove of the way that the Republicans [Democrats] are handling their job in Congress?" Responses ranged from "disapprove strongly" to "approve strongly" on a seven-point scale. The second item asked respondents, "How much trust and confidence do you have in the Republican [Democratic] Party when it comes to handling the nation's problems?" Response options ranged from "no confidence at all" to "a great deal of confidence" on a seven-point scale. The final item read, "We would like to get your general feelings about the Republican [Democratic] Party. Please rate the Republican [Democratic] Party with what we call a feeling thermometer by typing a number from 0 to 100. On this feeling thermometer, ratings between 0 and 49 degrees mean that you don't feel favorably toward the party and that you don't care too much for that party. Ratings between 51 and 100 degrees mean that you feel favorably and warm toward the party. If you don't feel particularly warm or cold toward the party you would rate it at 50 degrees." Those who answered "don't know" were set to the scale's midpoint for all three questions in the index.

Finally, the emotions respondents felt toward each party were measured through a series of seven questions. Subjects were asked, "How angry [afraid, frustrated, hopeful enthusiastic] do you feel when you think about the Republican [Democratic] party?" Responses were then added to form indices of positive (hopeful, enthusiastic) and negative (angry, afraid, frustrated) emotions, and each was rescaled to run from 0 to 1. The negative emotion index was then subtracted from the positive emotion index to form additional measures of global affect toward each party, each of which ran from −1 to 1. Factor analysis showed that the 10 emotion items line up on two distinct factors representing global affect toward each of the two parties (see Appendix Table 5.2).

Results

Table 5.2 illustrates the degree to which party identification changed between the time at which YouGov/Polimetrix obtained the first observation (t1) and the time at which the second observation was obtained during the study (t2). Bolded entries represent partisans whose party identity did not weaken from t1 to t2. Clearly, party identification varies over time, but the question remains whether this variation is random or systematic. Moreover, to the degree that party identification varies within surveys, what are the causes of this change, and why do partisans tend to revert back? Experiments are extremely useful when such dilemmas arise, because they allow for straightforward causal assessment.

This experiment was built on the premise that, in February of 2008, Republicans' own evaluations of the Republican and Democratic parties would put pressure on their party identity when made salient. Therefore, I began by first examining Republicans' attitudes toward the two parties relative to Democrats' attitudes toward the two parties. The idea was to determine whether Republicans' own attitudes were likely to threaten their party identification.

TABLE 5.2. *POST-TREATMENT PARTY IDENTIFICATION BY PRE-TREATMENT PARTY IDENTIFICATION*

Past Party Identification	Current Party Identification						
	Strong Dem	Weak Dem	Lean Dem	Indep	Lean Rep	Weak Rep	Strong Rep
Strong Dem	**83.3%**	7.4%	7.4%	1.9%	0.0%	0.9%	0.0%
Weak Dem	5.1%	**79.7%**	11.9%	1.7%	0.0%	0.0%	1.7%
Lean Dem	9.4%	0.0%	**87.5%**	3.1%	0.0%	0.0%	0.0%
Indep	2.0%	0.0%	15.7%	**74.5%**	5.9%	0.0%	2.0%
Lean Rep	0.0%	0.0%	0.0%	9.1%	**66.7%**	6.1%	18.2%
Weak Rep	0.0%	2.8%	0.0%	2.8%	5.6%	**83.3%**	5.6%
Strong Rep	0.0%	0.0%	0.0%	0.0%	4.1%	6.1%	**89.8%**

Note: Percentages were calculated so that rows sum to 100%.

As expected, when obtained prior to party identification, Republicans attitudes toward their own party (mean (M) = .131, standard deviation (SD) = .399) were less positive on average than Democrats' attitudes toward their own party (M = .339, SD = .414, $p < .01$). Republicans' attitudes toward the Democratic Party ($M = -.569$, $SD = .367$) were also less negative than Democrats' attitudes toward the Republican Party ($M = -.681$, $SD = .305$; $p < .10$). Therefore, priming either of these attitude dimensions was likely to put more pressure on Republicans' party identification than on that of Democrats.

Table 5.3 displays the effects of the attitude primes on party identification among Republicans, Democrats, and Independents.[6] Whereas Democrats and Independents do not seem to have been affected, the priming manipulation does appear to have put pressure on the party identity of Republicans, as expected. In particular, priming attitudes toward the Democratic Party weakened Republicans' identification with their own party. As illustrated in Figure 5.1, the predicted probability of maintaining a strong Republican identity from t1 to t2 dropped from 90% in the control condition to 72% in the Democratic Party attitude prime condition. The coefficient on the Republican Party attitude prime was in the expected direction but quite far from reaching statistical significance.[7] It appears that this prime either aroused less dissonance or that the dissonance it caused was easier to defend against.

6. The Republican and Democrat categories included those who initially identified as Independents but admitted to leaning toward one party or the other. The category of Independents therefore includes only "pure" Independents.
7. These priming effects do not appear to be moderated by the attitudes elicited by the priming stimuli (see Appendix Table 5.1). This suggests that the effect elicited

TABLE 5.3. *EFFECT OF ATTITUDE PRIMING ON PARTY IDENTIFICATION (ORDERED PROBIT)*

	Republicans—Party Identification (t2)	Democrats—Party Identification (t2)	Independents—Party Identification (t2)
	(N = 118)	(N = 145)	(N = 45)
	B	B	B
	(SE)	(SE)	(SE)
Republican Party Prime	−.194 (.286)	−.062 (.253)	.060 (.427)
Democratic Party Prime	−.706** (.294)	.062 (.245)	.016 (.402)
Party Identification (t1)	1.40*** (.169)	1.36*** (.153)	NA
Cut 1	−.627 (.484)	−3.50 (.419)	−2.03 (.481)
Cut 2	.061 (.375)	−2.11 (.375)	−.907 (.309)
Cut 3	1.63 (.366)	−.311 (.365)	1.44 (.356)
Cut 4	2.92 (.414)	.166 (.446)	2.09 (.494)

Note: The reported coeficients (B) and standard errors (SE) come from ordered probit regression. Republican, Democrat, or Independent status was determined using party identification at t1. "Leaners" were included with Republicans or Democrats; the Independents category contains only "pure" Independents.

***$p < .01$; **$p < .05$; *$p < .10$

from the Democratic prime was not driven by those Republicans whose attitudes toward the Democratic Party were most positive but was instead driven by an equal weakening of party identity across all Republicans. However, this null moderating effect may mask the moderating effect of attitude *change*. In other words, the priming effect may be driven by those Republicans whose attitudes toward the Democratic Party changed the most from t1 to t2 rather than being driven by those Republicans who had the most positive attitudes toward the Democratic party at the outset of the study. Unfortunately, YouGov/ Polimetrix does not keep measures of attitudes toward parties on record, so the potential moderating effect of attitude change cannot be tested. We simply know that Republicans' attitudes toward each of the parties were less extreme than those held by their Democratic counterparts.

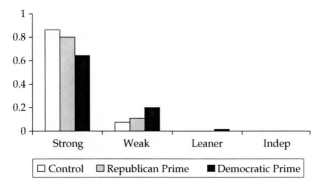

Figure 5.1 The figure illustrates the probability of each level of Republican Party identification at t2 after identifying as a strong Republican at t1.

Next, I examined how partisans reacted to the psychological pressure induced by the attitude primes (or at least the attitudes toward Democrats prime). We have seen that Republicans updated their identity to reflect primed attitudes toward the Democratic Party, but is this all that happened? The saliency hypothesis suggests that attitudes obtained after party identification should show evidence of identity justification as a result of Republicans' attempts to undo their party identification change. Therefore, I examined the difference between attitudes obtained before and after party identification. Table 5.4 illustrates how the simple question order manipulation affected Republicans' attitudes toward the parties. The results suggest that attitude priming triggered attitudinal bolstering on whichever dimension was measured immediately after party identification. Specifically, on a scale running from −1 to 1, attitudes toward the Democratic Party obtained after party identification were .161 lower than when they were obtained before party identification. Likewise, Republicans reported attitudes toward the Republican Party that were slightly (but nonsignificantly) higher when obtained after reporting their party identification.

In short, it appears that the priming manipulation triggered accuracy motivation. In order to maintain the belief that their identity was rooted in pragmatism, Republicans felt that they must update their identity to reflect their attitudes, and they did so in the Democratic prime condition. However, this conflicted with their partisan motivation. Republicans did not show significant evidence of identity change when attitudes toward their own party were primed, but this left the cognitive inconsistency between their attitudes and identity unresolved. Therefore, in both cases, Republicans felt compelled to justify their identity by bolstering their attitudes on whichever dimension

TABLE 5.4. *REPUBLICANS' ATTITUDES TOWARD PARTIES*

	Attitudes Toward Republican Party (N = 83) M (SE)	Attitudes Toward Democratic Party (N = 83) M (SE)
Measured Before Party Identification	.131 (.062)	−.569 (.057)
Measured After Party Identification	.225 (.065)	−.730 (.043)
Difference	.094 (.090)	−.161** (.071)

Note: The table shows mean differences (*M*) between attitudes measured before and after party identification. The table also reports the standard errors (*SE*) associated with these estimates. The attitude dimension obtained before party identification served as the prime.

***$p < .01$; **$p < .05$; *$p < .10$

was obtained after party identification.[8] No such effects emerged among Democratic respondents. This was expected, because Democrats' attitudes were more partisan to begin with, so the attitude prime did not cause them to experience cognitive dissonance and they did not weaken their party identity.

Although these effects provide clear support for the theory, another indicator of identity justification would make the case even stronger. Therefore, I examined subjects' emotions toward the Republican and Democratic parties. In addition to their cognitive component, attitudes have an emotional component or affective tag (see Eagly & Chaiken, 1993), and this may be the part an attitude that is most susceptible to motivational forces (see Westen, Blagov, Harenski, Kilts, & Hamann, 2006). In a study of social context effects on cognitive dissonance, Cooper and Mackie (1983) produced cognitive dissonance in members of a Republican student group by asking them to write a positive statement about a Democratic candidate. Typically, in such

8. Given the findings reported in Chapter 2, it is worth drawing attention to the fact that Republicans' dominant response to the Democratic attitudes prime was to update their party identity, whereas their dominant response to the Republican attitudes prime was to derogate the Democratic party. Therefore, it appears that they may have been more adept at generating lesser of two evils justifications than greater of two goods justifications.

a paradigm, subjects reduce cognitive dissonance arousal by changing their attitudes so that they are consistent with the statement they have written. In this case, however, because changing their attitudes to make them consistent with their statement would have conflicted with their Republican identity (and membership in the Republican student group), the students instead resolved their cognitive dissonance by reporting more negative feelings toward Democrats.

With this study in mind, Table 5.5 displays the effects of attitude priming on emotions toward the two parties. As expected, the emotional bolstering pattern appears strikingly consistent with the attitude bolstering pattern. When attitudes toward the Democratic Party were primed, Republicans reported more positive emotion toward Democrats ($B = .100$, $SE = .049$; $p < .05$) and less negative emotion toward their own party ($B = -.091$, $SE = .053$; $p < .10$). When attitudes toward the Republican Party were primed, Republicans reported less positive emotion toward their own party ($B = -.103$, $SE = .035$; $p < .01$) and more negative emotion toward the Democratic Party ($B = .075$, $SE = .047$; $p = .12$)—although the negative emotion effect narrowly missed the threshold for statistical significance at the $p < .10$ level. When the emotion items were combined into a single measure of bipolar affect, the Democratic prime led to a significant positive shift toward the Republican Party ($B = .184$, $SE = .063$;

TABLE 5.5. *ATTITUDE BOLSTERING IN RESPONSE TO ATTITUDE PRIMING AMONG REPUBLICANS*

	Positive Emotions Toward Reps	Negative Emotions Toward Reps	Total Emotions Toward Reps	Positive Emotions Toward Dems	Negative Emotions Toward Dems	Total Emotions Toward Dems
	(N = 116)	(N = 117)	(N = 116)	(N = 116)	(N = 116)	(N = 117)
	B	B	B	B	B	B
	(SE)	(SE)	(SE)	(SE)	(SE)	(SE)
Republican Party Prime	−.049 (.048)	.030 (.052)	−.086 (.086)	−.103*** (.035)	.075 (.047)	−.178** (.071)
Democratic Party Prime	.100** (.049)	−.091* (.053)	.184** (.087)	−.028 (.035)	−.013 (.048)	.021 (.072)
Constant	.605*** (.035)	.489*** (.039)	.117* (.063)	.292*** (.026)	.781*** (.035)	−.486*** (.053)

Note: The reported coeficients (*B*) and standard errors (*SE*) come from ordinary least squares (OLS) regression.

***$p < .01$; **$p < .05$; *$p < .10$

$p < .05$), and the Republican prime significantly shifted total affect toward the Democratic Party in a negative direction ($B = -.178$, $SE = .071$; $p < .05$). In other words, whichever dimension did *not* serve as the stimulus for partisan updating served as the basis for partisan justification. The effect of the Republican prime is particularly interesting, because it did not produce significant party identification change. Nonetheless, it appears that the prime did arouse cognitive inconsistency, which Republican subjects dealt with by derogating the Democratic Party.

Given Republicans' efforts to justify their identity in response to priming and partisan change, the question remains as to whether these efforts were successful in producing a rebound in party identification by the end of the study. Results from Table 5.6 suggest that they were indeed successful. After controlling for both of the prior party identification measures, both attitude primes were positively associated with party identification at t3—although only the effect of the Democratic attitude prime reached statistical significance. Recall that this was also the prime that significantly weakened party identification from t1 to t2. Substantively speaking, this finding suggests that the Democratic attitude prime produced a strengthening of party identification from t2 (immediately after the prime) to t3 (at the end of the 15-minute study). In other words, after initially weakening their identity in response to the Democratic attitude prime, this group of Republicans showed the greatest likelihood of rebounding by the end of the study.

The predicted probability of reverting back to strong Republican identification after initially weakening one's Republican identity is presented in Figure 5.2. The figure shows that, once their identity began to weaken, most Republicans in the control group maintained their weak identity (first observed at t2) or weakened their identity further. The probability of reverting back to strong party identification in the control group was only 7.8%, whereas the probability of further weakening was 44.3%. On the other hand, those exposed to the Democratic prime showed a higher probability of reverting back to strong identification with their party, rebounding 18.3% of the time, and a substantially lower probability of further weakening (26.7%). Finally, although exposure to the Republican prime did not significantly weaken party identification on average, strong partisans who did weaken their party identity showed a 12.3% chance of rebounding and a 35.4% chance of further weakening. Presumably, this identity rebounding resulted from the attitudinal and emotional bolstering demonstrated in Tables 5.4 and 5.5.

In order to establish that emotional bolstering mediated the rebound in party identification, the emotion measures obtained between the t2 and t3

TABLE 5.6. *EMOTION TOWARD PARTIES AS MEDIATORS OF PARTY IDENTIFICATION REBOUND AMONG REPUBLICANS*

	Party Identification (t3) (N = 118)	Party Identification (t3) (N = 116)	Party Identification (t3) (N = 116)
	B	B	B
	(SE)	(SE)	(SE)
Republican Party Prime	.254	.287	−.045
	(.268)	(.273)	(.285)
Democratic Party Prime	.513*	.390	.422
	(.280)	(.292)	(.288)
Party Identification (t1)	−.090	−.190	−.087
	(.192)	(.196)	(.199)
Party Identification (t2)	1.44***	1.41***	1.40***
	(.200)	(.205)	(.210)
Total Emotions Toward Republicans		1.06***	
		(.336)	
Total Emotions Toward Democrats			−1.28***
			(.399)
Cut 1	−1.33	−1.73	−1.27
	(1.00)	(.919)	(1.39)
Cut 2	−.543	−.967	−.191
	(.484)	(.520)	(.527)
Cut 3	.524	.194	.970
	(.382)	(.408)	(.417)
Cut 4	2.51	2.30	2.89
	(.429)	(.436)	(.460)
Cut 5	4.02	3.96	4.58
	(.497)	(.513)	(.561)

Note: The coeficients (*B*) and standard errors (*SE*) reported in the table come from ordered probit regression. To calculate the mediation effects reported in the text, identical models were run using ordinary least squares (OLS) regression. Results were substantively identical.

***p < .01; **p < .05; *p < .10

party identification measures were included in the model. As expected, inclusion of the measure of total affect toward the Republican Party reduced the size of the coefficients associated with exposure to the Democratic Party prime. A Sobel test for mediation established that emotions toward Republicans significantly mediated the relationship between the Democratic prime and party

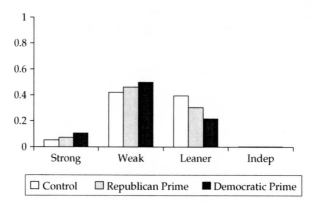

Figure 5.2 The figure represents the predicted probability of reporting each level of Republican Party identification at t3 after reporting a strong Republican identity at t1 and a weak Republican identity at t2.

identification at t3 ($p < .10$) (see Baron & Kenny, 1986). Turning to the other treatment, there was little room for identity rebound to occur, because exposure to the Republican Party prime did not significantly weaken party identification in the first place. However, when total affect toward the Democratic Party was included in the model, the nonsignificant coefficient associated with exposure to the Republican prime dropped even closer to zero.[9]

Discussion

Past research has posited that party identification varies largely as a result of measurement error and not as a result of short-term forces (Green & Palmquist, 1990, 1994; Green et al., 2002). This chapter examined the source of this measurement error. Devising survey questions to measure theoretical constructs is an inherently difficult task. Some degree of error must be expected when one is attempting to capture a given construct with a single survey item. However, as this chapter illustrates, this is not the only source of short-term fluctuation in survey responses. A large literature on question order effects demonstrates how responses to any given item can be influenced by considerations brought to mind by preceding questions. Although such effects may be construed as a type of measurement error, they do not result from the researcher's inability

---

9. In other words, if the rebound effect had been significant, we could have been confident that the effect was mediated by affect toward the Democratic Party.

to perfectly capture the construct but rather from the respondent's consideration of attitudes made salient by the survey.[10] This is a vital distinction, because when survey respondents change their party identity to reflect salient considerations, even if only for a moment, it reveals their responsiveness motivation.

As we have seen in previous chapters, partisans are also motivated to remain loyal to their team. Therefore, they may use subsequent survey responses to bolster their party identity and rationalize away inconsistencies between their responses. The results reported in this chapter demonstrate that when attitudes toward a party were made salient, partisans felt pressure to update their identity. To be good citizens and conform to norms of civic duty, they could not simply ignore considerations brought to mind during the survey. Just as in Chapter 2, partisans avoided changing their party identity (at least in the long term) by justifying their identity in two dimensions. As long as the respondent had more positive feelings toward her own party than toward the opposition party, stable party identification could be justified. In one treatment condition, participants reported weaker party identities but reverted back to their original identity after identity bolstering. In the other treatment condition, participants maintained a stable party identity throughout the study and resolved dissonance between the primed attitude dimension and their party identity by derogating the opposition party.

This chapter capitalized on the real-world political context of the 2008 primary election season, capturing Republican disaffection that culminated in their party's eventual lopsided defeat. This disaffection, of course, had been building for some time. According to Etheridge (2009), Republican identification declined across 25 of 26 demographic groups (i.e., every group except frequent churchgoers) between 2001 and 2009. By 2011, Republican identification had rebounded (Gallup, 2011),[11] but this short decline had significant electoral consequences.

By providing a window into the mind of Republican identifiers at this critical moment, the results reported here shed light on the complicated interplay between the fan and the good citizen within the mind of the partisan. Although partisan motivation clearly plays an important role in stabilizing

---

10. Memory-based models of survey response effects suggest that individuals construct their responses from salient attitudes (Zaller, 1992; Zaller & Feldman, 1992), but see footnote 1 for an explanation of why such models provide a poor fit in the case of party identification.

11. Includes "leaners."

party identification, it also appears that, under the right circumstances, partisans are driven to bring their identity into alignment with their attitudes. Still, the question remains as to whether this responsiveness motivation is rooted in the desire to identify with the party that best represents one's policy interests or whether it is embedded in the desire to conform to norms of civic duty and pragmatic partisanship. This question is taken up in Chapter 6.

CHAPTER 6

The Paradox of Partisan Responsiveness

Over several chapters, it has been established that partisans are motivated to maintain their party identity. Because party identity change entails a psychological cost, it tends to be avoided. Such results are consistent with theories dating back to Darwin (1890). Affection for one's group facilitates cohesion, and group living facilitates survival (Van Vugt & Hart, 2004; Van Vugt & Shaller, 2008). As a result, we instinctively feel a need to belong (Baumeister & Leary, 1995). Classic studies have shown that mere categorization into arbitrary groups can lead to identity formation (Tajfel, Billig, Bundy, & Falament, 1971), and intergroup competition only serves to solidify group delineations and heighten group-oriented behavior (Sherif, 1956). In fact, high identifiers have been shown to maintain group allegiance even when it means incurring individual costs, implying that to change teams would be even more costly (Van Vugt & Hart).

In short, we should not be surprised that individuals develop strong party attachments. Given the ongoing rivalry and perpetual antagonism between political parties, the group psychology literature tells us that this is inevitable. Once the fan develops a team allegiance, changing sides comes at a psychological cost. This chapter considers the implications of this cost for responsiveness motivation. In particular, under what conditions will responsiveness motivation be strong enough to outweigh this cost and produce party identity change?

Most revisionist works assume that individuals are driven to update their identity because they have a stake in political outcomes. These works argue that partisans change their identity to reflect their issue positions (Franklin, 1992; Franklin & Jackson, 1983; Jackson, 1975), party performance evaluations (Brody & Rothenberg, 1988; Fiorina, 1981; MacKuen, Erikson, & Stimson, 1989), and attitudes toward the candidates running for office (Brody & Rothenberg; Page & Jones, 1979). Such theories suggest that party identification serves an instrumental function. As long as partisans update their identity to reflect their evaluations of the world around them, they can rely on party cues to guide their decisions without fear of being led astray (Huckfeldt, Levine, Morgan, & Sprague, 1999; Popkin, 1991; Schaffner & Streb, 2002; Shively, 1979; Tomz & Sniderman, 2005).

The problem with this assumption is that, if there is any social or psychological cost to changing one's party identity, the motivation to attain policy benefits will likely be insufficient to overcome this cost. Downs (1957) explains that, in large-scale elections, abstention may be rational even for individuals who greatly prefer the policies of one party over another. Because each person can cast only a single vote, the probability of influencing the outcome of an election is extremely small. Therefore, the expected policy returns from voting are miniscule and unlikely to outweigh the cost of turnout (e.g., opportunity costs, effort). Likewise, if there is any cost to updating one's party identity, it may be rational to maintain a stable party identity regardless of the parties' issue positions, performance, and candidates for office. Again, because the probability of casting the decisive vote in any large-scale election approaches zero, the expected policy benefits to be derived from policy-oriented voting approach zero. Therefore, the expected policy benefits to be derived from updating one's party identity to reflect one's policy interests also approach zero. In other words, the well known paradox of voting may be a paradox of partisan responsiveness as well.

Still, we have seen in previous chapters that, under the right circumstances, individuals do update their identity. So what then motivates this responsiveness? Downs resolves the "paradox of voting" by arguing that there is a benefit to voting per se: "Rational men in a democracy are motivated to some extent by a sense of social responsibility relatively independent of their own short-run gains and losses" (p. 267). Riker and Ordeshook (1968) refer to this as the benefit of fulfilling one's civic duty and designate it as the "D-term" in their voter calculus model. They model the rewards to be derived from voting as a function of the probability of casting the decisive vote (p), the policy benefits to be gained from the preferred party winning (B), the cost of turning out to vote (C), and the expressive benefits of voting (D):

$$\text{Rewards} = pB - C + D$$

Therefore, as long as $pB + D > C$, a citizen will turn out to vote.

The same solution can be applied to the paradox of partisan responsiveness. Partisans update their identity, *not* because they want to identify with the party that offers the most policy benefits, but because they feel that it is their civic duty to conform to societal norms of pragmatism over partisanship. In Chapter 1, responsiveness motivation (R) was derived from the probability of one's vote determining the outcome of the election (p), the policy benefits associated with the preferred election outcome (*B*), and the expressive benefits that come from seeing oneself as a pragmatic citizen—an aspect of civic duty (*D*). The cost of partisan updating comes from acting against one's partisan motivation (*M*), given the ability to justify acting on that motivation (*J*). In short, because this cost is likely to overwhelm the expected policy benefits to be attained from changing one's party identity, responsiveness motivation is thought to be driven primarily by the desire for expressive benefits (see Equation 5, Chapter 1, p. 16).

According to the model, partisan identity weakening should occur only when $pB + D > MJ$. In Chapters 3 and 4, the *J*-term was experimentally manipulated (through cognitive load induction) to illustrate that individuals are more likely to report weaker party identities in response to disagreement with their party when their ability to justify (*J*) acting on their partisan motivation (*M*) is reduced. This chapter examines the other side of the inequality. Given a very small and constant *p*, party identification should be relatively unaffected by the policy benefits (*B*) at stake in a given election. However, increasing the salience of civic duty (*D*) should increase the probability of party identity weakening.

Duty Hypothesis:
Responsiveness motivation, and therefore partisan change, will be driven by the desire to appear unbiased and pragmatic, thereby conforming to norms of civic duty. Consequently, partisan identity updating will increase when norms of civic duty are made salient.

Stakes Hypothesis:
Party identification will *not* be affected by consideration of the policies the parties will attempt to enact upon taking power. Therefore, partisan identity updating will not increase when the policies at stake in an election are made salient.

CIVIC DUTY AND PARTISAN RESPONSIVENESS

In order to determine the effect of civic duty norms on partisan updating, it is first useful to consider what these norms actually entail. Two books by Schudson (1998) and Dalton (2008), both titled *The Good Citizen*, have examined the evolution of citizenship over time in America. Schudson traces norms of civic duty from the nation's founding to contemporary politics, finding that these norms have changed with political institutions. Of particular interest is the shift from turnout as the embodiment of civic duty during the heyday of machine politics, to informed and autonomous citizenship as the essence of civic duty after the Progressive Era and its reforms.

Although Dalton's (2008) quantitative approach is quite distinct from Schudson's historical analysis, both build on a broad and dynamic view of what

it means to be a good citizen. Traditionally, public opinion research has concep-
tualized civic duty quite narrowly. The civic duty measures included intermit-
tently in the American National Election Studies (ANES) are meant to capture
"the feeling that oneself and others ought to *participate* in the political process,
regardless of whether such political activity is seen as worthwhile or effica-
cious" (italics added) (Campbell, Gurin, & Miller, 1954). These are the measures
that Riker and Ordeshook (1968) famously used to capture their "D-term."

In contrast, Dalton (2008) delineates three norms of good citizenship in
addition to the *participation* norm: *solidarity, social order,* and *autonomy.* The
participation category involves a belief in the importance of voting and other
forms of political engagement. The *solidarity* category taps the idea that "good
citizenship includes a concern for others," and the *social order* category represents the recognition of authority and willingness to abide by laws. Finally,
autonomy entails the belief that responsible citizens should consider all available information—not just those ideas espoused by their fellow partisans—and
hold government accountable. This norm of political autonomy is of particular importance because it speaks to the elevation of pragmatism over partisanship that occurred in the wake of the Progressive Movement (Schudson
1998) and continues to shape our notions of civic duty today (Dalton, 2008;
Schudson, 1998). According to the duty hypothesis, citizens who endorse this
ideal should be more likely to hold their party accountable for the positions it
takes despite the psychological costs involved in doing so.

Measures

Dalton (2008) captured his four norms of civic duty using measures from the
2004 General Social Survey (GSS).[1] These measures, which I will also use in
this chapter, asked participants to respond to the following question:

> There are different opinions as to what it takes to be a good citizen. As far
> as you are concerned personally, on a scale of 1 to 7, where 1 is not at all
> important and 7 is very important, how important is it to…?

This was followed by a series of behaviors that were grouped into Dalton's
four categories. *Autonomy* was captured with two items: "Try to understand
reasoning of people with other opinions" and "Keep watch on actions of
government." The first item speaks to the importance of overcoming one's
biases and acting with an open mind, while the second item addresses the
duty of a citizen to act as an impartial judge of government performance. The
participation norm was captured with three items: "Always vote in elections,"

---

1. He also used the 2005 Citizens, Involvement, and Democracy Survey.

"Be active in social or political associations," and "Choose products for political, ethical or environmental reasons." These items pertain less to the notion of holding government accountable and more to the importance of participation for its own sake. In contrast to the autonomy category, the focus in the participation category was on behavior rather than intentions. *Solidarity* was also captured with two items: "Support people in America who are worse off than oneself" and "Help people in rest of the world who are worse off than oneself." These items obviously tap concern for others at home and abroad. Finally, *social order* was captured with three items: "Always obey laws and regulations," "Never try to evade taxes," and "Being willing to serve in the military in a time of need."

Dalton examined how these norms map onto the American population as well as the types of behavior with which they are associated. I examined how these various aspects of civic duty affect the relationship between party identification and issue positions.[2] As described earlier, I expected the relationship between party identification and issue positions to be stronger among those who endorse political *autonomy* as an important aspect of civic duty and criterion for good citizenship. Although this test did not allow for causal inference, it did allow me to determine whether the variables in question would move together in the expected direction.

As one might expect, the measures of civic duty obtained in the 2004 GSS were highly skewed in favor of endorsement: Skewedness = −1.514 (.064) (autonomy); −.828 (.065) (participation); −.658 (.064) (solidarity) −1.358 (.064) (social order). In other words, very few respondents considered participation, solidarity, social order, or autonomy to be unimportant.[3] To correct for skewedness, I averaged across the indices for each of the four variables and then consolidated the bottom quartile of each variable's distribution. This ensured that the small number of individuals who considered these norms to be unimportant (or perhaps reported this in error) did not disproportionately affect the analysis.

2. On the basis of a factor analysis, Dalton consolidated the four dimensions he laid out in his theory into two dimensions: engaged citizenship (comprised largely of autonomy and solidarity) and duty-based citizenship (comprised largely of social order and participation). However, because the theoretical distinction between autonomy and the other dimensions is important to my work, I chose to maintain the separation between the four categories. The survey analysis to follow suggests that participation and autonomy operate similarly to one another but, as the theory suggests, autonomy emerges as the clear driver.

3. Dalton (2008) also noted the very high means of the items used to tap these concepts (p. 30).

In addition to the civic duty measures laid out previously, respondents' *issue positions* also played an important role in my analysis. An *issue positions* index was created using a battery of items designed to tap respondents' views on how the federal government should allocate its budgetary resources (General Social Survey (GSS; 2004):

> "First I would like to talk with you about some things people think about today. We are faced with many problems in this country, none of which can be solved easily or inexpensively. I'm going to name some of these problems, and for each one I'd like you to tell me whether you think we're spending too much money on it, too little money, or about the right amount [or don't know]."

The battery contained 16 items ranging from space exploration to highways and bridges, the environment, and welfare.[4] Because many of these issues are not traditional cleavage issues, I selected the seven items that loaded most strongly onto the partisan cleavage dimension, using factor analysis.[5] In other words, I focused on the issues that Americans felt differentiated the parties.[6] Certainly, other issue dimensions exist, but the notion of bringing one's party identity into alignment with one's issue positions on a dimension that does not differentiate the parties is nonsensical (see Carsey & Layman, 2006; Dancey & Goren, 2010). A second factor analysis of only these seven items yielded a one-dimensional solution. These items were summed and rescaled to create

---

4. See Table 6.1 in Appendix. Question wording varied from form X to form Y. For the purpose of these analyses, the question types were combined.
5. See Appendix Table 6.1. Only variables with factor loadings on this dimension of .250 or greater were included in the index. The emergence of this dimension suggests that strong Republican identifiers tended to believe that too much money is spent on improving and protecting the environment (Form X)/the environment (Form Y), on welfare (Form X)/assistance for the poor (Form Y), on improving and protecting the nation's health (Form X)/health (Form Y), on dealing with drug addiction (Form X)/drug rehabilitation (Form Y), on improving the nation's education system (Form X)/education (Form Y), on assistance for child care (both forms), and on social security (both forms), whereas strong Democratic identifiers tended to believe that too little money is spent on these things.
6. The central question is whether partisans update their party identity when they realize that their party may not represent their issues positions as well as they originally thought (relative to the opposition party). As new cleavage issues emerge and partisans come to see the distinction, they should bring their party identity into alignment with their positions on these issues.

an *issue positions* measure that ran from the most liberal responses (–1) to the most conservative responses (1).

The standard seven-point measure of *party identification* served as the dependent variable. This variable was scaled to run from strong Democrat (–3) to strong Republican (3). Controls for age (18–89), education (years of school completed, 0–20), gender (dummy), race (dummies), and union membership (dummy) were also included in the model.[7]

Results

Table 6.1 displays the results of an ordered probit regression in which party identification was regressed on Dalton's four aspects of civic duty, respondents' issue positions, and the interactions between each aspect of civic duty and respondents' issue positions. As one would expect, *issue positions* have a strong positive relationship with party identity. Those with more liberal positions tend to identify as Democrats and those with more conservative positions tend to identify as Republicans, but this relationship is far from perfect. The question, of course, is whether this relationship is stronger among those who endorse norms of civic duty—in particular, political autonomy. The large positive interaction between *issue positions* and *autonomy* suggests that this is indeed the case. Those who support the norm of political autonomy hold party identities that better reflect their issue positions. In fact, the coefficient doubles in size.

Aside from *autonomy*issue positions*, the coefficients on each of the other interaction terms are small relative to the size of their standard errors. In other words, it appears that the norm of autonomy, but not any of the other norm of good citizenship, drives up the relationship between issue positions and party identification. In fact, aside from the control variables, the only other significant coefficient in the model is that of *social order*. As one might expect, those who endorse the norm of social order are more likely to identify with the Republican Party.

Figure 6.1 provides a substantive illustration of the impact of *autonomy* on the relationship between issue positions and party identification. The two graphs represent the probability of identifying with or leaning toward a party with which the respondent *disagrees*. For example, consider a person who takes the most liberal position possible on every issue measured. According to the figure, if this individual fails to endorse the norm of political autonomy, she

---

7. These controls are included because each has the potential to shape a person's conception of civic duty and most are also associated with party identification.

TABLE 6.1. *EFFECT OF ISSUE POSITIONS AND CONCEPTIONS OF CIVIC DUTY ON PARTY IDENTIFICATION*

	Party Identification B (SE) (N = 1210)
Issue Positions	1.01***
	(.175)
Autonomy	.219
	(.161)
Autonomy*Issue Positions	1.00**
	(.501)
Participation	−.013
	(.226)
Participation*Issue Positions	.394
	(.670)
Solidarity	−.255
	(.175)
Solidarity*Issue Positions	−.307
	(.516)
Social Order	.483***
	(.154)
Social Order*Issue Positions	−.363
	(.463)
Education	.001
	(.012)
Age	−.005**
	(.002)
Female	−.023
	(.062)
Black	−.380***
	(.139)

(*continued*)

TABLE 6.1. *(CONTINUED)*

	Party Identification B (SE) (N = 1210)
White	.318***
	(.119)
Union	−.099
	(.068)
Cut 1	−1.58
	(.243)
Cut 2	−.943
	(.239)
Cut 3	−.687
	(.239)
Cut 4	−.185
	(.239)
Cut 5	.110
	(.240)
Cut 6	.711
	(.243)

Note: The coefficients (*B*) and standard errors (*SE*) reported in the table were obtained via ordered probit models.

***$p < .01$; **$p < .05$; *$p < .10$

still has a 23% probability of identifying with or leaning toward the Republican Party. However, if she endorses the norm of political autonomy, this probability drops all the way down to 6%.

These results conform quite handsomely to the duty hypothesis. Those who endorse the norm of political autonomy hold party identities that better reflect their issue positions. Yet, as is often the case with survey analyses, one is left to consider the question of what causes what. From an empirical standpoint, the general stability of party identification relative to issue positions raises doubt as to whether issue positions could actually be causing autonomously minded individuals to update their party identity. However, from a theoretical standpoint, it is difficult to explain the reverse. In other words, it would be quite

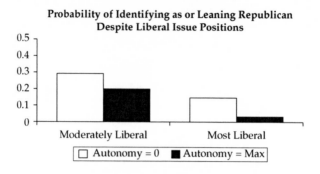

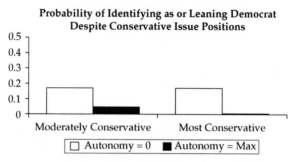

Figure 6.1 Predicted probabilities are based on ordered probit regression. For the purpose of prediction, all civic duty norms except autonomy were set to "0." Education (13.79) and age (45.45) were set to their means. Female was set to "1," and white, black, and union were set to "0." Differences between top and bottom panels are due largely to these settings. The most liberal respondent (i.e., one who has taken the most liberal position possible on every issue) corresponds to an issue position value of –1, and the most conservative to a value of 1. Moderately liberal and moderately conservative correspond to issue position values of –0.5 and 0.5, respectively.

strange if those who most adamantly endorsed the norm of political autonomy were also those who acted least autonomously—allowing their party identification to drive their issues positions. Still, additional evidence is needed before we can be confident in accepting the duty hypothesis. By experimentally inducing considerations of civic duty (specifically, political autonomy) and observing actual changes in party identification over time, the analyses that follow will provide much greater leverage over the issue of causality.

DUTY, STAKES, AND PARTY IDENTIFICATION CHANGE

An experiment was designed to manipulate the saliency of the norm of political autonomy versus the policy stakes of an upcoming election. The experiment complements the previous survey analysis by providing leverage over causality. Moreover, by measuring party identification before and after the experimental manipulation, it was possible to observe actual party identification change.

If party identification were found to be responsive, this would partially support revisionist claims. However, whereas most revisionist models portray party identification as serving an instrumental function in the quest for policy benefits, the dual motivations model suggests that the incentive to appear pragmatic and unbiased is likely to be the real driver of responsiveness. In other words, partisan updating is thought to serve an expressive function. When partisans change their identity to reflect their attitudes, they do so because they want to appear pragmatic and politically autonomous, not because they desire policy benefits.

The implications of this distinction are highly relevant to our understanding of democratic accountability. Scholars often draw analogies between democracy and markets. Voters are thought to demand policy from parties, just as consumers demand products from firms. To adapt Adam Smith's (1986) famous quote, it is not from the benevolence of the Republican or Democratic voter that we expect parties to be held accountable, but from their regard to their own interest. However, if partisan responsiveness is not driven by policy concerns but by civic duty, then benevolence is precisely what is needed to attain accountability.

Method

A sample composed of 1098 adult partisans and partisan "leaners" from across the United States was obtained over the Internet though YouGov/Polimetrix between July 29, 2008, and August 3, 2008. YouGov/Polimetrix matched subjects down to the known marginals of the general population of the United States on gender, age, race, education, and political interest. However, in this sample, partisan "leaners" were under-represented in the sample by a substantial margin relative to strong and weak partisans.[8] As in previous chapters,

---

8. The full sample was composed of two subsamples of 600 people surveyed from July 20 through July 31, 2008 and from August 1 through August 3, 2008, respectively. After the first sample was collected, it was realized that partisans "leaners" had mistakenly been left out of the sample. There was also concern regarding the length of subjects' responses to the stimulus. Therefore, a sentence was added to both treatment conditions asking participants to "Please explain your answer in a few sentences." The study was put back into the field the following day, and a new sample was collected—this time including partisan

"pure" Independents were excluded from analysis, because the purpose of the study was to determine what conditions lead partisans to defect from their party. Since "pure" Independents claim no partisan allegiance, it cannot be determined whether movement in their party identification constitutes movement toward or away from a favored party.

Procedure

This experiment employed a three-celled design in which subjects were primed to consider either the policy stakes of an upcoming election (i.e., instrumental concerns), the norms of civic duty and pragmatism (i.e., expressive concerns), or neither of the above. Both priming treatments were carried by a survey question administered near the beginning of the study. In all three conditions, subjects read the following introduction:

> "Experts predict that nearly 200 million people will vote in the November election. In addition to the presidential race, they will be casting votes for representatives and senators who will represent them in Congress.
>
> Most voters think of themselves as either a Republican or a Democrat, and most candidates are affiliated with one of those two parties."

In the control condition, respondents were not asked to comment. In the *policy stakes* condition, this introduction was followed by an open-ended question:

> "Think about what's at stake in the upcoming election. Do you believe the country and you personally will be seriously affected by which party wins this election? Please explain your answer in a few sentences."

In the *duty* priming condition, participants were asked:

> "Think about what it means to be a good citizen. Do citizens have a duty to consider the issues, or is it okay to just vote based on party? Please explain your answer in a few sentences."

Immediately after the prime, participants viewed a nonpartisan electronic voter guide outlining differences in the platforms of the Republican and Democratic parties. The voter guide discussed the economy, the war in Iraq/defense, education, healthcare, illegal immigration, abortion, and gun

---

"leaners." For the purposes of analysis, the two subsamples were combined. Neither the sampling issue nor the additional wording affected random assignment. Therefore, any differences that arose between experimental conditions can be attributed only to the priming stimuli and to no other factor.

control. The parties' positions were presented side by side in succinct statements (see Appendix Figure 6.1).

Measures

A variable corresponding to *past party identification strength* was created by simply folding the standard seven-point party identification measure in half. The new scale ran from 0 to 3. Strong Democrats as well as strong Republicans were coded as 3, weak partisans were coded as 2, leaners were coded as 1, and pure Independents were coded as 0. Because YouGov/Polimetrix uses sample matching to obtain nationally representative samples, they have party identification on record for everyone in their respondent pool. Thus, it was possible to avoid problems that would obviously result if party identification were obtained immediately prior to the treatment.

The primary dependent variable of interest in this study was *current party identification strength*. This variable was coded identically to *past party identification strength* except that those partisans who crossed over from one party to the other from pre-treatment to post-treatment were coded as having zero strength.

The measure of *issue distance* was based on subjects' assessments of the parties' positions relative to their own positions across a number of issues preceding party identification in the post-treatment instrument. Participants were asked to take positions on each of the issues discussed in the voter guide. They were then asked to place the Republican Party and Democratic Party on identical seven-point scales. These items were either taken directly from the ANES or modeled after ANES questions. (The actual wording of the measures appears in Appendix Figure 6.1.) These items were used to construct measures of each respondent's distance from his or her own (pre-test) party on each issue dimension (relative to the opposition party). Later in the survey, subjects were asked to rate the importance of each of these issues on a seven-point scale ranging from "not that important" to "extremely important." Each issue position was then weighted by the importance rating (rescaled to run from 0 to 1) assigned to it by the respondent.[9] These weighted values were then added together to form a single summary measure of issue distance and rescaled to run from −1 to 1.[10] Individuals whose weighted issue positions were

---

9. Carsey and Layman (2006) argued that partisans update their identity to reflect their issue positions when they are aware of differences between the two parties and when they consider the issue to be important. However, on issues they consider less important, they update their issue positions to reflect their party identity.

10. T-tests showed no significant differences in issue positions between conditions. Principal axis factor analysis of the seven issues resulted in a unidimensional solution with an Eigenvalue of 4.40.

equidistant from the two parties received a value of zero. Those who favored their own party's positions relative to the opposition party's positions received positive values. Those who favored the opposition party's positions received negative values.

Dummy variables were created to represent exposure to the *duty* prime condition or *policy stakes* prime condition. Subjects assigned to a treatment condition received a value of "1"; all others received a value of "0."

Results

I began by examining subjects' responses to the two priming questions. The experiment was built on the assumption that subjects assigned to the *stakes* condition would say that there was, indeed, something important at stake in the 2008 election. In the *norms* condition, they were expected to endorse the norm of voting on the issues as opposed to simply voting for one's party. As expected, 82.6% of subjects assigned to the *stakes* priming condition and 85.0% of respondents assigned to the *norms* priming condition responded in the expected manner.

Next, I checked random assignment to determine whether any chance associations existed between the treatment and any other variables related to party identification strength. Although no significant differences in previous party identification strength or political sophistication emerged between experimental conditions, differences in age and Democratic identification appear to have arisen between conditions by chance.[11] More specifically, before treatment, those assigned to the *policy stakes* condition showed a higher propensity to report party identity on the Democratic side of the scale (mean $(M) = .585$, standard deviation $(SD) = .026$) than those assigned to the control condition $(M = .484, SD = 0.251; p < .01)$.[12] In addition, subjects assigned to the *duty* prime were older on average $(M = 49.21, SD = 14.62)$ than subjects assigned to either the control group $(M = 47.15, SD = 15.64; p < .05)$ or the *policy stakes* prime $(M = 46.71, SD = 14.71; p < .05)$. These variables were therefore included as

---

11. Political sophistication was measured with the use of a seven-item battery. Therefore, the political sophistication variable ran from 0 (none correct) to 7 (all correct). This battery contained a variety of multiple choice questions about political figures and institutions. Respondents were asked to identify the jobs filled by Nancy Pelosi, John Roberts, Dana Perino, and Gordon Brown. Participants are also asked how many votes it takes to override a veto, which branch of government has the power to determine whether a law is constitutional, and which branch has the power of the purse.
12. Democratic identification was a dummy variable.

controls in the analyses that follows. Predicted values were estimated with age set to its mean, party identification strength set to "strong," and Democratic identification set to zero.

Past party identification and current party identification are cross-tabulated in Table 6.2. Although there was a clear tendency toward stability, there does appear to be variance in party identification to explain. However, the question is, of course, whether this variation constitutes experimentally induced systematic variation or just random measurement error (Green & Palmquist 1990, 1994; Green, Palmquist, & Schickler, 2002).

The first step was to examine the effects of both primes on current party identification while controlling for past party identification. I had hypothesized that the duty prime would weaken party identification whereas the stakes prime would have little effect. The probability of maintaining a strong party identity across experimental conditions is displayed by condition in Figure 6.2. As in previous chapters, these estimates were obtained with the use of ordered probit regression to account for potentially inconsistent intervals in party identification strength. Consistent with expectations, the results in Table 6.3 show that those exposed to the duty prime were less likely to maintain a strong party identity than those assigned to the control group ($p < .05$). On the other hand, the stakes prime had no effect on party identification whatsoever.

Although these results provide compelling evidence in favor of the duty and stakes hypotheses, it is possible that the duty prime simply encouraged closet partisanship. To be more specific, participants may have simply reported a weaker party identity in order to avoid the appearance of partisan

TABLE 6.2. *CROSS-TABULATION OF PAST PARTY IDENTITY AND CURRENT PARTY IDENTITY*

Past Party Identification	Current Party Identification						
	Strong Dem	Weak Dem	Leaning Dem	Indep	Leaning Rep	Weak Rep	Strong Rep
Strong Dem	**81.2%**	14.6%	2.1%	0.9%	0.3%	0.0%	0.9%
Weak Dem	7.6%	**74.1%**	10.6%	5.3%	1.2%	1.2%	0.0%
Lean Dem	5.6%	16.7%	**66.7%**	11.1%	0.0%	0.0%	0.0%
Indep	1.4%	2.8%	12.7%	**67.6%**	12.7%	2.8%	0.0%
Lean Rep	0.0%	0.0%	1.7%	15.5%	**65.5%**	6.9%	10.3%
Weak Rep	0.0%	2.7%	2.7%	5.9%	13.9%	**68.4%**	6.4%
Strong Rep	0.0%	0.0%	0.0%	1.1%	4.5%	10.4%	**84.0%**

Note: Percentages are calculated so that rows sum to 100%.

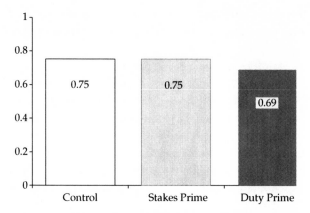

Figure 6.2 The figure illustrates the predicted probability of maintaining a strong party identity from pre-treatment to post-treatment. Predicted probabilities were based on ordered probit regression. For the purpose of prediction, past party identification strength was set at 3 (strong), Democrat identification at 0, and age at 47.54.

bias. They may not have actually brought their identity into alignment with their issue positions.

To determine whether the duty prime truly increased responsiveness motivation rather than merely eliciting closet partisanship, I examined whether issue positions moderated the effect of the duty prime. Although issue positions were measured after the stimulus, the results show that issue positions were entirely unaffected by the experimental manipulation. Therefore, they can safely be treated as exogenous for the purpose of testing the moderation prediction. To do this, the issue distance variable was interacted with each of the two treatment variables. The results presented in Table 6.4 indicate that the duty prime, but not the stakes prime, moderated the influence of issue positions on party identification. The results displayed in Figure 6.3 suggest that exposure to the duty prime led partisans to bring their identity into line with their issue positions. Those partisans whose issue positions were close to the positions of their own party, relative to the other party, tended to maintain their party identity regardless of condition. However, substantial differences emerged between conditions among those people who tended to disagree with their own party on the issues. Subjects in the stakes condition and in the control group who expressed more agreement with the opposition party than with their own party across a number of issues still managed to maintain a stable party identity approximately one-third of the time. This probability dropped to approximately one-twentieth in the *duty* priming condition. In sum, responsiveness motivation was increased by priming considerations of

TABLE 6.3. *EFFECTS OF DUTY PRIME AND STAKES PRIME ON PARTY IDENTIFICATION*

	Party Identification Strength
	B
	(SE)
	(N = 1083)
Duty Prime	−.189**
	(.089)
Stakes Prime	.010
	(.091)
Party Identification Strength (*t*–1)	1.38***
	(.059)
Democrat (*t*–1)	.112
	(.075)
Age	.007***
	(.003)
Cut 1	1.43
	(.186)
Cut 2	2.40
	(.188)
Cut 3	3.79
	(.206)

Note: Results are based on ordered probit regression. The coefficients (*B*) and standard errors (*SE*) reported in the table were obtained via ordered probit models.

***$p < .01$, **$p < .05$, *$p < .10$

duty and the virtue of pragmatism over partisanship. This led partisans to bring their identity into alignment with their issue positions.

On one hand, these results strongly support revisionist models of party identification by showing that, under at least some conditions, partisans will change their identity to reflect their issue positions. Thus, the "unmoved mover" portrayal of party identification appears to be a mischaracterization. On the other hand, these results provide a striking contrast with the general assumption that party identification is instrumental to the attainment of policy benefits. From these results, it appears that consideration of policy stakes has little or no influence on party identification. Instead, party identification change is driven by the incentive to express one's civic duty and pragmatism. Although the instrumentality of party identification cannot be

TABLE 6.4. *EFFECT OF ISSUE POSITIONS AND PARTY*
IDENTIFICATION MODERATED BY DUTY AND STAKES

	Party Identification Strength
	B
	(SE)
	(N = 1082)
Duty Prime	−.420
	(.302)
Stakes Prime	−.238
	(.297)
Issue Distance	1.45***
	(.296)
Duty Prime*Issue Distance	1.16***
	(.449)
Stakes Prime*Issue Distance	−.153
	(.421)
Party Identification Strength (t–1)	1.27***
	(.090)
Duty*Party Identification Strength (t–1)	−.017
	(.126)
Stakes*Party Identification Strength (t–1)	.124
	(.126)
Democrat (t–1)	.147**
	(.077)
Age	.004*
	(.003)
Cut 1	1.31 (.247)
Cut 2	2.34 (.248)
Cut 3	3.81 (.263)

Note: Results are based on ordered probit regression. The coefficients (*B*) and standard errors
(*SE*) reported in the table were obtained via ordered probit models.

***$p < .01$, **$p < .05$, *$p < .10$

ruled out on the basis of a single null finding, the correspondence between the
dual motivations theory and this result is noteworthy. A skeptic might argue
that individuals' party identities already reflected their concerns over policy
stakes coming into the experiment, so there was no room for partisans to bring
their identities into closer alignment with their issue positions. However, the

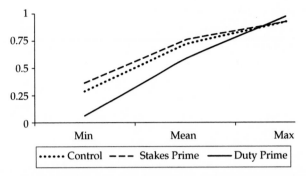

Figure 6.3 The figure illustrates the probability of maintaining a strong party identification from pre-treatment to post-treatment given one's issue positions. Predicted probabilities were based on ordered probit regression. For the purpose of prediction, past party identification strength was set at 3 (strong), Democrat identification at 0, age at 47.54, and word count at 14.35. The maximum negative issue distance was −.518 and the maximum positive issue distance was .857. These were the most extreme observed values in the data. Neutral issue distance was set at 0.

substantial effect of the duty prime suggests that partisans had plenty of room to move. Clearly, party identification was not in perfect alignment with issue positions coming into the study, and this relationship only increased in the *duty* priming condition—leading to weaker party identification.

Although individuals are motivated to see themselves as loyal partisans (and to avoid the cost of partisan disloyalty), they are also motivated to believe that their identity is issue-based and not merely rooted in partisan bias. The results reported here paint the image of a voter who is concerned with avoiding the appearance of partisan bias but not so concerned with maintaining the functionality of her party identity to facilitate the attainment of policy benefits.[13]

Discussion

This chapter asked the question, "To whatever degree partisans update their identity, what is their motivation for doing so?" Although a great

---

13. The parallel between these findings and those in the literature on racial prejudice is worth mentioning. Whereas racial attitudes can have a substantial influence on individuals' policy positions (Devine, 1989; Kinder & Sanders, 1996; Mendelberg, 2001; Valentino, Hutchings, & White, 2002), these influences are diminished when racial implications are made explicit, because they conflict with norms of egalitarianism (Devine; Mendelberg). In the cases of both party identification and racial prejudice, the influence of group bias appears to be reduced when conflict between biases and norms is made salient.

number of studies have examined the degree to which party identification changes, few have given attention to the motivations underlying party identification change. It is generally assumed that, because citizens have a stake in political outcomes, they will want to identify with the party that offers them the most policy benefits. However, this chapter demonstrates that, if there is any psychological cost associated with party identification change, expected policy benefits are unlikely to be great enough to outweigh this cost.

Because the American voter's motivation to attain policy benefits may not be sufficient to overcome her motivation to remain loyal to her party, we should, by implication, be wary of assuming that democratic accountability is guided by the invisible hand. Ironically, it appears that we may not be able to count on voters to act in their own policy interests (see also Caplan, 2007). Partisans appear motivated to act responsively—like good citizens—only when norms of civic duty are salient to them and not simply when their personal interests are at stake.

This also means that party identification may not function as an efficient shortcut for voters. For instance, consider a purely instrumental model in which party identification develops out of the need to make accurate political evaluations while minimizing information costs (Shively, 1979). For party identification to function efficiently, allowing relatively uninformed individuals to vote as if they had objectively weighed the available information, partisans would need to update their identity to reflect their issue positions. These results suggest that policy incentives are insufficient to offset the cost of partisan updating. Instead, it appears that the heuristic efficiency of party identification depends on instilling norms of civic duty through cultural socialization and civic education. Without such norms, partisans would have little incentive to hold their party accountable for its policies. To the degree that voters rely on their party identification to make decisions, these decisions would not accurately reflect their true preferences, and short-term democratic accountability would be threatened.

With this said, my intention has not been to argue that party identification is devoid of heuristic value. These results merely suggest that we should carefully consider how efficiently party identification actually operates as an information shortcut (also see Bartels, 1996). If there were no cost to updating one's party identity, we might safely assume that identification with responsible parties promotes democratic accountability by enabling relatively uninformed citizens to make sense out of a complicated political landscape. However, given the psychological cost of partisan updating, norms of civic duty may be the only thing preventing party identification from hopelessly biasing political assessments and undermining citizens' incentive to hold parties accountable. In short, good citizenship—at least as it pertains to party identification—is rooted in norms of civic duty and not in mere self-interest. Therefore, the promotion of these norms is vital if we want partisans to act like good citizens who hold parties accountable rather fans who support their team unconditionally.

CHAPTER 7

Motivation and Democracy

This book opened by asking whether team loyalties get in the way of voters' willingness to hold parties accountable for the policies they endorse and the way they perform while in power. In essence, it inquired whether partisans are good citizens or merely fans of a particular political team. Rival theories of party identification provide very different answers to this question. According to these models, partisans either hold parties accountable for their policy positions and performance, or they maintain their party allegiances regardless of the parties' positions and performance. Thus, party identification either serves as an efficient shortcut that allows relatively uninformed citizens to vote as if they were better informed, or it serves as a pervasive source of bias that leads relatively well-informed citizens to disregard information in order to maintain their party loyalty.

These divergent characterizations of party identification are rooted in the theories' underlying motivational assumptions. The Michigan model assumes that partisans are motivated to maintain and defend their identity (i.e., act like fans), whereas revisionist models assume that citizens are motivated to update their party identity in response to disagreements (i.e., act like good citizens). This, of course, leaves scholars of political behavior in an awkward predicament. We know that party identification is the most powerful predictor of voting behavior, but we cannot say whether this is good or bad for democracy.

The goal of this book has been to resolve this problem by building on the wisdom of both theories. The dual motivations theory, proposed here, argues that party identification is shaped by often competing motives. Partisans feel duty-bound to hold parties accountable for their issue positions and performance, but they are also motivated by party loyalty. As long as an individual can generate a justification for maintaining her identity despite disagreements with her party, this clash of motives results in stable party identification. Identity change occurs when continued identification cannot be justified or when responsiveness motivation comes to outweigh partisan motivation.

In Chapter 2 we saw that, after disagreement between study participants and their party was experimentally induced, individuals developed "lesser of two evils" justifications to rationalize maintenance of their party identity. In other words, study participants were able to maintain their identity by ensuring that their attitudes toward the opposition party remained more negative than their attitudes toward their own party. In general, liking the Democratic Party more was associated with liking the Republican Party less. However, as partisans' attitudes approached indifference between the two parties, they began to line up on a new dimension in which liking the Democratic party less was associated with liking the Republican party less as well. This same pattern emerged in data from the 1964–2008 American National Election Studies (ANES). When the economy performed poorly and the opposition party was in office, negative attitudes toward the opposition party were associated with positive attitudes toward one's own party. However, this relationship weakened when the economy was performing poorly during the tenure of one's own party. Just as in the experiment, partisans reported more negative attitudes toward the opposition party once their attitudes toward their own party could no longer be used to justify continued identification.

Chapter 3 provided additional evidence of party identity defense. In this case, partisans reduced inconsistency between their attitudes and their party identity by reprioritizing their issue positions to favor those that were consonant with their party identity. Across ANES surveys conducted between 1960 and 2000, when unemployment (or inflation) was high and the subject's own party controlled the presidency, partisans showed a substantially lower likelihood of reporting that unemployment (or inflation) was the nation's most important problem. On the other hand, when the opposition party was presiding over high unemployment (or inflation), partisans were happy to acknowledge its importance. This pattern was replicated in a national experiment designed to elicit disagreement between study participants and their party. However, these results were confined to Democrats. At the time of the study, the Republican Party was in the midst of turmoil. As a result, Republicans actually updated their party identity to reflect experimentally induced disagreement. Democrats, on the other hand, reprioritized their issue position to favor their party, shifting importance off of the dissonant issue and onto issues traditionally "owned" by their party. Importantly, however, Democrats' ability to justify continued identification in the face of disagreement seems to have been contingent on the availability of cognitive resources.

Chapter 4 continued this investigation by examining whether stable party identification is contingent on the availability of cognitive resources. Results suggest that partisans are able to maintain stable identities as long as they possess sufficient resources to justify these identities. When cognitive resources were in short supply, they became more susceptible to party identification change. Youth, lack of political sophistication, unaccommodating political context, and cognitive load all appeared to undermine party identity defense. These results contrast strikingly with the revisionist notion that individuals devote their cognitive resources to updating their party identity to reflect their issue positions and political evaluations. Instead, this type of rational updating appears only to occur *despite* partisans' best efforts to avoid it.

Chapter 5 considered the issue of measurement error. Donald Green and colleagues have argued in a series of important works that most of the observed change in party identification is simply the result of measurement error and does not constitute substantive change. However, if these short-term fluctuations are actually question order effects and do not result merely from the inherent difficulty of devising survey measures, these fluctuations may actually tell us a good deal about party identification. To examine the effects of question order on party identification, I conducted a national survey experiment during the 2008 primary season to capitalize on the widespread disaffection felt among Republicans at that time. Attitude primes administered at the start of the survey caused a chain reaction of responses—which in a standard survey context would likely be discounted as measurement error. When Republicans' attitudes toward the Democratic Party (which were relatively positive compared with Democrats' attitudes toward the Republican Party) were made salient to them, they responded to these considerations and reported a weaker party identity. However, because this conflicted with their partisan motivation, they quickly reverted back to their original identity by bolstering their feelings toward their own party. When Republicans were initially primed with attitudes toward the Republican Party, the pattern was identical except that no significant momentary shift in party identification occurred. Still, Republicans appear to have defended their identity in this latter situation by bolstering the negativity of their feelings toward the Democratic Party.

Chapter 6 shifted the focus to responsiveness motivation. Revisionist theories of party identification rest on the assumption that policy stakes motivate citizens to identify with the party that best represents their policy interests. The dual motivations theory argues that partisans' sense of civic duty, and specifically their desire to appear pragmatic and unbiased, motivates them to update their party identity. Thus, the revisionist model suggests that partisans are inherently motivated to hold parties accountable, whereas the dual motivations approach suggests that party accountability hinges on the norm of civic duty. Either way, if citizens fail to adjust their party identity to reflect the information they acquire, party cues may guide them to vote against their interests.

The duty and stakes hypotheses were tested using data from the 2004 General Social Survey and a national experiment in which considerations of either civic duty or policy stakes were primed. Survey results showed that, among those who endorsed the norm of political autonomy, the relationship between party identification and issue positions was considerably stronger. Even more to the point, partisans in the experiment changed their identity to more closely reflect their issue positions when primed to consider civic duty but not when primed to consider the policy stakes of the election. These results suggest that party identification change serves an expressive function rather than an instrumental function. Although party identification has the potential to operate as an efficient heuristic, this potential does not arise naturally from the desire to attain policy benefits but rests instead on the salience of civic duty and the norm of political autonomy.

By developing a dual motivations theory of party identification, this book has taken the first steps toward determining the conditions under which party identification helps versus harms democracy. Citizens are able to achieve democratic accountability when they demand effective policy, because this forces parties to compete for their support. If partisan motivation acts as a drag on citizens' willingness to respond to the positions parties take and the ways they perform while in office, accountability is threatened.[1] This raises the question of how we might increase responsiveness motivation and decrease partisan motivation. In the pages that follow, I consider the implications of the dual motivations theory of party identity and the role it suggests for parties in American government.

---

1. One might be tempted to argue that these errors should cancel out, so that this would be only a minor problem. However, because these are not random errors but rather systematic biases, this logic does not hold here as it does in other contexts (for example, see Page & Shapiro, 1992). For the systematic biases of Republicans and Democrats to cancel out, they would need to balance one another (i.e., the aggregate biases of the two parties would have to be identical). Assuming that these biases do not balance each other, then electoral outcomes will be systematically skewed in favor of one party—a circumstance that seems to fit the data quite well (see Bartels, 1996). Of course, even if these biases did balance one another, the political outcome would ride on the opinions of Independents (who tend to be far less knowledgeable and less engaged in politics than partisans) (Campbell et al., 1960; Lewis-Beck, Jacoby, Norpoth, and Weisberg, 2008).

PARTIES AS SHORTCUTS

Herbert Simon (1979) developed the notion of bounded rationality, arguing that individuals seek to maximize cognitive efficiency by expending the least amount of effort necessary to reach approximately correct decisions. Building on Simon's work, political scientists have investigated how citizens use information shortcuts, or heuristics, to achieve low-information rationality in political decision-making (for examples, see Lupia & McCubbins, 1998; Lupia, McCubbins, & Popkin, 2000; Popkin, 1991; Sniderman, Brody, & Tetlock, 1991). Given the relatively uninformed state of American public opinion (see Delli Carpini & Keeter, 1996) and the fact that political ignorance is theoretically rational (Downs, 1957), this is an important task. Still, although cognitive shortcuts give us great hope for the prospect of overcoming rational ignorance, we should also be cognizant of the limitations that heuristics might pose—a point that is central to the psychological literature on heuristics yet often overlooked in political research (Kuklinski & Quirk, 2000; Tversky & Kahneman 1974).

Before delving deeper into this literature, it is helpful to begin with a bit of conceptual clarification. Lupia, McCubbins, and Popkin (2000) emphasize that citizens rely on heuristics, not because they are "irrational," but because they are rationally reducing information costs. Humans have evolved the capacity for heuristic processing because it tends to be *efficient*. Dual processing capacity—the ability to engage in heuristic processing or systematic processing (see Eagly & Chaiken, 1993; Petty & Cacioppo, 1986)—allows humans to adapt to complex environments. Heuristic processing allows humans to conserve cognitive resources when errors in judgment have minimal consequences. However, when threats arise, judgmental accuracy becomes more advantageous, and our emotions trigger increased allocation of resources to information processing (Brader, 2006; Marcus, Neuman, & MacKuen, 2000). Whereas heuristics entail a loss of accuracy relative to more careful processing strategies, this loss is offset by the reduction in information costs. In fact, if the defining characteristic of a heuristic is its efficiency, any loss in accuracy must be offset by an equally large or larger reduction in information costs.

If individuals appear to be sacrificing information processing accuracy to such an extent that it can no longer be justified by information cost savings, these individuals' motives and the heuristics they are using should be questioned. Such an "irrational" sacrifice of information is likely to be motivated by the desire to reach a particular decision, rather than an accurate one, and therefore should be distinguished from heuristic processing. As discussed previously, partisan motivation is likely to be rooted in the evolutionary incentive to develop and preserve group bonds by avoiding disloyalty—a purpose quite distinct from that of heuristic processing. In short, people may follow party cues to reduce processing effort or to maintain group cohesion, but these are very different goals with very different implications for democracy.

The question of whether party identification acts as an efficient heuristic is particularly important given the centrality of both party identification and heuristics to our understanding of public opinion and political behavior. Some of the early work on partisanship implied a heuristic role quite clearly. Berelson, Lazarzfeld, and McPhee (1954) characterize partisanship as a "standing decision," a voting habit on which citizens rely in the absence of other information. Campbell, Converse, Miller, & Stokes (1960) draw an analogy between the uninformed consumer and the uninformed voter:

> Like the automobile buyer who knows nothing of cars except that he prefers a given make, the voter who knows simply that he is a Republican or Democrat responds directly to his stable allegiance without the mediating influence of perceptions he has formed of the objects he must choose between (p. 136).

Still, Campbell and colleagues (1960) are clear in their contention that party identification may provide uninformed voters with a basis on which to cast their ballot, but it is not necessarily an efficient shortcut if the end goal is to cast a vote that represents one's "true" policy interests. The authors explain:

> [T]he influence of party identification on attitudes toward the perceived elements in politics has been far more important than the influence of these attitudes on party identification itself (p. 135).

More recently, scholars have directly engaged the question of whether party identification functions as an efficient heuristic. Shively (1979) developed a functional theory of party identification, arguing that individuals with a desire to participate in politics and a motivation to reach accurate voting decisions identify with parties in order to reduce information costs. If citizens can determine which party generally represents their interests, they can avoid the cost of constantly monitoring politics.[2]

---

2. However, Downs (1957) specifically stated that reliance on parties as information shortcuts is irrational because parties' goals (i.e., to get elected) do not match those of citizens (i.e., to see policies passed that reflect their interests). Therefore, some monitoring of party positions must occur if party cues are to have heuristic value.

It seems more plausible, however, that the motivation to identify with parties—and with groups in general—results from natural selection, itself a utility maximization process that takes place over many generations. We identify with groups today because group bonds increased the likelihood of survival for our ancestors (Darwin, 1890; Van Vugt & Schaller, 2008). Therefore, while party identification may potentially serve a heuristic function, it seems unlikely that it developed specifically to fill this need.

Still, Shively's (1979) very clear and parsimonious model helps us to understand how a partisan heuristic might ideally operate. If partisan motivation is incorporated into Shively's model, party identification functions just as it does in the dual motivation model, serving as a useful voting heuristic as long as one's responsiveness motivation is greater than one's partisan motivation. However, when the opposite is true, party identification serves as a source of bias.

Several works have examined the heuristic utility of partisanship. In an innovative experiment, Rahn (1993) found that when party cues were available, participants relied less on issue positions and more on party identification to help them evaluate candidates. She discovered that this was true even when candidates took positions that conflicted with their party's ideology. Subjects dismissed these inconsistencies and evaluated candidates on the basis of their party affiliation. Rahn viewed these results as evidence that party cues serve as useful heuristics. However, given that subjects were able to make ideologically based judgments in the absence of party cues but then disregarded ideology in favor of party when cues were available, one might interpret these results as evidence that party identification biased candidate evaluations rather than serving as an effective shortcut.

This interpretation is bolstered by results from a series of similar experiments by Cohen (2003) in which party cues appeared to trump issues regardless of subjects' cognitive effort. Recent work by Bullock (2011) has also shown that party cues influence voters' opinions. But contrary to Rahn (1993) and Cohen, Bullock found that these cueing effects were relatively small compared to the effect of policy information. Importantly, neither Bullock nor Cohen found party cues to affect processing effort or recall. Instead, these cues affected the content of one's subsequent thoughts (Cohen). Thus, it appears that citizens follow party cues not simply to reduce cognitive effort (although they may do so under some circumstances) but to actively avoid disagreement with their party (see Gaines, Kuklinski, Quirk, Peyton, & Verkuilen, 2007).

Rather than assuming citizens are motivated to be responsive, Sniderman and colleagues explicitly allow partisan motivation to play a role in heuristic processing (Brady & Sniderman, 1985; Sniderman et al., 1991). They emphasize that citizens' feelings toward parties can act as a likeability heuristic that helps them determine on which side of an issue each party stands.[3] In other words, citizens' motivation to agree with their favored party and to distance themselves from the positions of the disfavored party serves as the basis by which many people attribute issue positions to parties.[4]

Although this "likeability" shortcut is theoretically innovative and more empirically plausible than models that assume an absence of partisan motivation, it stretches the definition of a heuristic. Party identification may help to constrain belief systems, but it seems less plausible that partisan biases allow individuals to behave more efficiently—the defining characteristic of a heuristic. For heuristic processing to function efficiently, individuals must, at a minimum, make use of the relevant information they possess. If partisans disregard information they know to be correct in favor of information they wish to be correct, then they cannot be said to be using information efficiently.[5]

Popkin (1991) provides a concise and persuasive argument for why heuristic reasoning is essential to American government, and in so doing also suggests exactly why heuristics are likely to have limited utility if they induce partisan biases:

> Given the many gaps in voters' information about government, and their lack of theory with which to make connections between government

---

3. Others have built on this idea by demonstrating that party cues (Schaffner & Streb, 2002) and accessible party identities (Huckfeldt, Levine, Morgan, & Sprague, 1999) facilitate the formation and durability of survey responses.
4. Individuals are thought to find a "balance" between their estimates of parties' true positions and their desire to believe that parties hold particular positions. In essence, Brady and Sniderman (1985) took a dual motivations approach to understanding how citizens attribute issue positions to parties. Under their model, the "balance" of these motivations is affected by a citizen's level of knowledge. Specifically, those with less knowledge about the parties' true positions rely more on their feelings toward the parties. Therefore, these feelings serve as a heuristic that citizens can fall back on in the absence of knowledge. By framing partisan bias as a heuristic, the authors implied that only those with low knowledge levels will act on these biases, but this is not necessarily the case. Well-informed partisans may be somewhat less affected by their feelings toward parties, but this does not mean that they would be acting objectively. The model still allows them to take positions that they know to be incorrect, simply because they are motivated to do so.
5. For a fascinating read and an important illustration of how Sniderman's views on party cueing have evolved, readers should see his most recent work (with Edward Stiglitz), *The Reputational Premium: A Theory of Party Identification and Policy Reasoning* (2012).

actions and their benefits, governments concerned primarily with gaining as many votes as possible have little incentive to maximize benefits to voters (p. 13).

Popkin's intent is clearly to point out why it is important for citizens to hold opinions and how heuristics can help, but he also makes the case for why these opinions must *accurately* represent voters' interests and not merely their partisan biases. If voters simply assume that their favored party supports their issue positions, as Brady and Sniderman suggested (1985), then elected officials can take any position they wish with little fear that their constituents will complain. In other words, a heuristic rooted entirely in one's biases does nothing to improve democratic accountability over the circumstances of a citizenry that learns no new information after socialization.

In an effort to determine whether heuristics allow uninformed citizens to function as if they are informed, Bartels (1996) examined actual public opinion in comparison to a hypothetical, fully informed version of public opinion imputed from demographic data. His results show that heuristics fall substantially short of this mark. Of course, some suggest that such a high standard is not necessary for the individual voter, because errors in opinion should cancel out in the aggregate (see Converse, 1990; Page & Shapiro, 1992). Therefore, Bartels also conducted an aggregate-level examination and found that, whereas aggregation closes the gap between observed and fully informed public opinion, incumbents and Democrats still perform better than they would in a fully informed electorate. Party cues might help to supplement information, but they do not appear to substitute for it (Althaus, 1998; Bartels, 1996). Of course, if one acknowledges that motivational biases prevent individuals from updating heuristics to reflect the information that they receive, this is exactly the pattern one would expect to observe.

In short, the fact that individuals follow party cues is not enough to warrant referring to party identification as an effective shortcut. Although party identification certainly has the potential to function as a heuristic, the group biases that tend to come along with identification undermine its utility. Rather than allowing individuals to function efficiently (as if they were fully informed), party identification may lead well-informed partisans to vote as if they were relatively uninformed.

PARTY INSTITUTIONS

Since the nation's founding, Americans have generally been skeptical of parties. James Madison famously addressed concern over factions (including parties) in Federalist No. 10 (Madison, 2003), and George Washington used his farewell address to warn against the danger of parties (which he witnessed developing within his own cabinet) (Washington, 1796/2008). Yet, in striking contrast, political scientists have developed an almost universal "commitment to the desirability, if not the absolute necessity of parties in a democratic system" (Epstein, 1986). In the famous words of E. E. Schattschneider (1942), democracy is "unthinkable save in terms of parties." But why is this so?

Aldrich (1995) explains that parties solve three fundamental problems in democracy: They regulate competition between ambitious office seekers; they alleviate social choice problems in the legislature; and they mobilize citizens to take collective action. However, the preceding chapters have drawn attention to an important shortcoming of parties: They nurture affective attachments that undermine citizens' motivation to hold them accountable.

In the United States, at least in the current era, politics are candidate-centered. Parties provide labels for candidates to run under, but parties have little control over their brand (Aldrich, 1995; Epstein, 1986). In other words, while parties have official platforms, their candidates are not bound to them. Whichever candidate wins the party's primary gets to carry the party's label regardless of his or her issue positions. Therefore, although party labels provide some information about a candidate's stances, there remains a substantial amount of uncertainty. Moreover, separation of powers, checks and balances, and the federated structure of American government make it difficult to determine who is ultimately responsible for the passage or failure of legislation. Parties' lack of brand control coupled with this institutional complexity allows elected officials to point fingers when things go badly and claim credit when things go well. In short, the American system of government is characterized by a substantial amount of ambiguity.

This ambiguity poses a clear concern for citizens' ability to obtain the information necessary to hold officials accountable, and it is even more troubling if we take into account that partisans may actually be motivated to *avoid* holding their party accountable in the first place. For the motivated partisan, ignorance is bliss. We have seen that partisans rationalize away disagreements with their party via lesser of two evils identity justifications and issue reprioritization. However, such effortful defense may not even be necessary in many cases. There is little pressure to change one's party identity when it is unclear what parties actually stand for. In such a system, "false consensus effects" (Ross, Greene, & House, 1977) can run rampant as citizens assume that their party and its candidates favor the positions that they themselves favor. And, when confronted with hard evidence that a candidate of one's own party has taken a position with which one disagrees, one can simply assume the candidate is not representative of the party as a whole (Marques & Yzerbyt, 1988). Even when it comes to party performance evaluations, officeholders' denials of responsibility remain quite plausible (Fiorina, 1980)—especially when partisans are motivated to believe them.

Proponents of the "doctrine of responsible party government" view stronger parties as the cure to this problem (see Ranney, 1954). These scholars see separation of powers, checks and balances, and federalism as antimajoritarian and argue that *majority rule* is the essence of democratic government. They propose a system in which government would be centered around at least (and preferably only) two *unified* and *disciplined* parties. Under such a system, they argue, a majority party would be directly accountable for all legislation passed while it was in power, and officials would be directly tied to the party. Thus, the system would be simple and unambiguous, allowing the public to hold officials responsible. To this end, they advocate reforms that would increase the discipline, influence, and centrality of parties in the American government (APSA Committee on Political Parties, 1950a, 1950b, 1950c).

Implicit in the doctrine of responsible party government is the notion that citizens are motivated to be responsive to parties' actions and not always loyal to their party. In other words, proponents of responsible parties take a very similar approach to those who write on the heuristic value of party identification, except that they focus on party institutions as opposed to voters. They view parties as a way to simplify voter decision-making. Such a system would also facilitate collective responsibility, making it somewhat more difficult for parties and candidates to deny responsibility when things go badly or claim credit when things go well (Fiorina, 1980). Moreover, by decreasing the ambiguity in politics, a responsible party system would likely increase the pressure to update one's identity in light of disagreements on issue positions. If it is clear where candidates and parties stand, it is more difficult to ignore inconsistencies between one's own issue positions and the stances of one's party.

However, this type of party system may well pose as many problems as solutions. When political debate is divided along a single, well-defined cleavage, it facilitates partisans' ability to avoid taking positions different from those of their party in the first place. Studies show that the influence of party identification is pervasive—even affecting assessments of the economy (Bartels, 2002; Duch, Palmer, & Anderson, 2000; Gerber & Huber, 2010). Moreover, partisan predispositions are particularly influential among those who are most informed about where their party stands on the issues (Converse, 1966; Zaller, 1992). More conclusive yet are experiments showing that ideology informs political evaluations unless party cues are available (Cohen, 2003; Rahn, 1993).[6] Once party cues are present, partisans disregard ideology and follow

---

6. Bullock (2011) argues that these effects are overstated. In an experiment, he found that party cues had an effect but policy considerations were more influential.

their party. In short, despite their apparent shortcomings, citizens do appear able to make use of information when it is available, but they tend to *disregard* that information when it conflicts with their party identity.

Recent research has shown that, in democratic systems with fewer and more disciplined parties, the propensity to identify with parties is greater—particularly among individuals with lower levels of education (Huber, Kernell, & Leoni, 2005). The question remains, however, whether higher rates of identification produce legislative outcomes that are more in line with citizens' "true" interests or less in line with them. This book's findings suggest that it may well be the latter. Although party identification may help those with less education to understand politics, it may also bias the judgments of those who are otherwise best equipped to hold parties accountable.

Contemporary American politics seems to bear out this concern. Research suggests that, in addition to allowing partisans to avoid ever disagreeing with their party, recurring confrontations along a single, well-defined cleavage should intensify intergroup conflict, polarization, and partisan bias (Sherif, 1956).

Such theoretical predictions conform all too well to our recent political experiences. Parties have become more unified and disciplined, as proponents of responsible party government advocate, yet many would argue that we are all the worse for it (Rae, 2007). Rather than these developments' facilitating citizens' ability to hold parties accountable for their platforms, voters, as Levendusky (2009) shows, are adjusting their ideology to fit that of their party—precisely the pattern uncovered in the experiments cited (Cohen, 2003; Rahn, 1993). Levendusky sees this as a positive development because it helps voters to constrain their belief systems. However, increased constraint is of little value in and of itself. Scholars have traditionally worried that without constrained belief systems, citizens have a difficult time holding government accountable (Converse, 1964). But, if constraint results from citizens' motivation to blindly follow their party wherever it leads them, it can hardly be said that accountability is better served.

How then might we decrease the ambiguity in American politics without exacerbating partisan biases? If responsible parties are not the answer, what is? Perhaps it is worth taking a second look at the role of interest groups in American politics. Pluralist theories of democracy (see, for example, Truman, 1993) lost favor in the mid-20th century as scholars came to realize that smaller and better-funded interests were advantaged relative to larger public interest groups (Lowi, 1979; Olson, 1971, 1982; Schattschnieder, 1975). Responsible parties came to be seen as a superior vehicle by which to aggregate citizens' interests, because they would be forced to vie to represent a true majority and not merely a coalition of narrow interests (Schattschneider, 1942). From the standpoint of the responsible parties thesis, the challenge was how to implement reforms that would transform American parties into responsible parties.

In contrast to the literature on responsible party government, some see "indigenous" American parties in a more favorable light. Epstein (1986) argues that parties have evolved to fit the circumstances of American government (also see Aldrich, 1995). He focuses on what he refers to as their "institutionalized porousness." By allowing entrance by individuals and groups who want to make use of their label rather than strict adherence to a particular platform, indigenous American parties bring together various interests in an effort to build winning coalitions. This is seen as a good thing because it forces adjustment and compromise between interests rather than ideological rigidity (Herring, 1940). Of course, the notion of adjustment and compromise between coalitions of interest groups does little to assuage the concerns of those who desire stronger parties precisely because they wish to stem the influence of special interests (see Schattschneider, 1975).

Nonetheless, some solace may be taken in the notion that interest groups are probably more diverse than their critics imply. Despite the inherent advantage of small groups, many larger, publicly oriented groups flourish. In his well-known interest group survey, Walker (1991) found that 56.4% of groups were either nonprofit (32.5%) or citizen groups (23.9%), whereas only 37.8% were profit sector groups, and 5.8% were mixed sector. He also found that different types of groups attempted to influence politics by different means. Profit sector groups engaged mostly in inside lobbying—directly petitioning legislators and bureaucrats, whereas citizen groups mostly engaged in outside lobbying—attempting to affect legislation via the public. Therefore, if our primary concern is with the relative advantage enjoyed by profit sector groups, we might consider how to bring lobbying out of the shadows (i.e., inside lobbying) and into the light (i.e., outside lobbying). This would allow groups to continue to check parties while making their actions transparent to the public. Such an arrangement is advantageous for several reasons.

First, parties exist not necessarily to promote issues but to help office seekers win power (Aldrich, 1995; Schumpeter, 1942); in contrast, interest groups exist specifically to promote polices. Sartori (1976) claimed that a party is "part of a whole attempting to serve the purposes of the whole, whereas a faction is only a part for itself." But the very nature of the system ensures that parties serve the purpose of the whole only if serving the whole constitutes a winning strategy. Individual politicians may be sincere in their desire to serve the

144 COMPETING MOTIVES IN THE PARTISAN MIND

public good, but they will never gain office unless serving the public good proves to be a winning strategy. In short, parties only serve the public good if the public demands that they do so. Because individual citizens have more incentive to enjoy the psychological benefits of loyal party identification than to make demands of parties, interest groups play an important role in filling the void.

Second, when interest groups force parties and candidates to take clear issue positions and then hold them accountable for those positions, democracy benefits from a reduction in ambiguity. Downs (1957) explained that, because parties have electoral goals whereas citizens have policy goals, it is irrational for citizens to trust parties for information. When it comes to parties, talk is cheap, because they have an incentive to tell citizens whatever they want to hear in order to get their vote (see Lupia & McCubbins, 1998; Sobel, 1985). On the other hand, because interest groups have clear policy goals, interest group cues convey much more reliable information. For example, when the insurance industry, the California Trial Lawyers Association, and a Ralph Nader–led consumer group all endorsed competing insurance reform initiatives in California, less informed citizens used endorsement cues to emulate the voting behavior of better-informed citizens (Lupia, 1994). Groenendyk and Valentino (2002) also show that citizens listen to interest groups. In their experiment, participants took notice when the Sierra Club criticized George W. Bush's environmental record. However, when Al Gore criticized Bush's environmental record in an identical appeal, the message fell on deaf ears.

The third reason interest groups serve as an effective check on parties is that interest group identification is not detrimental to democratic accountability. As previously stated, parties exist to win elections, but interest groups exist to promote policy agendas. Therefore, while parties have an incentive to take advantage of voters' loyalty as they constantly endeavor to build and maintain winning coalitions, interest groups have no such incentive. Because interest groups share the policy goals of their supporters, interest group identification does not undermine the heuristic value of interest group cues. Thus, voting one's interest group identity means voting one's policy interests.

If people come to identify with interest groups, these identities crosspressure their party identity, thereby checking partisan biases (Campbell et al., 1960). Take, for instance, a circumstance in which the Democratic Party criticizes the Republican Party. Not only does such communication constitute "cheap talk," but partisan motivation will drive Republicans to counter-argue against such criticisms even if they do find them credible. On the other hand, if the United States Chamber of Commerce criticizes the Republican Party or its candidates, it is likely to carry much greater weight with Republican voters.

Schattschneider (1942) argues that parties are like businesses in that laws are no more needed to make parties serve people than they are to make businesses serve consumers. The problem with this analogy is that in business, consumers demand high-quality goods, so producers must supply quality products if they hope to compete. In politics, voters' brand loyalties are so strong that they will often "buy" whatever policy package their party offers. Moreover, individual citizens have little incentive to demand that parties accommodate their interests, because they know that their individual vote has very little effect on policy outcomes. Instead, they engage in politics in large part because they develop "team" loyalties and enjoy watching the competition unfold. Interest groups are therefore needed to act as a check on parties and ensure that they are held accountable.

Just as well-regulated markets harness the self-interest of individuals to promote the public interest, a well-regulated democratic government can benefit by harnessing the self-interest of interests groups. The key is in effective regulation.[7] If interest group influence can be channeled through the public (i.e., outside lobbying as opposed to inside lobbying), interest groups may help to perform a vital service to democracy by informing the public about issues and mobilizing them to action. The tentative conclusion, then, is that we should not be so quick to extol parties and condemn interest groups. Although democracy might be "unthinkable" (Schattschneider, 1942) or at least "unworkable" (Aldrich, 1995) save parties, short-run party accountability may just be unattainable save interest groups.

A STATEMENT ON MOTIVATION

Understanding citizens' motivations is absolutely critical if we hope to build effective democratic institutions. Far too often, works rely on motivational assumptions that the literature has shown to be faulty. We know that voters have little incentive to become informed and that there are minimal policy benefits to be gained from political participation (Downs, 1957). So why, then, do we so often assume that political behavior is driven by voters' policy interests? In recent decades, scholars have made great strides by explicitly accounting for citizens' motivation (or lack thereof) to become informed about political matters and act in their own self-interest. Given citizens' lack of responsiveness motivation, our next step should be to more explicitly consider other sources of motivation. This book is an attempt to do just that.

---

7. In the wake of *Citizens United v. Federal Election Commission*, 558 U.S. 310 (2010), this is a particularly important concern.

If politics were merely about information and the motivation to attain it, there would likely be no party mascots, no team colors, no balloons, nor parades. And the horse race would be of little interest to voters, who would be looking for either substantive news or none at all. Of course, this is not the case. Parties and candidates do all they can to foster team spirit, because they know it works. And media outlets focus on the competitive drama, because that is what the public demands. Although some good citizens get involved in politics because they feel compelled to fulfill their civic duty, many others are drawn by the sporting nature of politics and the allure of cheering along with a team. For most citizens, politics involves an ongoing internal struggle to reconcile their motivation to be a good citizen with their motivation to be a good fan. Therefore, we must develop a clearer understanding of citizens' motivations and the conditions under which each drives behavior if we hope to harness these motivations in pursuit of greater democratic accountability.

The assumptions we make about citizens' motivations shape our judgments regarding institutional effectiveness. If citizens are driven to attain policy benefits, and parties aid them in this pursuit, then parties serve a useful function. However, if citizens are motivated to get involved in politics because they want to be part of something larger than themselves, and parties aid them in this pursuit, then we may want to be careful how we regulate these institutions. When citizens unconsciously place party loyalty above party accountability, they risk becoming puppets of party elites. And if party identification drives issue preferences, rather than vice versa, then parties are not being held accountable. With the rise of the Nazi regime in the 1930s, we witnessed what can happen when citizens get swept up in party movements led by charismatic politicians. This book is certainly not meant as an indictment of the public's qualifications for sovereignty. It is merely a plea to take into account citizens' competing motivations as we attempt to understand their behavior in politics.

THE EMERGING LITERATURE

Despite the longstanding debate over the nature and stability of party identification, exciting progress is being made in the literature. This book is not alone in its effort to develop a conditional model of party identification change, reconsider the efficiency of partisanship as an information shortcut, and unpack the implications of increased elite polarization. As mentioned in previous chapters Carsey and Layman (2006), discovered that partisans changed their identity to reflect their issue positions when they were aware of party differences on an issue and they deemed the issue to be important. Conversely, if they considered the issue to be unimportant, they changed their positions to reflect their party identity. Similarly, Dancey and Goren (2010) found that increased media coverage strengthened the link between party identification and issue positions in both directions.

Still, questions remain as to what drives this behavior and how we should understand the implications of these important findings. Are partisans motivated to be responsive and therefore identify with the party that best represents their positions? If so, given awareness of differences in party positions, they should update their party identity to reflect *all* of their issue positions and simply weight important issues more heavily. In other words, issues positions should influence party identity, but not vice versa. Responsive partisans might use party cues as a shortcut when forming their *initial* positions on unimportant issues, but both Carsey and Layman (2006) as well Dancey and Goren (2010) examined attitude *change*, not attitude formation. To take a position on an issue and then change that position to reflect the party line connotes partisan motivation. If a person has already taken a position on an issue, changing that position to reflect the party's stance takes more cognitive effort, not less.

The dual motivations approach provides additional insight into these findings. It appears that responsiveness motivation may increase when an issue is considered to be important. However, without this increase in importance, partisan motivation dominates. When an issue receives media attention, it increases its importance to some people but not to everyone. As a result, Dancey and Goren (2010) found reciprocal effects. By focusing on individual-level differences, Carsey and Layman (2006) were able to show that the direction of causality actually switches depending on a respondent's perception of the issue's importance. This implies that party identification may serve as an efficient voting heuristic with regard to important issues, but voters may end up casting ballots that conflict with their views on a range of less important issues (also see Arceneaux, 2008). Of course, Carsey and Layman assume that issue importance is exogenous—an assumption that was called into question in Chapter 3. Given that issue importance is itself affected by partisan and responsiveness motivation, additional research must be conducted before this relationship can be fully delineated.

Like these authors, Lavine, Johnston, and Steenbergen (2012) have also made exciting advances through their examination of partisan ambivalence. This concept is defined as a state of internal conflict between one's party identity and one's attitudes toward that party: "Whether it is a negative evaluation of one's own party, a positive evaluation of the other party, or both, the outcome is that identity and evaluation do not point in the same direction" (p. 4). The primary objective of their book was to compare the attitudes and behaviors of ambivalent partisans with those of "univalent" partisans (i.e., individuals whose attitudes and party identity are consistent with one another). To do this, they primarily treat ambivalence as an exogenous variable, focusing largely on its effects rather its determinants. The dual motivations approach is somewhat complementary. By examining attitudes and identities separately rather than combining them into a single ambivalence variable, it provides a theory of how tensions between party identification and political attitudes are managed.

Lavine and colleagues (2012) show that ambivalent partisans come much closer to approximating the "ideal citizen" than do univalent partisans.[8] However, after extended periods of ambivalence, partisans eventually bring their identities into alignment with their evaluations and cease to be ambivalent. But does this mean that they become bad citizens? This confusion results from the choice to distinguish between types of partisans (ambivalent versus univalent) rather than distinguishing between types of motivation that coexist within the mind of all partisans (responsiveness versus partisan motivation). A person could be univalent because she has acted on her responsiveness motivation and changed her identity to reflect her attitudes, or she could be univalent because she has acted on her partisan motivation and changed her attitudes to reflect her identity (see earlier discussion of Carsey and Laymen's [2006] article). Both are univalent, but the former has acted on her biases, whereas the latter has held her party accountable. In short, the strategy of comparing ambivalent partisans with univalent partisans facilitates Lavine and colleagues' ability to distinguish the important behavioral differences between these groups—the primary goal of their book—but inhibits their ability to determine the implications of these effects. To do this, one must consider the interplay among partisans' motivations.

From the perspective of the dual motivations theory, Lavine et al.'s (2012) findings suggest that partisan ambivalence may undermine partisan motivation. Thinking back to Chapter 2, we saw that partisans avoided crossing over the indifference threshold (i.e., reporting attitudes inconsistent with their party identity) by engaging in lesser of two evils identity defense. Ambivalent partisans are operationalized as those who have failed to avoid inconsistency between their attitudes and party identity and yet have maintained their party identity. Lavine and colleagues demonstrate that, before eventually giving in

---

8. Arceneaux and Vander Wielen (2013) also see some partisans as being predisposed toward good citizenship and others as predisposed to act with bias. However, they see this distinction as arising from differences in need for cognition versus need for affect.

to responsiveness motivation and changing their identity, ambivalent partisans start to act more responsive compared with univalent partisans. Thus, whereas they show how inconsistencies between attitudes and identity can affect behavior, the dual motivations theory illustrates the process by which partisans attempt to avoid ambivalence in the first place.

In yet another exciting recent book, Levendusky (2009) investigated the effect of elite polarization on party identifiers, finding that the clearer ideological distinction between parties in Congress has led partisans in the electorate to sort along ideological lines (also see Abramowitz, 2010). However, as discussed earlier in this chapter, citizens appear to be primarily changing their ideologies to reflect their party identity rather than changing their party identity to reflect their ideologies: Republicans have become conservatives, and Democrats have become liberals. Levendusky (2009, 2010) argues that this sorting is desirable because it facilitates the heuristic efficiency of parties. Because "party is the vehicle through which ordinary voters can connect their underlying values to a vote choice ... [s]orting helps voters vote 'correctly.' Simply put, sorting makes for better citizens" (Levendusky, 2009, p. 138).

Although these findings provide a valuable contribution to the literature, Levendusky's (2009) conclusion seems misplaced. Rather than helping citizens vote "correctly," Levendusky's results seem to suggest that party identification pulls voters away from their true ideological commitments and therefore drains party identification of meaningful content. Thus, despite the conclusion he draws, his findings conform nicely to the predictions of dual motivations theory and reinforce the concerns expressed earlier regarding elite polarization. In short, a clearer line in the sand between parties exacerbates partisan motivation and actually undercuts citizens' drive to vote "correctly."

In a similar vein, Sniderman and Stiglitz (2012) conducted a series of elegant and deceptively simple experiments that demonstrate the pervasive influence of partisanship in the new era of polarized parties and sorted voters. Rather than favoring candidates whose positions were closer to their own, citizens inferred candidates' party associations from their relative placement on the issues and aligned themselves with the candidate on "their side." In other words, Democrats tended to favor the candidate to the left, and Republicans tended to favor the candidate to the right, regardless of which candidate was actually closer to their own ideal point. However, this was true only among those who understood that Republicans tend to take conservative positions and Democrats tend to take liberal positions (an increasingly large portion of the electorate).

In a separate study, participants were provided party cues. In this case, individuals who were unaware of the link between party and ideology followed party cues even when the Republican candidate took a position to the left of the Democratic candidate. On the other hand, participants who were sophisticated enough to grasp the link between party and ideology did not allow their party identity to influence their preferences when candidates took positions out of order with their ideology. Still, as long as the Republican candidate took a position to the right of the Democratic candidate, respondents discounted Downsian spatial considerations and supported the candidate from their own party. In other words, they favored the candidate from their party even when the candidate from the other party took a position unambiguously closer to their own. Candidates were penalized only if the Republican candidate took a position to the left of the Democratic candidate (or vice versa) and the voter was sophisticated enough to realize that this pattern was inconsistent with the current ideological alignment of the parties.[9]

Sniderman and Stiglitz (2012) see these results as a mixed blessing. On one hand, absent clear information regarding candidates' positions, such reasoning may help voters to determine which candidates will best represent their interests. On the other hand, when voters simply align themselves with whichever candidate is on "their side" rather than favoring the candidate who takes the position closest their own, candidates are provided with a great deal of latitude in the positions they take. Moreover, if the electorate has sorted as a result of voters' changing their ideologies to match their party identities rather than vice versa (Levendusky, 2009), then even the small amount of observed ideological accountability is an illusion, and partisan motivation is the real driver of preferences.

Taken as a whole, the emerging literature has begun to shed new light on our understanding of party identification. After years of debating the nature of party identification, a conditional notion of partisan stability is beginning to take hold (Carsey & Layman, 2006; Dancey & Goren, 2010). Moreover, rather

---

9. From a dual motivations perspective, it would be difficult for a Republican [Democrat] to justify aligning herself with a candidate who has taken a position to the left [right] of the Democratic [Republican] candidate. In other words, lack of support for a candidate does not necessarily mean lack of motivation to support that candidate. This result is entirely consistent with a dual motivations approach. Moreover, it would be quite easy for a Republican [Democrat] to justify aligning herself with a candidate who has taken an extreme right-wing [left-wing] position over a Democratic [Republican] candidate who has taken a position closer to her own ideal point. In other words, to take such a position does not necessarily connote heuristic processing. Partisans may be actively avoiding disagreement with their party.

than focusing narrowly on the issue of party identification change versus stability, scholars are considering the implications of these models for what constitutes good citizenship (Lavine et al., 2012; Levendusky, 2009). And as our understanding of party identification continues to develop, scholars are asking how well today's polarized politics are working for us (Abramowitz, 2010; Levendusky, 2009; Sniderman & Stiglitz, 2012). In proposing the dual motivations theory of party identification, it is my hope to build on the foundation laid by these scholars and to continue to develop our understanding of the nature of party identification, its efficacy as an information shortcut, and the implications of contemporary polarization.

FUTURE DIRECTIONS

Whereas this book has focused exclusively on the American two-party system, future work should consider how a multiparty context might affect the motivational dynamics underlying party identification. As mentioned during the discussion of responsible party government, intergroup conflict is likely to be intensified when political competition occurs repeatedly along a single cleavage, as it does in two-party systems (Sherif, 1956). And recent research suggests that the propensity to identify with parties decreases with the effective number of parties—particularly among those with less education (Huber et al., 2005). Therefore, one might speculate that partisan motivation is weaker in multiparty systems.

Still, when one looks within multiparty systems and focuses on traditional cleavage parties, partisan attachments appear strong, and hostility toward opposition parties is common (Richardson, 1991). Therefore, it seems that partisan motivation may vary among partisans in multiparty systems. If this is the case, cleavage party identifiers, given disagreement with their party, should show a greater propensity to avoid identity change and instead seek a justification for their existing party identity—just like their counterparts in the United States. This should allow traditional cleavage parties to have greater policy and performance latitude than their non-cleavage party counterparts. Future work should, therefore, examine the relative ability of cleavage and non-cleavage parties to retain seats during periods of poor performance.

Additionally, although I have focused largely on individual-level dynamics in party identification, it is important to understand how these processes aggregate. In particular, how does the dual motivations theory help us to understand realignments in party identification? As suggested earlier, I suspect that an important part of the story may be explained by fluctuations in partisan motivation among large segments of society. Green, Palmquist, and

Schickler (2002) argue that realignments occur not as a result of changing political attitudes but rather as a product of changing social group imagery associated with parties. Recent work by Hutchings, Walton, and Benjamin (2010) reinforces this conclusion. During the Civil Rights Era, and particularly after the 1964 election, the image of the Democratic Party held by many Southerners began to change. As this occurred, the South drifted gradually in a Republican direction until finally becoming a Republican stronghold.

Green and colleagues' (2002) account meshes quite nicely with the framework of the dual motivations theory in this case. Throughout this book, partisan identifiers have been found to be motivated to maintain and defend their partisan allegiances. However, there is no reason that such motivation must be constant. Party imagery is critical to the motivation to maintain one's identity. Therefore, as this imagery evolves, the motivation to maintain one's party allegiance may change as well. After all, if partisanship is truly an identity, the images associated with one's party are associated with the self.[10]

With regard to the realignment of the American South, the very fact that so many conservative Southerners identified with the Democratic Party for so many years despite their ideological differences with the party speaks to the power of partisan motivation. As long as the image of the Democratic Party remained associated with Southern culture and pride, many Southerners remained motivated to maintain their loyalty to the party. However, during the 1960s this symbolism was forever altered, and so the partisan motivation of many Southern Democrats declined. Southern Democrats had maintained their partisan allegiance despite important differences prior to the Civil Rights Era and the 1964 election, but these differences had not fundamentally changed the party's image in the minds of Southerners. The decline in partisan motivation in the 1960s left Southerners open to persuasion on issues across the board and allowed full-scale regional realignment to occur.

In the current political landscape with polarized elites and partisans sorted by ideology, electoral realignment seems unlikely. Nonetheless, although the growing distinction between party brands seems likely to increase partisan motivation, this may not be true for everyone. If the Republican Party allows its brand to become too closely associated with NASCAR and country music, wealthy northern Republicans may find themselves less motivated to defend their party identities. Likewise, if the Democratic Party allows its brand to become too closely associated with organic foods and wine-tasting parties,

---

10. See Philpot (2004, 2007) for a fascinating study of changing party images in recent American politics.

working-class Democrats may become more receptive to Republican appeals. Future studies should continue to investigate trends in party identification with particular attention to causal processes. Of special interest is whether priming associations between parties and certain social images (e.g., NASCAR, country music, organic foods, wine-tasting parties) weakens partisan motivation and makes it easier to persuade partisans on unrelated issue dimensions.

In addition to investigating the dynamics of party identification itself, we should also consider the effects of partisan justification.[11] When a president makes controversial decisions, his party usually stands behind him. However, this means that the party must provide a justification for average party identifiers who might be struggling to defend the president's decision to themselves, their friends, and their neighbors. Parties do this by disseminating prepackaged "talking points" in press briefings and television appearances. But what effects do these justifications have on future discourse?[12] When the justification for the Iraq War shifted from the need to eliminate weapons of mass destruction to the need to protect the Iraqi people from tyranny, did Republicans' attitudes toward nation building change? If so, has this affected Republicans' foreign policy attitudes more generally, and how might acceptance of the Bush administration's justification for war affect Republicans' attitudes on future foreign policy issues? Likewise, did Democrats' opposition to the war affect their attitudes toward nation building? And how will this affect their future attitudes on foreign policy matters?

Although the justification for the Iraq War provides a useful example of how such justifications may have long-term repercussions for public opinion and even political ideology, this is only one example of a more common theme. Politicians must justify their actions, and their supporters have a strong incentive to accept these justifications in order maintain their loyalties. Therefore, to the degree that it exists, attitudinal constraint may be shaped in important ways by partisan justification. Future work should examine whether justification can have a domino effect on other attitudes, thereby shaping the trajectory of ideology.

---

11. See McGraw (1990, 1991, 1998) and McGraw, Timpone, and Bruck (1993) for a fascinating examination of the effect of elite justifications (and excuses) on public opinion.

12. Recent research has demonstrated that, once exposed to a particular issue frame, citizens selectively expose themselves to that same frame, decreasing the effect of counter-frames on their opinions (Druckman, Fein, & Leeper, 2012). But are these citizens similarly drawn to these recognized frames when they are used by elites to discuss other issues? Do they redeploy these frames themselves when considering other issues?

Appendices

CHAPTER 2

Figure A2.1 The figure contains screen shots and captions from the advertisement used in the experiment. The version displayed comes from the party cues condition. The advertisement used in the disagreement condition was identical except that party cues were removed from the ad and shown to participants in the same video format after reporting their opinion on the bill.

CHAPTER 3

EDITORIAL: NEW LEGISLATION OFFERS REFUGE FROM GROWING OUTSOURCING PROBLEM

By LARRY STOCKTON
Published: April 17, 2007

WASHINGTON, April 16—As globalization continues, Americans are becoming increasingly worried about job security. Though outsourcing originally concerned blue collar sectors of the economy, white collar jobs are now being shipped overseas as well. With many college educated workers in countries like India willing to work for near minimum wage, companies stand to save millions through outsourcing. Moreover, those businesses that choose not to engage in outsourcing will simply not be able to compete.

Once a single firm begins to outsource, other companies face a huge competitive disadvantage if they do not do the same. Companies that refuse to outsource jobs will eventually go under and be replaced by firms willing to take advantage of this cheap labor. In other words, we cannot simply ask firms not to outsource. Without legislation, their hands are essentially tied. This is why the U.S. government needs to step in and pass the Common Sense in Outsourcing Bill to give companies an incentive to keep jobs in the U.S.

This is not a conspiracy theory, but a simple application of Economics 101. Liberals and conservatives are nearly in universal agreement on these facts.

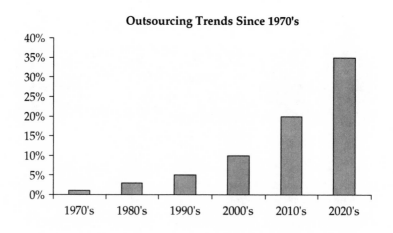

Over the coming years, millions of Americans will lose their jobs to outsourcing. The question is how to deal with this growing problem. The Common
Sense in Outsourcing Bill would provide tax incentives for corporations to
keep jobs on American soil.

Opponents of this bill argue that outsourcing is just an inevitable part
of the globalization process, and we should not attempt to get in its way.
However, supporters argue that this bill is in no way anti-globalization legislation. It merely provides incentives for companies to continue to employ
American workers.

While nearly everyone agrees that there are long-term benefits to globalization, it is the short-term costs that have many Americans concerned. Future
generations will likely benefit from a globally integrated economy, but that
does not mean that this generation and the next should be forced to pay all
the transition costs. If globalization is left completely unimpeded, economists
agree that we are likely to face record unemployment levels over the next 20
years. The Common Sense in Outsourcing Bill is simply an attempt to avoid
such massive unemployment and ease the transition into a globally integrated
economy.

The Common Sense in Outsourcing Bill would also prevent the U.S. government from contracting with foreign companies. Since foreign companies
are able to take advantage of cheaper labor, they are often able to underbid
U.S. firms for contracts with the federal government. For obvious reasons,
defense contracts are already regulated in this way. However, many less
publicized government contracts are increasingly going to foreign firms. For
example, the federal government spends millions of dollars on paper each
year, but this paper comes from Canada. Additionally, as the federal government continues to expand, bureaucratic work is being sent overseas. For
instance, the Internal Revenue Service is currently looking into contracting
with an Indian telecommunications company to outsource phone calls. Soon
you may have to talk to someone in India to get a question answered about
your taxes.

Clearly something needs to be done to provide Americans with economic security during this initial phase of globalization. These are clearly
tumultuous times in politics, and there are many important issues to consider. Nonetheless, as we listen to the 2008 presidential candidates laying
out their platforms, we must keep jobs in mind. Without legislation, companies will have an ever increasing incentive to send American jobs overseas.
Therefore, passing the Common Sense in Outsourcing Bill must be among
our top priorities.

CONGRESS CONSIDERS OUTSOURCING BILL

By ARNOLD HENSON
Published: April 24, 2007

WASHINGTON, April 23—Legislation entitled the "Common Sense in Outsourcing Bill" will soon come up for a vote in the Senate. If passed, the bill would provide tax incentives for companies to employ American workers rather than outsourcing jobs to foreign shores. Supporters of the bill contend that market based solutions through tax incentives are the way to go in easing the transition into a global economy. To date, the bill has received a mixture of support and opposition from Republicans and Democrats alike.

The bill's sponsors argue that outsourcing is a growing problem that deserves our attention. "American workers need our support, and if we don't do something soon the problem will only get worse," said Jack Phillips, founder of a bi-partisan advocacy group called the Business and Labor Partnership for America's Future. Supporters also point out that the bill is not a tax cut for corporations, but rather a restructuring of the corporate tax code. In other words, the bill would shift the tax burden to companies that outsource the most jobs. This essentially amounts to a tax cut for firms that outsource the fewest jobs and a tax increase for corporations that outsource the most jobs.

Asked where they stand on the outsourcing bill, respondents in a recent Gallup poll appear supportive. What impact this bill will have on the 2008 presidential election is a point of debate among media pundits. Since none of the contenders for the Republican and Democratic nomination have yet taken a public stance, its potential impact remains a point of speculation.

DEMOCRATS TO OPPOSE OUTSOURCING BILL

By ARNOLD HENSON
Published: April 24, 2007

WASHINGTON, April 23—The Republican sponsored "Common Sense in Outsourcing Bill" will soon come up for a vote in the Senate, and Democrats are digging their heels in for a fight. If passed, the bill would provide tax incentives for companies to employ American workers rather than outsourcing jobs to foreign shores, but Democrats complain that there is no room in the budget.

Republicans, on the other hand, argue that outsourcing needs to be a priority, and the bill would cost the federal government very little in tax revenue. "American workers need our support, and if we don't do something soon the problem will only get worse," said Senate Minority Leader Mitch McConnell (R). Republican supporters also point out that the bill is not a tax cut for corporations, but rather a restructuring of the corporate tax code. In other words, the bill would shift the tax burden to companies that outsource the most jobs. This essentially amounts to a tax cut for firms that outsource the fewest jobs and a tax increase for corporations that outsource the most jobs.

Asked where they stand on the outsourcing bill, Democratic presidential hopefuls appear to be toeing the party line. Hillary Clinton, Barack Obama, and John Edwards have all pledged that they will vote no when the bill reaches the floor. What impact this will have on their presidential aspirations is a point of debate among media pundits. Still, with Republican contenders united in support of the bill, things could be building toward a showdown over outsourcing in the 2008 general election.

REPUBLICANS TO OPPOSE OUTSOURCING BILL

By ARNOLD HENSON
Published: April 24, 2007

WASHINGTON, April 23—The Democrat sponsored "Common Sense in Outsourcing Bill" will soon come up for a vote in the Senate, and Republicans are digging their heels in for a fight. If passed, the bill would provide tax incentives for companies to employ American workers rather than outsourcing jobs to foreign shores, but Republicans complain that there is no room in the budget.

Democrats, on the other hand, argue that outsourcing needs to be a priority, and the bill would cost the federal government very little in tax revenue. "American workers need our support, and if we don't do something soon the problem will only get worse," said Senate Majority Leader Harry Reid (D). Democratic supporters also point out that the bill is not a tax cut for corporations, but rather a restructuring of the corporate tax code. In other words, the bill would shift the tax burden to companies that outsource the most jobs. This essentially amounts to a tax cut for firms that outsource the fewest jobs and a tax increase for corporations that outsource the most jobs.

Asked where they stand on the outsourcing bill, Republican presidential hopefuls appear to be toeing the party line. Rudi Giuliani, John McCain, and recent contender Fred Thompson have all spoken out against the bill. What impact this will have on their presidential aspirations is a point of debate among media pundits. Still, with Democratic contenders united in support of the bill, things could be building toward a showdown over outsourcing in the 2008 general election.

CHAPTER 4

TABLE A4.1. *EFFECT OF DISAGREEMENT ON STRENGTH OF PARTY IDENTIFICATION*

	No Cognitive Load	No Cognitive Load	Cognitive Load	Cognitive Load
	B	*B*	*B*	*B*
	(SE)	*(SE)*	*(SE)*	*(SE)*
Disagreement	−.142	−.108	−.268	−.300*
	(.201)	(.205)	(.174)	(.176)
Party ID Strength (*t*−1)	1.85***	1.97***	1.12***	1.19***
	(.169)	(.180)	(.118)	(.123)
Over 35 Years Old		−.044		−.048
		(.244)		(.200)
Sophistication		.163***		.120**
		(.052)		(.050)
Democrat		.328		−.117
		(.213)		(.178)
Cut 1	1.26	2.42	−.126	.527
	(.301)	(.506)	(.265)	(.418)
Cut 2	2.70	3.92	1.24	1.90
	(.331)	(.537)	(.252)	(.407)
Cut 3	4.41	5.73	2.58	3.27
	(.433)	(.634)	(.294)	(.445)

Note. Results were obtained using ordered probit regression. The table reports probit coefficients (*B*) and the standard errors (*SE*) associated with these coefficients.

***$p < .01$, **$p < .05$, *$p < .10$

TABLE A4.2. *EFFECT OF AGE AND DISAGREEMENT ON STRENGTH OF PARTY IDENTIFICATION*

	No Cognitive Load B (SE) (N = 161)	Cognitive Load B (SE) (N = 187)
Disagreement	−.223 (.423)	−.793** (.317)
Over 35 Years Old	.979 (.687)	−.792 (.524)
Disagreement*Over 35	.053 (.483)	.757** (.380)
Party ID Strength (*t*–1)	2.24*** (.322)	.950*** (.200)
Party ID Strength (*t*–1)*Over 35	−.491 (.331)	.279 (.231)
Cut 1	2.02 (.614)	−.667 (.442)
Cut 2	3.47 (.694)	.705 (.433)
Cut 3	5.19 (.676)	2.08 (.452)

Note. Results were obtained using ordered probit regression. The table reports probit coefficients (*B*) and the standard errors (*SE*) associated with these coefficients.

***$p < .01$, **$p < .05$, *$p < .10$

TABLE A4.3. *EFFECTS OF COGNITIVE LOAD, AGE, AND DISAGREEMENT ON PARTY IDENTIFICATION*

	Party Identification Strength
	B
	(SE)
	(N = 348)
Disagreement	−.221
	(.415)
Over 35 Years Old	.958
	(.684)
Disagreement*Over 35	.059
	(.475)
Party ID Strength (t−1)	2.12***
	(.305)
Party ID Strength (t−1)*Over 35	−.480
	(.330)
Cognitive Load	2.62***
	(.743)
Cognitive Load*Disagreement	−.613
	(.523)
Cognitive Load*Over 35	−1.78**
	(.859)
Cognitive Load*Disagreement*Over 35	.738
	(.610)
Cognitive Load*Party ID Strength (t−1)	−1.13***
	(.355)
Cognitive Load*Party ID Strength (t−1)*Over 35	.764*
	(.403)
Cut 1	1.92 (.605)
Cut 2	3.33 (.615)
Cut 3	4.83 (.635)

Note. Results were obtained using ordered probit regression. The table reports probit coefficients (*B*) and the standard errors (*SE*) associated with these coefficients.

***p < .01, **p < .05, *p < .10

TABLE A4.4. *EFFECT OF POLITICAL SOPHISTICATION AND DISAGREEMENT ON STRENGTH OF PARTY IDENTIFICATION*

	No Cognitive Load B (SE) (N = 161)	Cognitive Load B (SE) (N = 187)
Disagreement	−1.40** (.602)	−.430 (.543)
Sophistication	−.271 (.177)	−.025 (.164)
Disagreement*Sophistication	.239** (.106)	.029 (.094)
Party ID Strength ($t-1$)	1.22*** (.455)	.828* (.438)
Party ID Strength ($t-1$)*Sophistication	.137* (.077)	.061 (.072)
Cut 1	−.175 (1.05)	−.241 (1.01)
Cut 2	1.33 (1.06)	1.13 (1.00)
Cut 3	3.19 (1.08)	2.51 (1.01)

Note. Results were obtained using ordered probit regression. The table reports probit coefficients (*B*) and the standard errors (*SE*) associated with these coefficients.

***$p < .01$, **$p < .05$, *$p < .10$

TABLE A4.5. *EFFECTS OF COGNITIVE LOAD, POLITICAL SOPHISTICATION, AND DISAGREEMENT ON PARTY IDENTIFICATION*

	Party Identification Strength
	B
	(SE)
	(N = 348)
Disagreement	−1.23**
	(.578)
Sophistication	−.245
	(.173)
Disagreement*Sophistication	.209**
	(.102)
Party ID Strength (t−1)	1.09**
	(.444)
Party ID Strength (t−1)*Sophistication	.128*
	(.076)
Cognitive Load	.125
	(1.44)
Cognitive Load*Disagreement	.784
	(.800)
Cognitive Load*Sophistication	.218
	(.240)
Cognitive Load*Disagreement*Sophistication	−.181
	(.139)
Cognitive Load*Party ID Strength (t−1)	−.218
	(.240)
Cognitive Load*Party ID Strength (t−1)*Sophistication	−.064
	(.105)
Cut 1	−.141 (1.04)
Cut 2	1.29 (1.04)
Cut 3	2.83 (1.05)

Note. Results were obtained using ordered probit regression. The table reports probit coefficients (*B*) and the standard errors (*SE*) associated with these coefficients.

***$p < .01$, **$p < .05$, *$p < .10$

TABLE A4.6. *EFFECT OF DEMOCRATIC IDENTIFICATION AND DISAGREEMENT ON STRENGTH OF PARTY IDENTIFICATION*

	No Cognitive Load	Cognitive Load
	B	*B*
	(SE)	*(SE)*
	(N = 161)	*(N = 187)*
Disagreement	−.724**	−.315
	(.304)	(.245)
Democrat	−.517	−.508
	(.571)	(.485)
Disagreement*Democrat	1.07***	.086
	(.415)	(.348)
Party ID Strength (*t*–1)	1.88***	1.07***
	(.217)	(.157)
Party ID Strength (*t*–1)*Democrat	.090	.149
	(.258)	(.213)
Cut 1	1.02	−.358
	(.411)	(.351)
Cut 2	2.54	1.02
	(.434)	(.331)
Cut 3	4.34	2.37
	(.524)	(.362)

Note. Results were obtained using ordered probit regression. The table reports probit coefficients (*B*) and the standard errors (*SE*) associated with these coefficients.

***$p < .01$, **$p < .05$, *$p < .10$

TABLE A4.7. *EFFECTS OF COGNITIVE LOAD, DEMOCRATIC IDENTITY, AND DISAGREEMENT ON PARTY IDENTIFICATION*

	Party Identification Strength B (SE) (N = 348)
Disagreement	−.668**
	(.297)
Democrat	−.498
	(.566)
Disagreement*Democrat	.980**
	(.404)
Party ID Strength (t−1)	1.72***
	(.192)
Party ID Strength (t−1)*Democrat	.091
	(.257)
Cognitive Load	1.32**
	(.515)
Cognitive Load*Disagreement	.334
	(.385)
Cognitive Load*Democrat	−.037
	(.745)
Cognitive Load*Disagreement*Democrat	−.886*
	(.533)
Cognitive Load*Party ID Strength (t−1)	−.586**
	(.235)
Cognitive Load*Party ID Strength (t−1)*Democrat	−.065
	(.334)
Cut 1	.926 (.398)
Cut 2	2.37 (.408)
Cut 3	3.87 (.436)

Note. Results were obtained using ordered probit regression. The table reports probit coefficients (*B*) and the standard errors (*SE*) associated with these coefficients.

***$p < .01$, **$p < .05$, *$p < .10$

CHAPTER 5

TABLE A5.1. *EXPLORATORY FACTOR ANALYSIS OF ATTITUDE PRIMING QUESTIONS*

	Component 1	Component 2
Republican Feeling Thermometer	−.403	.832
Trust Republican Party	−.319	.886
Approve of Republicans in Congress	−.200	.816
Democratic Feeling Thermometer	.828	−.410
Trust Democratic Party	.931	−.277
Approve of Democrats in Congress	.806	−.235
Eigenvalue	4.21	1.09
Variance Explained	70.14%	18.23%

Note. Eigenvalue cutoffs were set to 1.0 (Kaiser's rule). Cattel's scree test yields the same number of factors, as indicated by the Eigenvalues. Extractions were based on principal axis factoring with varimax rotation.

TABLE A5.2. *EXPLORATORY FACTOR ANALYSIS OF EMOTION ITEMS*

	Component 1	Component 2
Enthusiasm—Republican Party	.549	−.574
Hope—Republican Party	.577	−.602
Anger—Democratic Party	.896	−.095
Afraid—Democratic Party	.861	−.283
Frustrated—Democratic Party	.852	−.113
Enthusiasm—Democratic Party	−.743	.495
Hope—Democratic Party	−.715	.491
Anger—Republican Party	−.138	.923
Afraid—Republican Party	−.274	.822
Frustrated—Republican Party	−.154	.826
Eigenvalue	6.34	1.70
Variance Explained	63.36%	16.97%

Note. Eigenvalue cutoffs were set to 1.0 (Kaiser's rule). Cattel's scree test yields the same number of factors, as indicated by the Eigenvalues. Extractions were based on principal axis factoring with varimax rotation.

TABLE A5.3. *MODERATING EFFECT OF ATTITUDES ON THE RELATIONSHIP BETWEEN ATTITUDE PRIMING AND PARTY IDENTIFICATION AMONG REPUBLICANS*

	$N = 118$ B (SE)	$N = 118$ B (SE)
Republican Party Prime	−.194 (.286)	−.392 (.311)
Democratic Party Prime	−.706** (.294)	−.886* (.511)
Attitudes Toward Republican Party		.593 (.394)
Attitudes Toward Democratic Party		−.839* (.461)
Republican Party Prime*Attitudes Toward Republican Party		−.434 (.629)
Democratic Party Prime*Attitudes Toward Democratic Party		−.128 (.718)
Party Identification (t1)	1.40*** (.169)	1.28*** (.185)
Cut 1	−.627 (.484)	−.428 (.604)
Cut 2	.061 (.375)	.301 (.504)
Cut 3	1.63 (.366)	1.76 (.493)
Cut 4	2.92 (.414)	3.10 (.536)

Note. Results were obtained using ordered probit regression. The table reports probit coefficients (*B*) and the standard errors (*SE*) associated with these coefficients.

***$p < .01$, **$p < .05$, *$p < .10$

CHAPTER 6

Issue Positions Battery (2004 General Social Survey):
Space exploration program (Form X)/Space exploration (Form Y)
Improving and protecting the environment (Form X)/The environment (Form Y)
Improving and protecting the nation's health (Form X)/Health (Form Y)
Solving the problems of the big cities (Form X)/Assistance to big cities (Form Y)
Halting the rising crime rate (Form X)/Law enforcement (Form Y)
Dealing with drug addiction (Form X)/Drug rehabilitation (Form Y)
Improving the nation's education system (Form X)/Education (Form Y)
Improving the conditions of Blacks (Form X)/Assistance to Blacks (Form Y)
The military, armaments and defense (Form X)/National defense (Form Y)
Foreign aid (Form X)/Assistance to other countries (Form Y)
Welfare (Form X)/Assistance for the poor (Form Y)
Highways and bridges (Both forms same)
Social Security (Both forms same)
Mass transportation (Both forms same)
Parks and recreation (Both forms same)
Assistance for childcare (Both forms same)

Issue Positions Battery (Experiment):
There is much concern about taxes. Some people argue that people should be taxed at higher rates as their income increases, because people who make more money can more easily afford to pay taxes than people who make less money. This is known as a graduated tax system. Suppose these people are at one end of a scale, at point 1. Others argue that everyone should be taxed at the same rate. This is known as a flat tax system. Those who favor a flat tax argue that a graduated tax system reduces the incentives to be productive and therefore hurts the economy. Suppose these people are at the other end, at point 7. And, of course, some other people have opinions somewhere in between, at points 2, 3, 4, 5, or 6. Where would you place yourself [the Republican Party, the Democratic Party] on this scale?

There is much concern about jobs. Some people feel the government in Washington should see to it that every person has a job and a good standard of living. Suppose these people are at one end of a scale, at point 1. Others think the government should just let each person get ahead on their own. Suppose these people are at the other end, at point 7. And, of course, some other people have opinions somewhere in between, at points 2, 3, 4, 5, or 6. Where would you place yourself [the Republican Party, the Democratic Party] on this scale?
There is much concern about the War in Iraq. Some people feel that we should stay and fight until order is restored and Iraq can govern itself. Suppose these

people are at one end of a scale, at point 1. Others argue that the war cannot be won through military means, and we should withdraw from Iraq immediately. Suppose these people are at the other end, at point 7. And, of course, some other people have opinions somewhere in between, at points 2, 3, 4, 5, or 6. Where would you place yourself [the Republican Party, the Democratic Party] on this scale?

There is much concern about the rapid rise in medical and hospital costs. Some people support a government insurance plan which would cover all medical and hospital expenses for everyone. Suppose these people are at one end of a scale, at point 1. Others feel that all medical expenses should be paid by individuals through private insurance plans like Blue Cross or other company paid plans. Suppose these people are at the other end, at point 7. And, of course, some other people have opinions somewhere in between, at points 2, 3, 4, 5, or 6. Where would you place yourself [the Republican Party, the Democratic Party] on this scale?

There is much concern about illegal immigration. Some people feel that we should provide illegal immigrants who already live in the United States with a path to citizenship. This would bring illegal immigrants out of hiding so that the government could keep track of them and tax their income. Suppose these people are at one end of a scale, at point 1. Others argue that that citizenship should not be granted to anyone who has come into the country illegally. They argue that illegal immigration is a crime and it should be punished not rewarded. Suppose these people are at the other end, at point 7. And, of course, some other people have opinions somewhere in between, at points 2, 3, 4, 5, or 6. Where would you place yourself [the Republican Party, the Democratic Party] on this scale?

There is much concern about abortion. Some people feel that unborn infants have a fundamental right to life and that abortions should be illegal. Suppose these people are at one end of a scale, at point 1. Others feel that women should have the right to choose whether or not to have an abortion, and that this is a private matter that the government should not interfere with. Suppose these people are at the other end, at point 7. And, of course, some other people have opinions somewhere in between, at points 2, 3, 4, 5, or 6. Where would you place yourself [the Republican Party, the Democratic Party] on this scale?

There is much concern about gun control. Some argue that greater restrictions should be placed on gun ownership. They argue that assault rifles and armor piercing bullets should be banned, and they support a waiting period before a gun can be purchased. Suppose these people are at one end of a scale, at point 1. Others argue that Americans have the right to own guns and that restrictions on gun ownership violate the Second Amendment of the

Constitution. Suppose these people are at the other end, at point 7. And, of course, some other people have opinions somewhere in between, at points 2, 3, 4, 5, or 6. Where would you place yourself [the Republican Party, the Democratic Party] on this scale?

There is much concern about education. Some people feel that the best way to improve our education system is to promote competition between schools. They feel that if parents were provided with school vouchers that could be used to send their children to any public or private school, schools would be forced to compete. Suppose these people are at one end of a scale, at point 1. Others argue that public funds should only be used for public schools and not private schools. They feel that school vouchers would just funnel money away from public schools that need the funding. Suppose these people are at the other end, at point 7. And, of course, some other people have opinions somewhere in between, at points 2, 3, 4, 5, or 6. Where would you place yourself [the Republican Party, the Democratic Party] on this scale?

TABLE A6.1. *2004 GENERAL SOCIAL SURVEY ISSUE FACTOR LOADINGS*

Factor	Final Group	Initial Group				
		1	2	3	4	5
Environment	.553	.478		.425		
Welfare	.493	.470				.304
Health	.645	.678				
Drug Addiction	.523	.293	.580			
Education	.666	.646				
Child Care	.610	.489				
Social Security	.549	.601				
Crime	NA		.620		−.350	
Foreign Aid	NA					.826
Defense	NA				−.821	
Space	NA		−.372	.466		.365
Cities	NA		.576	.263		
Aid to Blacks	NA		.428		.306	.368
Highways	NA			.582		
Mass Transit	NA			.660		
Parks	NA			.457		
Party Identity	NA	.334			.550	
Eigenvalue	2.355	3.151	1.466	1.415	1.119	1.017

Note. The table displays results from two separate factor analyses. The first column illustrates the factor loadings of the issues used in the analysis. The other columns illustrate the factor loadings when all issues were included in the analysis. Results were based on principal-component analysis with varimax rotation. Factors loadings greater than .250 are displayed.

VOTER GUIDE

Every four years, the Republican and Democratic parties re-write their party platforms. A party's platform lays out that party's positions on the important issues of the time. While the platforms will not be officially ratified until the party conventions later this summer, the drafting process has already begun. To aid voters, expected highlights of party platforms appear below.

FIGURE 6.1

Democrats	Republicans

	Democrats	Republicans
Economy	*A Graduated Tax System to Protect Lower and Middle Class Americans* • Maintain current tax rates for families making less than $250,000 and raise taxes for families making $250,000 or more • Maintain the estate tax • Raise capital gains taxes *Protect American Jobs and American Workers* • Renegotiate NAFTA to protect American jobs • Keep jobs in America • Raise the minimum wage	*A Flatter Tax System to Promote Economic Growth* • Make expiring tax cuts permanent • Abolish the Alternative Minimum Tax (AMT) • Repeal estate taxes under $10 million • Lower corporate tax rate • Keep capital gains taxes low to increase incentive to save • Simplify the tax code *Promote Free Markets and Promote the American Dream* • Support NAFTA
War in Iraq/ Defense	*Bringing the Troops Home and Building Our Reputation Abroad* • Immediate withdrawal • Work through UN to negotiate an end to sectarian violence and stabilize Iraq's economy • Increased diplomacy	*A Free Iraq and a Safer World* • Establish stable government in Iraq • Continue surge strategy • Get Iraq's economy back on its feet • Call for increased international pressure on Iran and Syria

(continued)

FIGURE 6.1 *(CONTINUED)*

	Democrats	**Republicans**

	Democrats	**Republicans**
	Keeping America Safe and Secure • Target homeland security federal funding toward high-risk areas (cities)	*A Strong Defense and a Safer America* • Development of a national missile defense system
Education	*Improving our Schools and Giving Every Child a Chance to Succeed* • Raise teacher pay • Expand Head Start program • Oppose vouchers for private schools • Increase federal grants for college	*Excellence, Choice, and Competition in American Education* • Increase local control • Increase competition between schools through vouchers and school choice • Teacher testing and training • Increased federal grants for college
Healthcare	*Healthcare for every Man, Woman, and Child* • Universal healthcare • Mandatory healthcare for children	*Affordable Healthcare without Big Government* • Make private health insurance more accessible to lower income Americans • Lower costs through medical liability reforms
Illegal Immigration	*Reforming our Immigration System* • Provide a path to citizenship for illegal immigrants	*Securing our Borders* • Increased border security
Abortion	*Protecting a Woman's Right to Choose* • The right to privacy is protected by the Constitution, and there is nothing more private than a woman's decision regarding whether or not to terminate a pregnancy	*Respecting the Sanctity of Life* • Roe v. Wade is a flawed decision by an activist court attempting to pass public policy from the bench. There is no Constitutional basis for the right to have an abortion

(continued)

FIGURE 6.1 *(CONTINUED)*

Democrats	Republicans

	Democrats	Republicans
Gun Control	*Keeping Deadly Firearms Off America's Streets*	*Protecting Second Amendment Rights*
	• Support restrictions on assault rifles • Support a five day waiting period between purchase and attainments of a firearm • Make armor-piercing bullets illegal • Support criminal background checks • Support gun lock requirements	• Oppose restrictions on so called "assault rifles" • Oppose restrictions on ammunition • Oppose waiting periods on gun purchases • Support criminal background checks • Support gun lock requirements

References

Abelson, R. P. (1959). Modes of resolution of belief dilemmas. *Journal of Conflict Resolution, 3*(4), 343–352.

Abramowitz, A. I. (2010). *The disappearing center.* New Haven, CT: Yale University Press.

Abramowitz, A. I., & Saunders, K. L. (2008). Is polarization a myth? *Journal of Politics, 70*(2), 542–555.

Achen, C. H. (1992). Social psychology, demographic variables, and linear regression: Breaking the iron triangle in voting research. *Political Behavior, 14*(3), 195–211.

Achen, C. H. (2002). Parental socialization and rational party identification. *Political Behavior, 24*(2), 151–170.

Akerlof, G. A., & Kranton, R. E. (2000). Economics and identity. *Quarterly Journal of Economics, 15*(3), 715–758.

Aldrich, J. H. (1995). *Why parties?: The origin and transformation of political parties in America.* Chicago, IL: University of Chicago Press.

Allport, G. W. (1954). The nature of prejudice. Reading, MA: Addison-Wesley.

Allsop, D., & Weisberg, H. F. (1988). Measuring change in party identification in an election campaign. *American Journal of Political Science, 32*(4), 996–1017.

Althaus, S. L. (1998). Information effects in collective preferences. *American Political Science Review, 92*(3), 545–558.

Alvarez, M. R. (1990). The puzzle of party identification: Dimensionality of an important concept. *American Politics Quarterly, 18*(4), 476–491.

Alwin, D. F., & Krosnick, J. A. (1991). Aging, cohorts, and the stability of sociopolitical orientations over the life span. *American Journal of Sociology, 97*(1), 169–195.

American Political Science Association, Committee on Political Parties. 1950a. The need for greater party responsibility. *American Political Science Review, 44*(3), 15–36.

American Political Science Association, Committee on Political Parties. 1950b. Proposals for party responsibility. *American Political Science Review, 44*(3), 37–84.

American Political Science Association, Committee on Political Parties. 1950c. The prospect for action. *American Political Science Review, 44*(3), 85–96.

Amodio, D. M., & Devine, P. G. (2006). Stereotyping and evaluation in implicit race bias: Evidence for independent constructs and unique effects on behavior. *Journal of Personality and Social Psychology, 91*(4), 652–661.

Arceneaux, K. (2008). Can partisan cues diminish democratic accountability? *Political Behavior, 30*(2), 139–160.

Arceneaux, K., & Vander Wielen, R. J. (2013) The effects of need for cognition and need for affect on partisan evaluations. *Political Psychology, 34(1),* 23–42.

Baldassarri, D., & Gelman, A. (2008). Partisans without constraint: Political polarization and trends in American public opinion. *American Journal of Sociology, 114*(2), 408–446.

Barabas, J. (2004). How deliberation affects policy opinions. *American Political Science Review, 98*(4), 687–701.

Bargh, J. A., & Chartrand, T. L. (1999). The unbearable automaticity of being. *American Psychologist, 54*(7), 462–479.

Baron, R. M., & Kenny, D. A. (1986). The moderator-mediator variable distinction in social psychological research: Conceptual, strategic, and statistical considerations. *Journal of Personality and Social Psychology, 51*(6), 1173–1182.

Barry, B. (1970). *Sociologists, economists, and democracy.* London: Collier-Macmillan.

Bartels, L. M. (1996). Uninformed votes: Information effects in presidential elections. *American Journal of Political Science, 40*(1), 194–230.

Bartels, L. M. (2002). Beyond the running tally: Partisan bias in political perceptions. *Political Behavior, 24*(2), 117–150.

Bassi, A., Morton, R. B., & Williams, K. C. (2011). The effects of identities, incentives, and information on voting. *Journal of Politics, 73*(2), 558–571.

Baumeister, R. F., & Leary, M. R. (1995). The need to belong: Desire for interpersonal attachments as a fundamental human motivation. *Psychological Bulletin, 117*(3), 497–529.

Behr, R. L., & Iyengar, S. (1985). Television news, real-world cues, and changes in the public agenda. *Public Opinion Quarterly, 49*(1), 38–57.

Berelson, B. R., Lazarsfeld, P. F., & McPhee, W. N. (1954). *Voting: A study of opinion formation in a presidential campaign.* Chicago, IL: University of Chicago Press.

Berinsky, A. J. (2009). *In time of war: Understanding American public opinion from World War II to Iraq.* Chicago, IL: Chicago University Press.

Boninger, D. S., Krosnick, J. A., & Berent, M. K. (1995). Origins of attitude importance: Self-interest, social identification, and value relevance. *Journal of Personality and Social Psychology, 68*(1), 61–80.

Box-Steffensmeier, J. M., & Smith, R. M. (1996). The dynamics of aggregate partisanship. *American Political Science Review, 90(3),* 567–580.

Brader, T. (2006). *Campaigning for hearts and minds: How emotional appeals in political ads work.* Chicago, IL: University of Chicago Press.

Brader, T., & Tucker, J. A. (2001). The emergence of mass partisanship in Russia, 1993–1996. *American Journal of Political Science, 45*(1), 69–83.

Brady, H. E., & Sniderman, P. M. (1985). Attitude attribution: A group basis for political reasoning. *American Political Science Review, 79*(4), 1061–1078.

Brody, R. A., & Rothenberg, L. S. (1988). The instability of partisanship: An analysis of the 1980 presidential election. *British Journal of Political Science, 18*(4), 445–465.

Bullock, J. G. (2011). Elite influence on public opinion in an informed electorate. *American Political Science Review, 105*(3), 496–515.

Campbell, A., Converse, P. E., Miller, W. E., & Stokes, D. E. (1960). *The American voter*. New York, NY: Wiley.

Campbell, A., Gurin, G., & Miller, W. E. (1954). *The voter decides*. Evanston, Ill: Row.

Caplan, B. (2007). *The myth of the rational voter: Why democracies choose bad policies*. Princeton, NJ: Princeton University Press.

Carmines, E. G., & Stimson, J. A. (1989). *Issue evolution: Race and the transformation of American politics*. Princeton, NJ: Princeton University Press.

Carsey, T. M., & Layman, G. C. (2006). Changing sides or changing minds? Party identification and policy preferences in the American electorate. *American Journal of Political Science, 50*(2), 464–477.

Cohen, G. L. (2003). Party over policy: The dominating impact of group influence on political beliefs. *Journal of Personality and Social Psychology, 85*(5), 808–822.

Cohen, J. E. (1995). Presidential rhetoric and the public agenda. *American Journal of Political Science, 39*(1), 87–101.

Conover, P. J., Feldman, S., & Knight, K. (1987). The personal and political underpinnings of economic forecasts. *American Journal of Political Science, 31*(3), 559–583.

Converse, P. E. (1964). The nature of belief systems in mass publics. In D. Apter (ed.), *Ideology and discontent (pp. 206–261)*. New York, NY: Free Press.

Converse, P. E. (1966). Information flow and the stability of partisan attitudes. In A. Campbell, P. E. Converse, W. E. Miller, & D. E. Stokes (Eds.), *Elections and the political order (pp. 136–158)*, New York, NY: Wiley.

Converse, P. E. (1969). Of time and partisan stability. *Comparative Political Studies, 2*(2), 139–171.

Converse, P. E. (1976). *The dynamics of party support: Cohort analyzing party identification*. Sage: Beverly Hills, CA.

Converse, P. E. (1990). Popular representation and the distribution of information. In J. A. Ferejohn & J. H. Kuklinski (Eds.), *Information and democratic processes (pp. 369–388)*. Chicago, IL: University of Illinois Press.

Converse, P. E., & Markus, G. B. (1979). Plus ça change...: The new CPS election study panel. *American Political Science Review, 73*(1), 32–49.

Cooper, J., & Mackie, D. (1983). Cognitive dissonance in an intergroup context. *Journal of Personality and Social Psychology, 44*(3), 536–544.

Cowden, J. A., & McDermott, R. M. (2000). Short-term forces and partisanship. *Political Behavior, 22*(3), 197–222.

Dalton, R. J. (2008). *The good citizen: How a younger generation is reshaping American politics*. Washington, DC: Congressional Quarterly Press.

Damasio, A. R. (1994). *Descartes' error: Emotion, reason, and the human brain*. New York, NY: G. P. Plenum.

Dancey, L., & Goren, P. (2010). Party identification, issue attitudes, and the dynamics of political debate. *American Journal of Political Science, 53*(3), 686–699.

Darwin, C. (1890). *The descent of man* (2nd ed.). London, United Kingdom: J. Murray.

Delli Carpini, M. X., & Keeter, S. (1996). *What Americans know about politics and why it matters*. New Haven, CT: Yale University Press.

Dennis, J. (1988). Political independence in America—Part II: Towards a theory. *British Journal of Political Science, 18*(2), 197–219.

Devine, P. G. (1989). Stereotypes and prejudice: Their automatic and controlled components. *Journal of Personality and Social Psychology, 56*(1), 5–18.

Downs, A. (1957). *An economic theory of democracy*. New York, NY: Harper.

Druckman, J. N., Fein, J., & Leeper, T. J. (2012). A source of bias on public opinion stability. *American Political Science Review, 106*(2), 430–454.

Duch, R. M., Palmer, H. D., & Anderson, C. J. (2000). Heterogeneity in perceptions of national economic conditions. *American Journal of Political Science, 44*(4), 635–652.

Duckitt, J. (2003). Prejudice and intergroup hostility. In D. O. Sears, L. Huddy, & R. Jervis (Eds.). *Oxford handbook of political psychology (pp. 559–600)*. New York, NY: Oxford University Press.

Eagly, A. H., & Chaiken, S. (1993). *The psychology of attitudes*. Fort Worth, TX: Harcourt Brace Jovanovich College Publisher.

Epstein, L. (1986). *Political parties in the American mold*. Madison, WI: University of Wisconsin Press.

Erbring, L., Goldenberg, E. N., & Miller, A. H. (1980). Front-page news and real-world cues: A new look at agenda-setting by the media. *American Journal of Political Science, 24*(1), 16–49.

Etheridge, E. (2009, May 19). The Republican crackup, part the XXXVIth. *The New York Times*.

Evans, G., & Andersen, R. (2006). The political conditioning of economic perceptions. *Journal of Politics, 68*(1), 194–207.

Fein, S., & Spencer, S. J. (1997). Prejudice as self-image maintenance: Affirming the self through derogating others. *Journal of Personality and Social Psychology, 73*(1), 31–44.

Festinger, L. (1957). *A theory of cognitive dissonance*. Evanston, IL: Row.

Festinger, L., Rieken, H. W., Schachter, S. (1956). *When prophecy fails: A social and psychological study of a modern group that predicted the end of the world*. Minneapolis, MN: University of Minnesota Press.

Fiorina, M. P. (1976). The voting decision: Instrumental and expressive aspects. *Journal of Politics, 38*(2), 390–413.

Fiorina, M. P. (1980). The decline of collective responsibility in American politics. *Daedalus, 109*(3), 25–45.

Fiorina, M. P. (1981). *Retrospective voting in American national elections*. New Haven, CN: Yale University Press.

Fiorina, M. P., Abrams, S. J., & Pope, J. (2011). *Culture war? The myth of a polarized America* (3rd ed.). New York, NY: Pearson-Longman.

Fiorina, M. P., Abrams, S. A., & Pope, J. C. (2008). Polarization in the American public: Misconceptions and misreadings. *Journal of Politics, 70*(2), 556–560.

Fischle, M. (2000). Mass response to the Lewinsky scandal: Motivated reasoning or Bayesian updating? *Political Psychology, 21*(1), 135–159.

Franklin, C. H. (1984). Issue preferences, socialization, and the evolution of party identification. *American Journal of Political Science, 28*(3), 459–478.

Franklin, C. H. (1992). Measurement and the dynamics of party identification. *Political Behavior, 14*(3), 297–309.

Franklin, C. H., & Jackson, J. E. (1983). The dynamics of party identification. *American Political Science Review, 77*(4), 957–973.

Gaines, B. J., Kuklinski, J. H., Quirk, P. J., Peyton, B., & Verkuilen, J. (2007). Same facts, different interpretations: Partisan motivation and opinion on Iraq. *Journal of Politics, 69*(4), 957–974.

Gallup. *Presidential job approval in depth.* (2008). [Data]. Retrieved from http://www.gallup.com/poll/124922/Presidential-Job-Approval-Depth.aspx.

Gallup. (2011). *Party affiliation* [Data]. Retrieved from http://www.gallup.com/poll/15370/Party-Affiliation.aspx.

Gant, M. M., & Davis, D. F. (1984). Negative voter support in presidential elections. *Western Political Quarterly, 37*(2), 272–290.

Gant, M. M., & Sigelman, L. (1985). Anti-candidate voting in presidential elections. *Polity, 18*(2), 329–339.

Gerber, A., & Green, D. (1998). Rational learning and partisan attitudes. *American Journal of Political Science, 42*(3), 794–818.

Gerber, A., & Green, D. (1999). Misperceptions about perceptual bias. *Annual Review of Political Science, 2,* 189–210.

Gerber, A. S., Huber, G. A. (2010). Partisanship, political control, and economic assessments. *American Journal of Political Science, 54*(1), 153–173.

Gerber, A. S., Huber, G. A., & Washington, E. (2010). Party affiliation, partisanship, and political beliefs: A field experiment. *American Political Science Review, 104*(4), 720–744.

Goren, P. (2002). Character weakness, partisan bias, and presidential evaluation. *American Journal of Political Science, 46*(3), 627–641.

Goren, P. (2005). Party identification and core political values. *American Journal of Political Science, 49*(4), 881–896.

Goren, P. (2007). Character weakness, partisan bias, and presidential evaluation: Modification and extensions. *Political Behavior, 29*(3), 305–325.

Goren, P., Federico, C. M., & Kittilson, M. D. (2007). Source cues, partisan identities, and political value expression. *American Journal of Political Science, 53*(4), 805–820.

Green, D. P. (1988). On the dimensionality of public sentiment toward partisan and ideological groups. *American Journal of Political Science, 32*(3), 758–780.

Green, D. P., & Citrin, J. (1994). Measurement error and the structure of attitudes: Are positive and negative judgments opposites? *American Journal of Political Science, 38*(1), 256–281.

Green, D. P., & Palmquist, B. (1990). Of artifacts and partisan instability. *American Journal of Political Science, 34*(3), 872–902.

Green, D. P., & Palmquist, B. (1994). How stable is party identification? *Political Behavior, 16*(4), 437–466.

Green, D. P., Palmquist B., & Schickler, E. (2002). *Partisan hearts and minds: Political parties and the social identities of voters.* New Haven, CN: Yale University Press.

Green, D. P., & Schickler, E. (1993). Multiple-measure assessment of party identification. *Public Opinion Quarterly, 57*(4), 503–535.

Greene, S. H. (1999). Understanding party identification: A social identity approach. *Political Psychology, 20*(2), 393–403.

Greene, S. H. (2000). The psychological sources of partisan-leaning independence. *American Politics Quarterly, 28*(4), 511–537.

Greene, S. H. (2004). Social identity theory and party identification. *Social Science Quarterly, 85*(1), 136–153.

Greene, S. H. (2005). The structure of partisan attitudes: Reexamining partisan dimensionality and ambivalence. *Political Psychology, 26*(5), 809–822.

Groenendyk, E. W. (2012). Justifying party identification: A case of identifying with the "lesser of two evils." *Political Behavior, 34*(3), 453–475.

Groenendyk, E. W., & Valentino, N. (2002). Of dark clouds and silver linings: Effects of exposure to issue versus candidate advertising on persuasion, information retention, and issue salience. *Communication Research, 29*(3), 295–319.

Hastie, R., & Park, B. (1986). The relationship between memory and judgment depends on whether the judgment task is memory-based or on-line. *Psychological Review, 93*(3), 258–268.

Herring, P. (1940). *The politics of democracy.* New York, NY: W. W. Norton.

Hetherington, M. J. (2001). Resurgent mass partisanship: The role of elite polarization. *American Political Science Review, 95*(3), 619–631.

Hibbs, D. A., Jr. (1977). Political parties and macroeconomic policy. *American Political Science Review, 71*(4), 1467–1487.

Hibbs, D. A., Jr. (1979). The mass public and macroeconomic performance: The dynamics of public opinion toward unemployment and inflation. *American Journal of Political Science, 23*(4), 705–731.

Highton, B., & Kam, C. D. (2011). The long-term dynamics of partisanship and issue orientations. *Journal of Politics, 73*(1), 202–215.

Hilton, J. L., & von Hippel, W. (1996). Stereotypes. *Annual Review of Psychology, 47,* 237–271.

Huber, J. D., Kernell, G., & Leoni, E. L. (2005). Institutional context, cognitive resources, and party attachments across democracies. *Political Analysis, 13*(4), 365–386.

Huckfeldt, R., Levine, J., Morgan, W., & Sprague, J. (1999). Accessibility and the political utility of partisan and ideological orientations. *American Journal of Political Science, 43*(3), 888–911.

Hutchings, V. L., Walton, H., Jr., & Benjamin, A. (2010). The impact of explicit racial cues on gender differences in support for confederate symbols and partisanship. *Journal of Politics, 72*(4), 1–14.

Iyengar, S., & Kinder, D. R. (1987). *News that matters: Television and American opinion.* Chicago, IL: University of Chicago Press.

Jackson, J. E. (1975). Issues, party choices, and presidential votes. *American Journal of Political Science, 19*(2), 161–185.

Jennings, M. K., & Niemi, R. G. (1981). *Generations and politics.* Princeton, NJ: Princeton University Press.

Jessee, S. A. (2010). Partisan bias, political information and spatial voting in the 2008 presidential election. *Journal of Politics, 72*(2), 327–340.

Jost, J. T., Glaser, J., Kruglanski, A. W., & Sulloway, F. J. (2003). Political conservatism as motivated social cognition. *Psychological Bulletin, 129*(3), 339–375.

Jost, J. T., Hennes, E. P., & Lavine, H. (in press). Hot political cognition: Its self-, group-, and system-serving purposes. In D. Carlston (Ed.), *Oxford handbook of social cognition.* New York, NY: Oxford University Press.

Kam, C. D. (2005). Who toes the party line? Cues, values, and individual differences. *Political Behavior, 27*(2), 163–182.

Kam, C. D. (2007). When duty calls, do citizens answer? *Journal of Politics, 69*(1), 17–29.

Kamieniecki, S. (1988). The dimensionality of partisan strength and political independence. *Political Behavior, 10*(4), 364–376.

Katz, R. S. (1979). The dimensionality of party identification: Cross-national perspectives. *Comparative Politics, 11*(2), 147–163.

Kinder, D. R., & Sanders, L. M. (1996). *Divided by color: Racial politics and democratic ideals.* Chicago, IL: University of Chicago Press.

Kingdon, J. (1995). *Agendas, alternatives, and public policies* (2nd ed.). Boston, MA: Little Brown.

Kohut, A., Doherty, C., Dimock, M., & Keeter, S. (2007). Trends in political values and core attitudes: 1987–2007. Washington, DC: The Pew Research Center for the People and the Press.

Krosnick, J. A. (1988). The role of attitude importance in social evaluation: A study of policy preferences, presidential candidate evaluations, and voting behavior. *Journal of Personality and Social Psychology, 55*(2), 196–210.

Krosnick, J. A. (1990). Government policy and citizen passion: A study of issue publics in contemporary America. *Political Behavior, 12*(1), 59–62.

Kuklinski, J. H., & Quirk, P. J. (2000). Reconsidering the rational public: Cognition, heuristics, and mass opinion. In A. Lupia, M. D. McCubbins, & S. L. Popkin (Eds.), *Elements of reason: Cognition, choice, and the bounds of rationality* (pp. 153–182). New York, NY: Cambridge University Press.

Kuklinski, J. H., Quirk, P. J., Jerit, J., & Rich, R. F. (2001). The political environment and citizen competence. *American Journal of Political Science, 45*(2), 410–424.

Kunda, Z. (1990). The case for motivated reasoning. *Psychological Bulletin, 108*(3), 480–498.

Kunda, Z. (1999). *Social cognition: Making sense of people.* Cambridge, MA: MIT Press.

Kunda, Z., Davies, P. G, Adams, B. D., & Spencer, S. J. (2002). The dynamic time course of stereotype activation: Activation, dissipation, and resurrection. *Journal of Personality and Social Psychology, 82*(3), 283–299.

Kunda, Z., & Oleson, K. C. (1995). Maintaining stereotypes in the face of diconfirmation: Constructing grounds for subtyping deviants. *Journal of Personality and Social Psychology, 68*(4), 565–579.

Kunda, Z., & Sanitioso, R. (1989). Motivated changes in the self-concept. *Journal of Experimental Social Psychology, 25*(3), 272–285.

Kunda, Z., & Spencer, S. J. (2003). When do stereotypes come to mind and when do they color judgments? A goal-based theoretical framework for stereotype activation and application. *Psychological Bulletin, 129*(4), 522–544.

Lau, R. R. (1982). Negativity in political perception. *Political Behavior, 4*(4), 353–377.

Lau, R. R. (1985). Two explanations for negativity in political behavior. *American Journal of Political Science, 29*(1), 119–138.

Lavine, H., Johnston, C., & Steenbergen, M. (2012). *The ambivalent partisan: How critical loyalty promotes democracy.* New York, NY: Oxford University Press.

Lavine, H., Lodge, M., & Freitas, K. (2005). Authoritarianism, threat, and selective exposure to information. *Political Psychology, 26*(2), 219–244.

Lebo, M, J., & Cassino, D. (2007). The aggregated consequences of motivated reasoning and the dynamics of partisans presidential approval. *Political Psychology, 26*(6), 719–746.

Levendusky, M. (2009). *The partisan sort: How liberals became Democrats and conservative became Republicans.* Chicago, IL: University of Chicago Press.

Levendusky, M. (2010). Clearer cues, more consistent voters: A benefit of elite polarization. *Political Behavior, 32*(1), 111–131.

Lewis-Beck, M. S., Jacoby, W. G., Norpoth, H., & Weisberg, H. F. (2008). *The American voter revisited.* Ann Arbor, MI: University of Michigan Press.

Lewis-Beck, M. S., Nadeau, R., & Elias, A. (2008). Economics, party, and the vote: Causality issues and panel data. *American Journal of Political Science, 52*(1), 84–95.

Lodge, M., & Taber, C. (2000). Three steps toward a theory of motivated political reasoning. In A. Lupia, M. D. McCubbins, & S. L. Popkin (Eds.), *Elements of reason: Cognition, choice, and the bounds of rationality (pp.* 183–212). Cambridge, United Kingdom: Cambridge University Press.

Lodge, M, & Taber, C. S. (2013). *The rationalizing voter.* New York, NY: Cambridge University Press.

Lowi, T. J. (1979). *The end of liberalism: The second republic of the United States* (2nd ed.). New York, NY: Norton.

Lupia, A. (1994). Shortcuts versus encyclopedias: Information and voting behavior in California insurance reform elections. *American Political Science Review, 88*(1), 63–76.

Lupia, A., & McCubbins, M. D. (1998). *The democratic dilemma: Can citizens learn what they really need to know?* Cambridge, United Kingdom: Cambridge University Press.

Lupia, A., McCubbins, M. D., & Popkin, S. L. (Eds.). (2000). *Elements of reason: Cognition, choice, and the bounds of rationality.* New York, NY: Cambridge.

MacKuen, M. B., Erikson, R. S, & Stimson, J. A. (1989). Macropartisanship. *American Political Science Review, 83*(4), 1125–1142.

Macrae, C. N., Milne, A. B, & Bodenhausen, G. V. (1994). Stereotypes as energy-saving devices: A peek inside the cognitive toolbox. *Journal of Personality and Social Psychology, 66*(1), 37–47.

Madison, J. (1787/2003). The Federalist No. 10. In A. Hamilton, J. Madison, & J. Jay (Eds.), *The Federalist Papers.* New York, NY: Bantam Dell.

Maggiotto, M. A., & Piereson, J. E. (1977). Partisan identification and electoral choice: The hostility hypothesis. *American Journal of Political Science, 21*(4), 745–767.

Malhotra, N., & Kuo, A. G. (2008). Attributing blame: The public's response to Hurricane Katrina. *Journal of Politics, 70*(1), 120–135.

Marcus, G. (2000). Emotions in politics. *Annual Review of Political Science, 3,* 221–250.

Marcus, G., MacKuen, M., Wolak, J., & Keele, L. (2006). The measure and mismeasure of emotions. In D. P. Redlawsk (Ed.), *Feeling politics: Emotion in political information processing (pp. 31–45).* New York, NY: Palgrave MacMillan.

Marcus, G., Neuman, W. R., & MacKuen, M. (2000). *Affective intelligence and political judgment.* Chicago, IL: Chicago University Press.

Markus, G. B., & Converse, P. E. (1979). A dynamic simultaneous equation model of electoral choice. *American Political Science Review, 73*(4), 1055–1070.

Marques, J. M., & Yzerbyt, V. Y. (1988). The black sheep effect: Judgmental extremity towards ingroup members as a function of group identification. *European Journal of Social Psychology, 18*(1), 1–16.

McCarty, N., Poole, K. T., & Rosenthal, H. (2006). *Polarized America: The dance of ideology and unequal riches.* Cambridge, MA: MIT Press.

McCombs, M. E., & Shaw, D. L. (1972). The agenda-setting function of mass media. *Public Opinion Quarterly, 36*(2), 176–187.

McGraw, K. M. (1990). Avoiding blame: An experimental investigation of political excuses and justifications. *British Journal of Political Science, 20*(1), 119–131.

McGraw, K. M. (1991). Managing blame: An experimental test of the effects of political accounts. *American Political Science Review, 85*(4), 1133–1157.

McGraw, K. M. (1998). Manipulating public opinion with moral justification. *Annals of the American Academy of Political and Social Science, 560,* 129–142.

McGraw, K. M., Timpone, R., & Bruck, G. (1993). Justifying controversial political decisions: Home style in the laboratory. *Political Behavior, 15*(3), 289–308.

Mendelberg, T. (2001). *The race card: Campaign strategy, implicit messages, and the norm of equality*. Princeton, NJ: Princeton University Press.

Miller, W. E. (1991). Party Identification, realignment, and party voting: Back to the basics. *American Political Science Review, 85*(2), 557–568.

Miller, W. E., & Shanks, J. M. (1996). *The new American voter*. Cambridge, MA: Harvard University Press.

Monroe, R. K., Hankin, J., & Van Vechten, R. B. (2000). The psychological foundations of identity politics. *Annual Review of Political Science, 3*, 419–447.

Mutz, D. C. (1998). *Impersonal influence: How perceptions of mass collectives affect political attitudes*. Cambridge, United Kingdom: Cambridge University Press.

Nyhan, B., & Reifler, J. (2010). When corrections fail: The persistence of political misperceptions. *Political Behavior, 32*(2), 303–330.

Olson, M. (1971). *The logic of collective action: Public goods and the theory of groups*. Cambridge, MA: Harvard University Press.

Olson, M. (1982). *The rise and decline of nations: Economic growth, stagflation, and social rigidities*. New Haven, CT: Yale University Press.

Page, B. I., & Jones, C. C. (1979). Reciprocal effects of policy preferences, party loyalties and the vote. *American Political Science Review, 73*(4), 1071–1089.

Page, B. I., & Shapiro, R. Y. (1992). *The rational public: Fifty years of trends in Americans' policy preferences*. Chicago, IL: University of Chicago Press.

Petrocik, J. R. (1996). Issue ownership in presidential elections, with a 1980 case study. *American Journal of Political Science, 40*(3), 825–850.

Petrocik, J. R., Benoit, W. L., & Hansen, G. J. (2003–2004). Issue ownership and presidential campaigning, 1952–2000. *Political Science Quarterly, 118*(4), 599–626.

Petty, R. E., & Cacioppo, J. T. (1986). *Communication and persuasion: Central and peripheral routes to attitude change*. New York, NY: Springer-Verlag.

Philpot, T. S. (2004). A party of a different color? Race, campaign communication, and party politics. *Political Behavior, 36*(3), 249–270.

Philpot, T. S. (2007). *Race, Republicans, and the return of the party of Lincoln*. Ann Arbor, MI: University of Michigan Press.

Pool, G. J., Wood, W., Leck, K. (1998). The self-esteem motive in social influence: Agreement with valued majorities and disagreement with derogated minorities. *Journal of Personality and Social Psychology, 75*(4), 967–975.

Popkin, S. L. (1991). *The reasoning voter: Communication and persuasion in presidential campaigns*. Chicago, IL: University of Chicago Press.

Prior, M., & Lupia, A. (2008). Money, time, and political knowledge: Distinguishing quick recall and political learning skills. *American Journal of Political Science, 25*(1), 169–183.

Rae, N. C. (2007). Be careful what you with for: The rise of responsible parties in American national politics. *Annual Review of Political Science, 10*, 169–191.

Rahn, W. M. (1993). The role of partisan stereotypes in information processing about political candidates. *American Journal of Political Science, 37*(2), 472–496.

Rahn, W. M., Krosnick, J. A., & Breuning, M. (1994). Rationalization and derivation processes in survey studies of political candidate evaluations. *American Journal of Political Science, 38*(3), 582–600.

Ranney, A. (1954). *The doctrine of responsible party government, its origin and present state.* Urbana, IL: University of Illinois Press.

Richardson, B. M. (1991). European party loyalties revisited. *American Journal of Political Science, 85*(3), 751–775.

Riker, W. H., & Ordeshook, P. C. (1968). A theory of the calculus of voting. *American Political Science Review, 62*(1), 25–42.

Rokeach, M. (1960). *The open and closed mind.* New York, NY: Basic Books.

Rose, R., & Mishler, W. (1998). Negative and positive party identification in post-communist countries. *Electoral Studies, 17*(2), 217–234.

Ross, L., Greene, D., & House, P. (1977). The "false consensus effect": An egocentric bias in social perception and attribution processes. *Journal of Experimental Social Psychology, 13*(3), 279–301.

Rosema, M. (2006). Partisanship, candidate evaluations, and prospective voting. *Electoral Studies, 25*(3), 467–488.

Rudolph, T. J. (2003). Who's responsible for the economy? The formation of consequences of responsibility attributions. *American Journal of Political Science, 47*(4), 689–713.

Rudolph, T. J. (2006). Triangulating political responsibility: The motivated formation of responsibility judgments. *Political Psychology, 27*(1), 99–122.

Sanitioso, R., Kunda, Z., & Fong, G. T. (1990). Motivated recruitment of autobiographical memories. *Journal of Personality and Social Psychology, 59*(2), 229–241.

Sartori, G. (1976). *Parties and party systems* (Vol. 1). New York, NY: Cambridge University Press.

Schaffner, B. F., & Streb, M. J. (2002). The partisan heuristic in low-information elections. *Public Opinion Quarterly, 66*(4), 559–581.

Schattschneider, E. E. (1942). *Party government.* New York, NY: Rinehart & Company.

Schattschneider, E. E. (1975). *The semisovereign people: A realist's view of democracy in America.* Fort Worth, TX: Harcourt Brace Jovanovich College Publishers.

Schudson, M. (1998). *The good citizen: A history of American civic culture.* Cambridge, MA: Harvard University Press.

Schuessler, A. A. (2000). *A logic of expressive choice.* Princeton, NJ: Princeton University Press.

Schuman, H., & Presser, S. (1981). *Questions and answers in attitude surveys: Experiments on question form, wording, and context.* New York, NY: Academic Press.

Schumpeter, J. A. (1942). *Capitalism, socialism, and democracy* (2nd ed.). New York, NY: Harper and Brothers.

Schwarz, N. (1999). Self-reports: How the questions shape the answers. *American Psychologist, 54*(2), 93–105.

Sears, D. O., & Levy, S. (2003). Childhood and adult political development. In D. O. Sears, L. Huddy, & R. Jervis (Eds.), *Oxford handbook of political psychology (pp. 60–109)*. New York, NY: Oxford University Press.

Sears, D. O., & Valentino, N. A. (1997). Politics matters: Political as catalysts for preadult socialization. *American Political Science Review, 91*(1), 45–65.

Sherif, M. (1956). Experiments in group conflict. *Scientific American, 195*(5), 54–58.

Sherif, M. (1966). *Group conflict and co-operation: Their social psychology*. London: Routledge & Kegan Paul.

Sherman, J. W., Lee, A. Y., Bessenoff, G. R, & Frost, LA. (1998). Stereotype efficiency reconsidered: Encoding flexibility under cognitive load. *Journal of Personality and Social Psychology, 75*(3), 589–606.

Sherman, J. W., Stroessner, S. J., Conrey, F. R., & Azam, O. A. (2005). Prejudice and stereotype maintenance processes: Attention, attribution, and individuation. *Journal of Personality and Social Psychology, 89*(4), 607–622.

Shively, W. P. (1979). The development of party identification among adults: Exploration of a functional model. *American Political Science Review, 73*(4), 1039–1054.

Sigelman, L., & Gant, M. M. (1989). Anticandidate voting in the 1984 presidential election. *Political Behavior, 11*(1), 81–92.

Simon, H. A. (1979). *Models of thought*. New Haven, CT: Yale University Press.

Smith, A. (1986). *Inquiry into the nature and causes of the wealth of nations* (Vol. 1). New York, NY: Penguin.

Sniderman, P. M., Brody, R. A, & Tetlock, P. E. (1991). *Reasoning and choice: Explorations in political psychology*. New York, NY: Cambridge University Press.

Sniderman, P. M., & Stiglitz, E. H. (2012). *The reputational premium: A theory of party identification and policy reasoning*. Princeton, NJ: Princeton University Press.

Sobel, J. (1985). A theory of credibility. *Review of Economic Studies, 52*, 557–573.

Spencer, S. J., Fein, S., Wolfe, C. T., Fong, C., & Dunn, M. A. (1998). Automatic activation of stereotypes: The role of self-image threat. *Personality and Social Psychology Bulletin, 24*(11), 1139–1152.

Steele, C. M. (1988). The psychology of self-affirmation: Sustaining the integrity of the self. In L. Berkowitz (Ed.), *Advances in experimental social psychology (Vol. 21, pp. 261–302)*. San Diego, CA: Academic Press.

Stoker, L., & Jennings, M. K. (2008). Of time and the development of partisan polarization. *American Journal of Political Science, 53*(3), 619–635.

Sundquist, J. (1983). *Dynamics of the party system: Alignment and realignment of political parties in the United States*. Washington, DC: Brookings Institution.

Taber, C. S., & Lodge, M. (2006). Motivated skepticism in the evaluation of political beliefs. *American Journal of Political Science, 50*(3), 755–769.

Taber, C. S., Lodge, M., & Glathar, J. (2001). The motivated construction of political judgments. In J. H. Kuklinski (Ed.), *Citizens and politics: Perspective from political psychology (pp. 198–226)*. New York, NY: Cambridge University Press.

Tajfel, H., Billig, M. G., Bundy, R. P., & Flament, C. (1971). Social categorization and intergroup behavior. *European Journal of Social Psychology, 1*(2), 149–178.

Tetlock, P. E., & Kim, J. I. (1987). Accountability and judgment processes in a personality prediction task. *Journal of Personality and Social Psychology, 52*(4), 700–709.

Tetlock, P. E., Skitka, L., & Boettger, R. (1989). Social and cognitive strategies for coping with accountability: Conformity, complexity, and bolstering. *Journal of Personality and Social Psychology, 57*(4), 632–640.

Theriault, S. (2008). *Party polarization in Congress.* New York, NY: Cambridge University Press.

Tilley, J., & Hobolt, S. B. (2011). Is the government to blame? An experimental test of how partisanship shapes perceptions of performance and responsibility. *Journal of Politics, 73*(2), 316–330.

Tomz, M., & Sniderman, P. M. (2005). *Brand names and the organization of mass belief systems.* Unpublished manuscript. Stanford University Press, Palo Alto, CA.

Truman, D. B. (1993). *The governmental process: Political interests and public opinion* (2nd ed.). Berkeley, CA: Institute of Governmental Studies.

Tversky, A., & Kahneman, D. (1974). Judgment under uncertainty: Heuristics and biases. *Science, 185*(4157), 1124–1131.

Valentine, D. C., & Van Wingen, J. R. (1980). Partisanship, independence, and the partisan identification question. *American Politics Quarterly, 8*(2), 1965–1986.

Valentino, N. A., Hutchings, V. L., & White, I. K. (2002). Cues that matter: How political ads prime racial attitudes during campaigns. *American Political Science Review, 96*(1), 75–90.

Valentino, N. A., & Sears, D. O. (1998). Event-driven political communication and the preadult socialization of partisanship. *Political Behavior, 20*(2), 127–154.

Van Vugt, M., & Hart, C. M. (2004). Social identity as social glue: The origins of group loyalty. *Journal of Personality and Social Psychology, 86*(4), 585–598.

Van Vugt, M., & Schaller, M. (2008). Evolutionary approaches to group dynamics: An introduction. *Group Dynamics, 12*(1): 1–6.

Walker, J. L. (1991). *Mobilizing interest groups in America: Patrons, professions, and social movements.* Ann Arbor, MI: University of Michigan Press.

Washington, G. (2008). *Washington's farewell address 1796.* Lillian Goldman Law Library, Yale Law School. Retrieved from http://avalon.law.yale.edu/18th_century/washing.asp.

Weinschenk, A. C. (2010). Revisiting the political theory of party identification. *Political Behavior, 32*(4), 473–494.

Weisberg, H. F. (1980). A mulitdimensional conceptualization of party identification. *Political Behavior, 2*(1), 33–60.

Weisberg, H. F., & Christenson, D. P. (2007). Changing horses in wartime? The 2004 presidential election. *Political Behavior, 29*(2), 279–304.

Weisberg, H. F., & Christenson, D.P. (2010). Partisan defection and change in the 2008 US presidential election. *Journal of Elections, Public Opinion, and Parties, 20*(2), 213–240.

West, D. M. (2010). *Ad wars 1952–2008* (5th ed.). Washington, D C: CQ Press.

Westen, D., Blagov, P. S., Harenski, K., Kilts, C., & Hamann, S. (2006). Neural bases of motivated reasoning: An fMRI study of emotional constraints on partisan political judgment in the 2004 U.S. presidential election. *Journal of Cognitive Neuroscience, 18*(11), 1974–1958.

Yzerbyt, V. Y., Coull, A., & Rocher, S. J. (1999). Fencing off the deviant: The role of cognitive resources in the maintenance of stereotypes. *Journal of Personality and Social Psychology, 77*(3), 449–462.

Zaller, J. (1992). *The nature and origins of mass opinion.* Cambridge, United Kingdom: Cambridge University Press.

Zaller, J., & Feldman, S. (1992). A simple theory of survey response: Answering questions versus revealing preferences. *American Journal of Political Science, 36*(3), 579–616.

INDEX

Note: Page numbers followed by n, *f* and *t* refer to notes, figures and tables.

CPSIA information can be obtained at www.ICGtesting.com
Printed in the USA
BVOW03s1427090916

461647BV00002B/3/P